Gabriele Crespi

THE ARABS
IN EUROPE

Introduction by
Francesco Gabrieli

RIZZOLI
NEW YORK

First published in the United States of America in 1986 by
RIZZOLI INTERNATIONAL PUBLICATIONS, INC.
597 Fifth Avenue, New York, NY 10017

© 1979
Editoriale Jaca Book, Milano

First Italian Edition
October 1982

Iconographic contributions:
Oronoz Photographic Archives, Madrid,
Giovanni Piotti, Gabriele Crespi,
Eduard Olivella.
The source for 13 photographs in the
present work is the volume «The Arabs in Italy»
and associated photographic archives of the
«Antica Madre» series. These are reproduced by
kind permission of «Credito Italiano» - Milan
and of «Libri Scheiwiller s.r.l.»
via G. Sacchi, 3 - Milan,
who hold the world copyrights.
Photographs for which no provenance is
indicated in the captions were supplied
by Gabriele Crespi and Giovanni Piotti

Front Cover
Cordoba. East Front of the Great Mosque

Library of Congress Cataloging -in -Publication Data

Crespi Gabriele.
    The Arabs in Europe.

    Translation of: Gli Arabi in Europa.
    Bibliography: p.
    1. Muslims--Europe--History.   2. Europe--History--
476-1492.   3. Civilization, Occidental--Islamic
influences.   4. Art, Islamic--Europe.   5. Art--Europe.
I. Title.
DS36.96.C7313   1986   940'.04924   85-30180
ISBN 0-8478-0707-X

Table of Contents

Introduction

All the historical events dealt with in this book took place outside the Arab peninsula, the cradle of the people among whom Islam originated and whence it spread out over two continents. The scope of these preliminary pages is to provide the reader with an outline of the origins, the characteristics and the circumstances of the Arabs before they entered world history with their new faith, together with a brief introduction to the essential nature of this faith and the fruits it bore: the culture and civilization of which the Arabs themselves, throughout Asia, Africa and Europe, were the repositories.

The prehistory of this people in its peninsula homeland before the unifying religion of Muhammed propelled it onto the vast scene of its diaspora is long, monotonous and obscure. In the pre-Islamic period, which the Muslims refer to as *Giahiliyya* (religious ignorance or barbarism), the nomadic Arabs played a marginal role as auxiliaries, mobile flanking troops and raiders among the powers that fought one another for supremacy in the Near East, Assyrians, Seleucids, Romans, Byzantines and Persians. Only to the north and south of the peninsula were there to be found permanent settlements and forms of state organization such as were the kingdoms of the Nabates and the Palmirenes, both subjugated by Rome, and the sedentary kingdom of Southern Arabia (*Arabia Felix* or Yemen) that enjoyed such prosperity as derives from an advanced agricultural economy and from spice trading. But the prevalent way of life in the heart of the peninsula, *ab antico*, was nomadism, expanding steadily in the early centuries of the Christian era, together with the associated phenomenon of tribal cleavage. The life of the Arabs, if one makes exception for the religious centre of Mecca and the urban settlement of Yathrib (the future Medina), was the wretched hand to mouth existence of the desert dweller: scattered tribal groups and subgroups, reliant on a pastoral economy, fighting both among themselves and against the inclemencies of nature; in a state of constant strife over the arid grazing grounds, their wells and their livestock. Although in their great majority they were averse to or incapable of any form of social cohesion that transcended the genealogical ties of the tribe, nonetheless embryonic buffer states did come into being on the perimeter of the desert — the Ghassanids on the Syrian *limes* and the Làkhmids on the

Euphrates — vassal states of, respectively, Byzantium and Sassanian Persia. Here, in contact with superior civilizations, the untrammelled bedouin way of life was tempered and submitted to refining influence. Everywhere else the Arabs remained in a primitive state, both socio-economic and spiritual. Rising above this, obscure of genesis and development, is their cult of poetry that has been aptly described as the archives of Arab splendor, the reflection of their passions and strifes and the legacy of Arab paganism to the Arab civilization still to come.

The religion of this primitive society took the form of an elementary polydemonism, marked by a plethora of idols that separately might often be the cult object of a single tribe but whose images were collectively installed within the Meccan Ka'aba. The notion of a superior divinity, an Allah or a preeminent Lord God, was not wholly absent but since the relation of such an entity to the world and to mankind was uncertain, the concept remained vague and elusive. Worship was simple and sporadic, confined to sacrifice and divinatory oracles. The common factor and motive for fraternal feeling was the annual pilgrimage to Mecca, where the aerolite, the Black Stone built into the Ka'aba was worshipped and three female divinities, Allàt, Manàt and al-Uzza were the object of civic devotion and, on specific occasion, of the homage of bedouin pilgrims. In the absence of any precise belief in otherworldly survival, the religious life of pagan Arabia was accounted for in these simple rites and resolved itself in a rough-hewn materialistic humanism while there rose to eminence before it the representatives of the two great monotheistic faiths, Judaism and Christianity, both present in pre-Islamic Arabia as much in the small urban settlements as in separate tribes in the desert. Unassimilated to either and almost a portent of what Islam would become, isolated figures of *homines religiosi* emerge from Arab tradition, the so-called *hanìf*, emblematic of the craving for a monotheism that was as yet beyond the reach of theological formulation.

At the start of the seventh century this poverty-stricken warrior race, socially divided and discordant, lukewarm if not indeed indifferent to religious sentiment, produced the figure and the work of its Prophet, the Meccan Muhammad, whose name on Western lips became *Machometus*, Mahomet. It is not our task here to examine the events of this life in detail: the dawning within him of the dominant concept of the One God, the Creator and Lord of the Universe, his Judge at the moment of the Supreme Judgment; the long, tenacious struggle, first with his fellow Meccans, then with all the Arabs of the Higiàz and of the entire peninsula to gain acceptance for this new faith as it had been revealed to him and by him set down in the Koran; the passion of the Vigil, the flight to Medina (in 622, the start of the Muslim era), the transformation from isolated propagandist of a personal belief to head of a community and of a State welded together by the new faith of Islam; the final victory of this faith and of its Prophet over the diffidence of the pagan Meccans and bedouins; Mahomet's triumphal return to his birthplace, the purification of the Ka'aba by the expulsion of all idolatrous cult and the solemn transmutation of a pagan rite into the Muslim pilgrimage, still today the greatest unitary expression of that faith. It suffices to recall that the triumph of Mahomet at Mecca took place in 630 and that only two years later, in 632, his death at Medina set the seal on that extraordinary career of chosen messenger and codifier of a new Word to

8

his entire people and, contrary to all initial forecast, to so great a part of the rest of humanity.

Let us briefly remind ourselves of the essence of Islam as it is expressed in the lapidary formula of the *shahada*, or profession of faith: «There is no other god but Allah, Muhammad is the Messenger of Allah.» This is repudiation of pagan polytheism and assent to undeviating observance of monotheism; the rejection of every concept of divine descent (Christianity) and at the same time the recognition of the Arab Prophet as the messenger by divine mandate of the Supreme Truth; his sacred Book, of unsurpassing beauty and efficacy, the Koran, the direct and literal word of God. The principal requisites of the cult, headed by the aforesaid *shahada*, are simple, comprising the five «pilasters» of the new faith: the canonical fivefold daily observance of prayer (*salàt*), elaborate of formulas and gestures of adoration in conformity with a strictly prescribed ritual, but soon becoming second nature to every believer; compulsory almsgiving (*zakàt*), to be made to prescribed charitable causes and in payment of taxes; fasting in the sacred month of ramadan, requiring total abstention from food and drink, smoking and sexual relations from sunrise to sunset; in ultimate, the pilgrimage (*hagg*) in the chosen month to that most ancient of Arab sanctuaries, the Ka'aba at Mecca, astutely «Islamized» by Mahomet, who incorporated it into his faith. Believers were all brothers in the faith; the ties of religion thus replaced all other genealogical and tribal bonds that had previously governed the collective existence of the Arab people. As far as the status of the Prophet himself is concerned in that new society or community (*umma*), from the initial phase of apostle of a new creed it passed to the other, more demanding in complexity and responsability, of head of state and model for believers, establishing laws not only by means of divine revelation but also through his own attitudes and injunctions (*sunna*). These were expressed and passed on in countless short «loghia» (*hadìth*) the compilation of which must have been for centuries one of the main intellectual activities of the Muslim community. The dignity of Prophet Elect (with certain derived prerogatives, especially in the field of matrimony) never obscured Mahomet's awareness of his human origin nor his proclamation of it within limits that only the zeal of a much later veneration by the faithful has ever conspired to override: the constant evocation of the One (*tawhid*), of the transcendent, absolute Lord of the Universe, remained throughout Islam's history the nexus of her evolution. Islam's radical rejection of the native polytheism spread and deepened in antithesis to the other two monotheistic faiths to which she was kin but which were judged to be inadequate and corrupt: Judaism, as the exclusivist faith of a tiny people with debased scriptures, and Christianity, by reason of her trinitarian doctrine, as a defection from the absolute monotheism of Abraham upheld solely by the Islam of Muhammad.

While paganism was totally banished, the status of tolerated cults was accorded to the followers of Judaism and Christianity in that they were «People of the Book,» endowed that is to say with sacred scriptures. This stand taken by the new Arab faith in respect of her own precedents and her predecessors is linked to the problem of Islamic particularism or universalism, which bears some analogy with the development and spread of Christianity. Initially, Muhammad certainly intended his word for the ears of his own people, spreading out from his birthplace in ever-widening circles to the surrounding Higiàz, ultimately to embrace the entire peninsula, seat of the Arab peoples in their as yet circumscribed field of action. This «national» vision of Islam was probably intended to extend beyond the confines of Arabia even in the lifetime of the Prophet himself for an eye to other horizons can be detected in his preaching and deeds. This thesis is substantiated by his letters and diplomatic missions to the neighbouring sovereigns of Arabia (those of Byzantium, Persia and Abyssinia), and in the raids and military expeditions organized or planned by Mahomet himself towards the end of his life, chiefly directed at the frontiers with Byzantium. In this culminating phase of his career and of his life itself, Mahomet was no longer satisfied it would seem to bequeath his victorious faith to the Arab people alone (as solemnly proclaimed by Allah in what was perhaps the last Koranic revelation: «I have been pleased to give you Islam as a religion»), instead, his eyes looked beyond the desert homeland to other lands and empires, to foreign faiths that the Arab faith he had proclaimed might replace. In other words, the universalism of Islam, while not explicitly formulated as such, was already germinating in the final phase of Mahomet's work, once the faith had been definitively established in the Peninsula. The Prophet's first successors and lieutenants, the Caliphs, merely gave explicit expression to a tendency to universalism already existing in outline when they set in motion the conquests by reason of the expansion of the young Arab State and, contemporaneously, of the propagation of its faith. The frank and lucid explanation of Arab historians for the dynamics of the conquests is summed up in the binomial «plunder and holy war», an illustration on the one hand of the perpetuation on vaster horizons of the old bedouin instinct for plunder and robbery and, on the other, the development at an international level of the fulfillment of obligations towards the *gihàd* (combat or struggle, that is to say armed attack) inculcated by the Koran in defense of and for aggression by the Muslim community in respect of its enemies: the Meccans and other pagan Arabs in the first place and subsequently the States and peoples outside Arabia with whom the young theocratic State came into contact. This *gihàd* or holy war, while not included among the recorded pilasters of the faith has, nonetheless, for centuries, been one of the primary motives underlying the expansionistic belligerency of Islam. Even today, thirteen centuries away from its Meccan origin, it characterizes the struggle for independence of the Muslim peoples (with their *mugiahidìn* or fighters of the *gihàd*) against the encroachment and oppression of foreign powers.

Shortly after the death of the Prophet therefore, young Arab Islam swarmed off to war beyond the confines of its Peninsula. A part of this conquering diaspora, the part concerning the Western Mediterranean, is the subject of this book; but the opposite direction, to the East, should not be overlooked for in less than a century the Arabs had placed as much distance between themselves and their point of departure as in the West, having penetrated Central Asia almost to the borders of China. A people that had previously been confined to the deserts of the Peninsula fanned out in one vast sweeping curve that extended from Chinese Turkestan to the Atlantic Ocean: it, or rather that part of it that migrated, fought and established itself on conquered territory (altogether, at the outset, some hundreds of thousands of men, inclusive of fighters and respective families) took with it its language, traditions and native discordances, held in check but not entirely suppressed by Islam, together with its most precious and fruitful endowment, this new faith that immediately revealed its extraordinary attraction and proselytizing potential. The familiar image of the spread of Islam «by the sword» is wholly inexact and quite inadequate to explain the rapidity with which it was embraced by peoples of different ethnic origins, of different faiths, cultures and civilizations. It has already been said that to those who were «People of the Book,» that is to say in possession of their own sacred scriptures (Jews, Christians and Zoroastrians), the victors in the name of the Prophet accorded freedom of worship and protection in exchange for a payment of tribute. One of the main incentives for conversion was certainly exoneration from this obligation and escape from the subordinate status of «protectee» by entering the egalitarian community of the victors and in the course of a couple of centuries this created a Muslim majority (old and new) in countries of non-Arab ethnic background (Persia, Iraq, Syria and Palestine, Egypt, North Africa and Spain) in which the combined force of Arabism and Islamism put down deep and, almost everywhere, ineradicable roots. Only Persia wholly assimilated Islam, but blended it with its own language and national traditions, while Spain, after a centuries-long struggle, ended by rejecting both Islam and the Arabs. In the middle of the eighth century, while violence reigned at the summit of the Islamic empire where the Abbasids were replacing the 'Umayyads as Caliphs, the Arab peoples had attained their maximum diffusion from East to West, to which the subsequent Mediterranean conquests and raids (Sicily, France and Italy) could add but little by way of territory, and a vast field lay open, for centuries, to contacts and cultural cross-fertilization.

In the light of these foregoing points let us consider the Arab diaspora, no longer through the eyes of its protagonists — the Arabs themselves, their historians, jurists, scientists and poets who all extol the dynamic, irresistible expansion of their faith — but instead, through those of their adversaries, essentially, the representatives of Greek and Latin Christianity who, in part surrendered and submitted to the invasions, in part put up tenacious resistance to them. We shall see that the «Saracens» (the term used in our early Middle Ages to refer to the Arabs and the Muslims generally) were viewed as a scourge of God, aggressors and looters, agents of desecration of whatever values, religious, social or civic. This is on a par with the «abomination of desolation» applied in biblical tones by the patriarch of Jerusalem, Sophronius, to Arab presence in the Holy City; they are the recurrent deprecations of Byzantine, Frankish and Italian chroniclers commenting Arab-Muslim raids and conquests on Christian soil. The first wave of Arab offensive, whether aimed at permanent settlement or in the nature of a short-lived raid, always engendered violent devastation; nor could it have been otherwise since the sword had an effective primary function if not in the conversion, then in the subjugation of the peoples and the States struck down by Arab invasion; this remained true wherever the Arabs, in accordance with their juridico-religious distinction, felt themselves to be in the «seat of war» (*dar al-harb*), pursuant in their struggle of the familiar two-fold objective of booty and *gihàd*. But wherever the «seat of war» was transformed by consolidated conquest into «territory of Islam» (*dar al-Islam*), in other words into territory where pacific acceptance of Muslim occupation existed, the dynamics of aggression were replaced by the fruitful development of their faith, civilization and culture, the armed encounter by the encounter and cross-fertilization of cultures; the Saracen looter became the magnanimous and magnificent emir, scholar, poet, craftsman and artist. All the ambivalence of Arab-Islamic encroachment or domination outside Arabia is revealed in this contrast.

If the Koran had been the sole viaticum of progressive Islam, had its followers remained the sole protagonists of the new course of history, there would be nothing more to say because the Book of God met their every intellectual and spiritual need (this, according to legend, is the motive attributed to the Caliph Omar for his alleged destruction of the Library of Alexandria). But due to what we may call, in the manner of the Arabs, a «ruse of Allah,» or, in a blend of Christian thought and *Historismus*, an act of Providence, the authority of the sacred Book, albeit representing the supreme instance for believers, was no obstacle to their receptiveness to the cultures of their subject people nor did it prevent them from adopting alongside their own ancient but meagre national tradition those infinitely richer traditions of other superior cultures that they encountered in the course of their diaspora. From such impartiality and fruitful encounters sprung the composite Arab-Islamic civilization that flourished in the early Middle Ages of the East and also shone its beneficial rays on the vanquished Christian West.

Besides the profound religious experience of their faith (founded by the Prophet, the third religion in descent from Abraham), the Arabs' contribution to this cultural «pool» was their poetry, the sole enduring fruit of their modest spiritual life in the pre-Islamic age. So profoundly rooted in the Arab psyche was this that the canonical forms and themes of the pagan period were still pursued, virtually unchanged, in the Islamic age.

Arab-Islamic civilization held the cultivation of national poetry in high esteem both for its intrinsic merit and in the interests of interpretation of the sacred Book, the Koran, written in a language substantially that of the poetic *koiné*, uncontaminated by idiomatic expression. Ancillary to philology and sacred exposition alike, grammar evolved as the Arab national science, and here the foundation work was supplied by both Arabs and non-Arabs such as the Persian Sibawaih. It is important to remember that the true common denominator of Arab-Islamic culture and civilization in its classical era was not ethnic in character but linguistic and cultural, from which it follows that by reason of the use of the language and expressed allegiance to Arabism (opposed, but in Arabic, by the nationalistic movement of the *Shu'ubiyya*), alien Muslims felt themselves to be «Arabs,» Iranians or Syrians or Turks by origin they might be, but all placed on an equal footing by Islam and assimilated by language and culture to the, initially, preeminent Arab people. Such, for example was the great Biruni, the foremost Scientist of the Islamic Middle Ages, such too, were the philosophers al-Farabi and Avicenna, together with a pleiad of men of letters, jurists and scientists, all of whom wrote in Arabic, thus testifying to the unquestionable primacy of the language and to the rapidly achieved international standing of the Islamic faith. «Arab,» used in this sense is therefore the equivalent of, to coin a term, «Arabophone,» an important distinction to make if one is not to detract from the pride that attaches to the purity or ethnic origin of certain representatives of that common culture, such as the «philosopher of the Arabs» al-Kindi, and in the Maghrib and in Spain, great thinkers and pure Arabs such as Averroes, Ibn Tufail and Ibn Khaldùn.

But by mention of philosophers, historians and scientists we are already transported from the territory of Arab literary-linguistic tradition to the field to which there accretes, during the Muslim Middle Ages, the vestiges of other great foreign civilizations. It is here that the fruitful encounter between Arabism and the ancient cultures of the Near East takes place, initially with the Iranian and Hellenistic traditions. *Persia capta* conquers in its turn the rude victors, with its own cultural tradition in which purely Iranian elements are blended with Indian influences. The Arab-Islamic world's acquisition of this Indo-Iranian cultural patrimony that surfaces in the fabulized *Kalila and Dimna*, in gnomology and in the narrative form (the older parts of *The Thousand and One Nights*) is one of the most fascinating chapters of Eastern Muslim civilization. Through the mediation of such genial figures as Ibn al Muqaffa', this Middle-Eastern cultural patrimony pervaded Arab-Islamic culture and from here was further transposed to the Muslim West and beyond, to Christian Europe. In analogous manner Arab-Islamic culture was the go-between for the other great stream of Hellenistic studies (in philosophy and the sciences) and the Western world, competing with and complementing the direct mediation of Byzantium. The body of disciplines referred to by the Arabs as *'ulùm al-awà'il* or *'ulùm al-qudamà* (the sciences of the Ancients), in antithesis to those of their national tradition embraced not only philosophy but mathematics and astronomy, medicine and the natural sciences: the effective patrimony of the Hellenistic heritage (with the exclusion of poetry, eloquence and Greek historiography) that in response to an insatiable cultural thirst in the eighth to tenth centuries of our era was to be decanted (following the usual channels of intermediary Syrian versions) from Greek into Arabic, there to meet with further elaboration. This was the path taken by the philosophy of Plato, Aristotle and Plotinus, and by the science of Hippocrates, Dioscorides and Galen, to penetrate Arab-Islamic culture, to influence the work of Farabi and Avicenna, al-Khuwarizmi and ar-Razi, by Biruni in the East and Zahrawi in the West to cross the Mediterranean from one end to the other, to be taken up by Arab Spain and thence be surrendered to the Latin Middle Ages.

This mediatory function of Arab-Islamic civilization (in which the Christians of the East played a large part, but through the Arab language, in conformity with the characteristic of Arabism we noted earlier) is, in our eyes, one of its indisputable claims to glory. And this is not to deny the originality and creativity of its own intrinsic merits. In the field of literature, one such, and authentically Arab, is the splendid flowering of poetry that, according to much debated theories, exerted a formative influence on Romance poetry; and in the field of the figurative arts, notwithstanding the burden of its uncompromising rejection of images, there is the conspicuous contribution of Islam to the artistic patrimony of humanity.

The story of the «Arabs in Europe» to which the following pages are devoted offers concrete evidence of this transmigratory process, this dissemination of culture that proves to be richer and noble by far than one might have supposed from the arbitrary image of the «Saracen Despoilers» that has been common currency around our Mediterranean shores for centuries.

THE ARABS
IN EUROPE

CHAPTER ONE

THE CONQUEST OF
THE MEDITERRANEAN

The Mediterranean at the Dawn of Islam

In the year 610 the emperor Heraclius was crowned at Constantinople. His accession brought to an end a period of anarchy that had set in after the disintegration of the system introduced by Justinian little more than a half century earlier. Under Justinian the *Imperium Romanum Christianum* had invested itself with leadership of the Mediterranean world. It viewed itself as the harbinger, not only of a mature civil conscience but also of the tidings of Christian salvation, whose authenticity was vouched for in the person of the emperor, the living symbol of divine power.

But the course of history pointed elsewhere, compelling Byzantium to measure itself both against the tradition and forms of life of the ancient Mediterranean world and against the new forces gathering momentum in the Arab peninsula.

In the second half of the sixth century the empire, already weakened by internal strife, found itself obliged to take defense measures against external aggression — a situation which, without diminishing its artistic and cultural stature, was prejudicial to its image and role in the Mediterranean.

Justinian's reconquests proved to be short-lived.

The tide of Slav movement in the Balkans could not be checked and it soon reached Macedon. A few years after the victorious conclusion of the Gothic war, Lombard penetration of Italy began and the peninsula was divided between the new occupants and the empire. This new division left the empire in control of the islands, the exarchate of Ravenna, the duchy of Rome, certain minor coastal areas in the south, Calabria (Apulia) and Bruzio (Calabria).

The Visigoths in Spain gradually recovered all their lands from the Byzantines, bringing this new conquest to a conclusion in 629. Yet while they had resorted to every means to combat its political presence on Spanish soil, Byzantium clearly remained a model and the Visigoths, in consequence, adopted the power symbols of Roman tradition. Under Reccared I (586-601) they converted from Arianism to Catholicism, and at the Council of Toledo in 589 a majority of their bishops embraced the Roman faith. This provided the Visigothic Kingdom with a mediator in its relations with Byzantium — the papacy, whose political and cultural importance was growing in the West.

On the eve of the rise of Islam, such was the number and diversity of political, ethnic and religious components fluctuating between alliance and strife, it could only be a matter of conjecture which of the many courses open to it the evolution of Mediterranean Europe might take.

In the East an ancestral hostility such as had once existed between Romans and Persians afflicted relations between Byzantium and the Sassanian empire. Both Byzantines and Persians created buffer states on the borders of the Arab peninsula to curb the turbulent and growing movement of the Arab tribes tempted by the fertile plains of the Euphrates and Syria. Such states were the Ghassanid kingdom, a vassal of Byzantium, the kingdom of the Lakhmids, a Persian vassal, and that of Kinda, owing allegiance to Himyar, whose history had often stirred pre-Islamic poets.

In the first decades of the seventh century Sassanian hostility toward Byzantium intensified: Damascus fell in 613, Jerusalem in 614, and in 626 Constantinople was under siege. Heraclius succeeded in reversing the situation, turning the tide in Byzantine favor. The Sassanians were definitively crushed and the victorious emperor entered Jerusalem in 630. This was the year of Muhammad's conquest of Mecca; without anyone being aware of it an extremely dynamic and potent religious, political and military reality had arisen in a nation that the outside world had merely deigned to keep in check by the creation of bordering states. In a few short years it was to be a commanding presence on the Mediterranean, irrevocably altering the political and cultural equilibrium of the entire basin.

Islam Victorious and the Caliphate of Damascus

When the Prophet died on the 13 rabî I of the year II (8 June 632), revolts broke out everywhere, a movement of centrifugal forces that led to the secession from Islam of many tribes (*ridda*)[1] and to the formation of various parties.

The task of putting down these revolts fell to Abû Bakr, the first in the line of the four orthodox caliphs to be so involved. Bringing back peace to the heart of the peninsula and launching the wars of conquest fell to Khâlid ibn al-Walîd, who bore the title of Sayd Allâh (The Sword of Allah). In 633, with order restored among the tepid Muslims of Central Arabia, he moved towards the Euphrates and, crossing the border, easily took possession of the southern provinces of the Sassanian empire.

But Muslim interests in this period were concentrated on Syria[2] where the Christian Arabs of the borderlands had repeatedly requested Medina's aid in protest against the Emperor Heraclius who in that period had withdrawn the periodic subsidies by which he hoped to win the favors of his less important allies. In the autumn of 633 small reconnoitering detachments were sent to Syria, quickly followed by reinforcements in the form of Khâlid's crack cavalry regiments from the Euphrates.

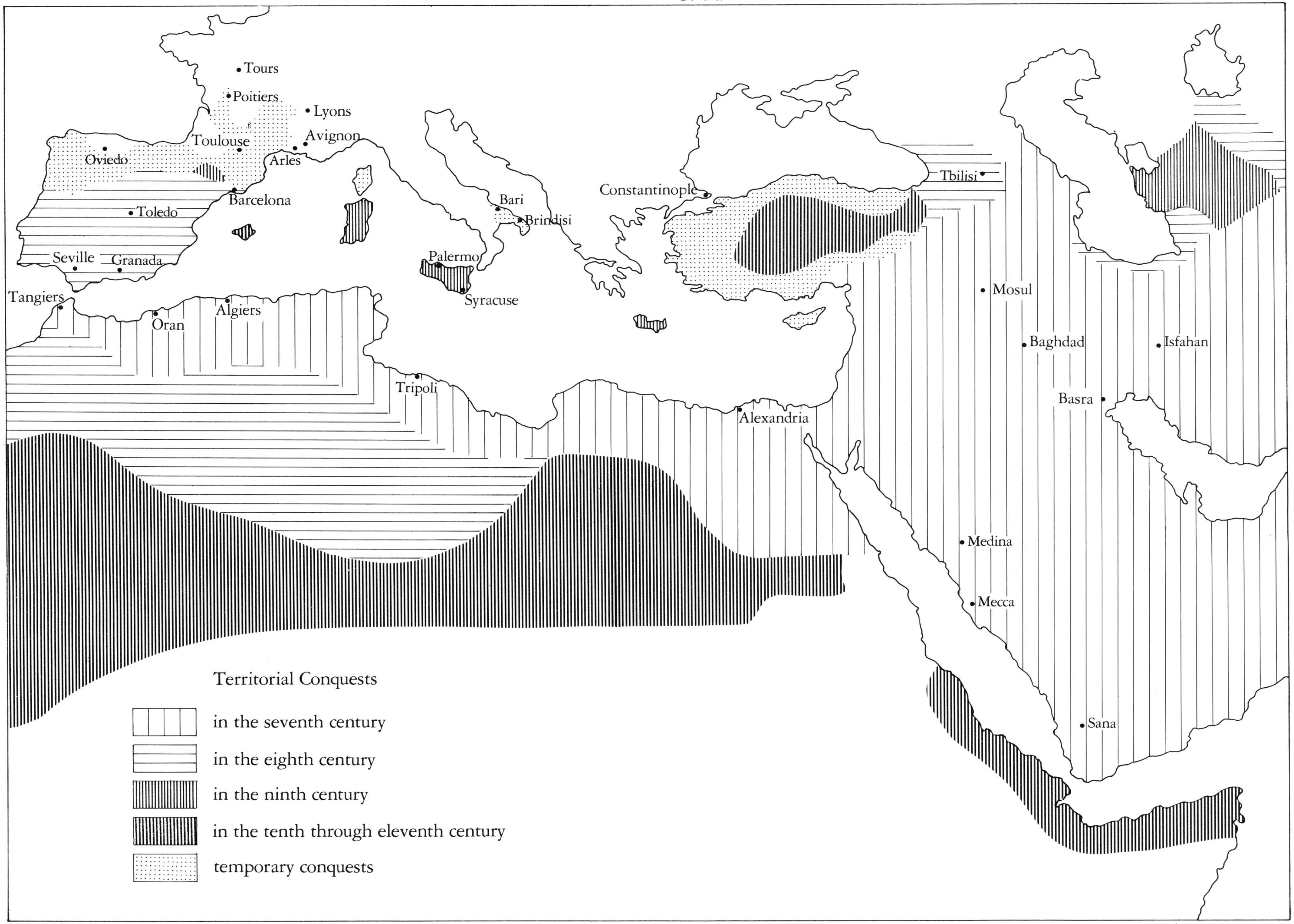

The growth of Arab expansion from the seventh through eleventh centuries

BARR GARDNER ASSOCIATES, LTD.

Territorial Conquests

in the seventh century

in the eighth century

in the ninth century

in the tenth through eleventh century

temporary conquests

Tours
Poitiers
Lyons
Avignon
Arles
Toulouse
Barcelona
Oviedo
Toledo
Seville
Granada
Tangiers
Oran
Algiers
Tripoli
Syracuse
Palermo
Bari
Brindisi
Constantinople
Tbilisi
Alexandria
Mosul
Baghdad
Basra
Isfahan
Medina
Mecca
Sana

The defeated emperor withdrew to Antioch and the Syrian ports were opened; a few months later the Arab horsemen appeared beneath the walls of Damascus and the town, probably betrayed by the civil authorities, surrendered in September 635. At the end of the same year Emesa fell too. Heraclius however, had no intention of leaving the country; feverish activity resulted in the formation of Armenian and Arab mercenary troops at Antioch and Edessa. The clash took place to the east of the Jordan, in the deep Yarmûk valley, the most fertile region of Syria. Here, at the center of the communication lines connecting the region with central Palestine, the Byzantine army was crushed in August 636. Syria's fate was sealed. Khâlid pushed north in the company of Abû 'Ubaida, expressly sent to Syria by the second caliph, 'Umar, to keep an eye on his all too powerful general, and took possession of Baalbek and Antioch. Jerusalem, recently reconquered by the Byzantines, surrendered in 638 and Cesarea in 640.

Meanwhile, alarmed by the serious losses suffered by the Byzantines, the Persians[3] had crossed the Euphrates intent on halting Arab progress. Sa'd ibn Abî Waqqâs, one of the Companions to whom Muhammad had promised paradise, met them on the Qâdisîya plain in the summer of 637 and on this occasion it was the Persian army that was defeated. The victors marched on towards the Tigris and conquered Ctesifonte. The caliph gave orders for the military base of Kûfa, in the vicinity of Hîra, to be raised to the dignity of capital of the newly conquered territories. It was subsequently to become one of the great centers of Muslim culture, as was, at a later date, the other military base of Basra. The last king, Yezdegerd, made a desperate attempt at resistance at Ecbatana but was forced to flee to the shores of the Caspian Sea, where he was murdered by one of his satraps.

The image of Islam no longer evoked the state of Medina; it now stood for the ideal of a universal Muslim empire. From this moment the expeditions became systematic conquests. An early example of this was the occupation of Mesopotamia[4] and in 641, the conquest of Mosul, a strategic link between Syria and the Iraqi provinces. Ten years later the conquest of Fars, present-day Persia, was accomplished and the Arabs reached Khorâsân.

Meanwhile there was apprehension among the Arabs that the Byzantines might attempt to re-invade Syria from their bases in Egypt, not an impossible undertaking in that the imperial fleet was anchored in the harbours of Alexandria and Klysma. It was this fear, comforted by the fame of the legendary riches of Egypt that inspired the Arabs to attack. The commander of the invading forces was 'Amr ibn al-'Âs, a man of great authority and prestige, with a talent moreover for organization. In December 639 he turned up on the weakly garrisoned eastern frontier and a month later entered Pelusium where he was joined by Zubair, one of the Companions of the Prophet. Together they defeated the Byzantines in the battle of Heliopolis in July 640.

Heraclius died the following year, and the Arabs took possession of the citadel of Babylon, thus opening up the Upper-Nile route to Alexandria. When the great Mediterranean port succumbed to them, in 642, Egypt was lost. But not even Alexandria was chosen as the capital of the new state. 'Amr founded the military base of al-Fustât, on the site of the former Babylon, on the east bank of the Nile. As had been the case with his colleague Khâlid, he too was flanked by a trusty of the caliph, 'Abd Allâh ibn Sa'd ibn Abî Sarh, who proved his worth in the field of administration and finances while governing the country.

In the meantime, especially during the reign of 'Umar, the Muslim empire began to acquire organizational skills. In occupied territories the administrative systems of their predecessors were maintained, together with the familiar officials in their usual places. A *walî*, the caliph's military and political governor, was given charge of every province, assisted by an *'âmil*, an official responsible for keeping finances in good order. As a security measure, a policy of donating lands to the Arabs was pursued; this created a class of landowners ready to defend the territories in which their properties lay. The army played an important role, organized in *giund*: outposts scattered over the single provinces or large concentrations of troops in the new military bases. Coexisting with the Muslims was the *ra'aya* class, those of the conquered peoples that by rejecting conversion had become liable, as protectees (*dhimmî*), to the payment of tribute money. This was later to become a polltax known as *gizya*, whose entity varied according to the circumstances of the protectee. A tax known as *kharâg* was levied on properties that remained in the hands of their owners. Where unconditional surrender had taken place, lands might simply be confiscated or left provisionally in the hands of the proprietors, usually in exchange for payment of this tax. Bishops continued to run the civil affairs of their communities. In this way, the theocratic empire that gradually took shape under the caliphate of 'Umar came to be made up of two classes divided by reason of religious and, consequently, of political outlook. The Muslims formed the military caste and its generals and, as governors for the caliph and heads of the community, led prayer. Only civil administration was in the hands of an official directly responsible to central power.

The only tax payed by Muslims was the *zakâ*. One fifth of the booty of war was levied by the state, in addition to lands abandoned by the proprietors. What remained, inhabitants included, was divided among the soldiers who had taken part in the conquest.

A fierce struggle centered on the caliphate in this period, exposing the discords that characterized the Muslim world. The great problem was that of caliphal succession. In 644, at the height of his activity, 'Umar was stabbed to death by a slave. The ruler elected to replace him after much hesitation was Uthmân, an 'Umayyad of the ancient Meccan aristocracy, who had long opposed the Prophet and only allied himself to the Muslims of Medina at the last moment. In 655, 'Uthmân in his turn was killed and the same day 'Alì was elected caliph. Only Syria refused to acknowledge his authority. The hostility of the Prophet's widow overcome and the support of Egypt certain, 'Alì seemed to have fate on his side when the clash came with the governor of Syria, Mu'âwiya, head of the 'Umayyad clan and a relative of the deceased caliph.

The battle took place at Siffîn in 657: all seemed lost for Mu'âwiya when, on the advice of the old Ibn al'-As, the Syrian soldiers hoisted pages of the Koran in the air on the tips of their lances. Such was the piety of 'Alì that he laid down his weapons and began negotiations. Many of his followers broke away from him at this point and moved over to the camp of Harûrâ, taking the name of Khawârig (Those who broke away). They were to become his fiercest enemies. The results of this arbitration are not known to us, but Mu'âwiya proclaimed himself caliph in Jerusalem in 660. Six months later 'Alì was assassinated in the mosque of Kûfa by a kharigite. His followers were to form the *shî'at 'Alì*, the party of 'Alì, and become known as

Shi'ites, that is to say those who at all cost remain faithful to 'Alì and his descendants, accepting the principles of the imamate. Imam, a title that rightfully belonged to 'Ali and his descendants, unlike the Sunnite caliph, did not indicate merely the temporal head of a politico-religious community in as much as the divine inspiration of the Prophet was perpetuated through the holder of this title. The temporal authority of the caliph in no way invalidated that of the Alid imam, a title that, if legitimately held, carried with it an aura of infallibility.

The 'Umayyads came to power with Mu'âwiya, and the capital was transferred to Damascus; the caliphate, while preserving the fiction of election, became hereditary. Notwithstanding the disturbance created by struggles with the Shiites and the hostility between the two powerful Qaisid and Kalbite tribes, by the time the caliph 'Abd al-Malik died in 705 peace reigned in the empire with the provinces reunited under steady administration, the monetary system consolidated and trade flourishing with India, east Africa and distant China. This era of peace lasted throughout the reigns of al-Walîd, Sulaymân and 'Umar ibn 'Abd al-'Azîz and the empire attained its maximum degree of expansion; the Arabs penetrated the Maghrib, conquered Spain and pushed on over the Pyrenees; they penetrated the Punjab and Central Asia, and reached the frontiers of China. Towns were built, contacts with the conquered peoples enriched, and Arabic was recognized as the dominant tongue; centers of intellectual activity arose in Syria and Iraq, while the theological sciences flourished at Medina.

Strife returned to the empire under Yazîd II and Hishâm. The death knell sounded for the dynasty when Al-Walîd II, who had succeeded to Hishâm in 743, was murdered in his castle at Bakhra, south of Palmyra. Its authority had been shattered in the East by Alid preaching, encouraged, especially in Khorâsân, by the 'Abbasids. Their prestige was derived from an ancestor, 'Abd Allâh ibn 'Abbas, cousin both to the Prophet and to 'Alì. A descendant of his had laid claim to the Shi'ite imamate, a title subsequently inherited by his son Ibrâhîm who, in 746, now sent the Iranian-born Abû Muslim to Khorâsân where he acquired a large following, especially among the peasants. Kûfa became the centre of 'Abbasid agitation. In 750, the last 'Umayyad caliph, Marwân II, was defeated on the right bank of the Great Zâb and fled to Egypt with his enemies in pursuit; the Syrian towns fell without opposing resistence. This was a triumph for the black banners of Abû l-'Abbâs al-Saffâh, Ibrâhîm's son, who ordered the massacre of the 'Umayyad family entire. It was also the victory of the Persian element and, in general, of the non-Arabs of recent conversion who brought to government an official aristocracy, an aristocracy based not on religious merit or noble lineage, but on the authority conferred by the prince. The absolutist empire of the 'Abbasids was to change the course of the evolution of the history of Islam.

The Conquest of the Maghrib

The history of Arab expansion in Africa and in the extreme Maghrib is markedly different from that of the conquest of Egypt and Asia. The crucial factor contributing to this is the diversity of composition of the population. The authority of Byzantium had never made itself felt over North Africa in its entirety: it terminated with the meridian of Shatt-al-Hadan, to the west, and resumed only at Ceuta (Sabta). The rest of the country was under Berber control. Some of the Berbers had submitted to the influence of Carthage and later to that of Rome, but the great majority of them had had no contact at all with either of the two civilizations; theirs was a patriarchal and essentially pastoral way of life untouched by urbanization and formed of an infinite number of tiny political entities representing the tribes and villages.

The predominance of the Berber component had been one of the obstacles in the path of Justinian's imperial restoration. The exarchs were continually obliged to deal with uprisings that could only be quelled from the towns, whose walls often set the limit to their authority and to the garrisons' capacity to keep order. From the outset the difficulties the Arabs met with in their own conquest of Africa came not from the Byzantines but from the Berbers.

The complete conquest of Ifrîqiya was a late venture because the first caliphs viewed the undertaking with disfavor. «As long as my eyes can shed tears I shall send no one» was 'Umar's reply to 'Amr's request for permission to continue his march to the West. Only after the establishment of the 'Umayyad dynasty in the East did systematic conquest begin under 'Uqba ibn Nâfi', a figure soon to enter legend as the symbol of Fighting Islam.

Constans II, emperor of Byzantium, had just been assassinated and his successor, Constantine Pogonot, with all available troops engaged against a usurper in Sicily, had left Africa ungarrisoned. Lack of protection from the Greek garrisons gave 'Uqba his first triumph, over the Berber Christians, who were unprepared for resistance. It was he who created, in 43/664, the first permanent Muslim settlement in the Maghrib — Kairouan, built on a treeless plain and destined to remain the capital of the Muslim West for centuries.

'Uqba suffered a period of disgrace, but on returning to power in 681, he captured Kusaila, leader of the Auraba Berbers, and dragged him in chains to Tlemsen. With Kusaila in captivity, he proceeded from Tlemsen to Tangiers where the waves of the Atlantic Ocean prevented him, to his regret, from carrying the Truth any further. But a martyr's death awaited him on his return journey in 683 at Tahuda in the vicinity of Biskra, to the southwest of the Auras mountains. Here Kusaila, newly escaped from captivity, attacked, and a massacre took place. At the head of Berbers and Byzantines Kusaila entered Kairouan, to remain its master for three years. The Arabs had to abandon all territories extending beyond Barqa, while the Byzantine garrisons consolidated their positions at Susa, Annâba, and in a number of citadels in the interior. Newly converted to Islam, the Berbers gave themselves over to apostasy. An abortive attempt at reconquest by Zuhair ibn Qays, a former companion of 'Uqba, came to nothing, and the Muslims remained excluded from Africa.

Meanwhile, the Auraba had been supplanted as leaders of Berber resistance by the Giarâwa tribe, members of the great Zenata family. Nomad camel drivers with no experience of the Byzantines, the Giarâwa lived in the eastern regions of the Auras under the rule of a queen. This woman, al-Kâhina, a figure no less legendary than Kusaila, was to bring new strategies to the struggle. As a consequence, seven years later, Hassân ibn al-Nu'mân set out from the West to reconquer the lost province. The Berber prophetess defeated him on the banks of the river Nini, not far from Bagai, and forced him to beat a retreat to Tripoli. Shortly after, with the aid of a great fleet that overpowered that of the Byzantines, Carthage was taken by assault. From that moment the rulers of the waves in the western Mediterranean were the Arabs. Al-Kâkina continued her policy of systematic devastation of the countryside and demolition of the towns until, possibly in 702, the Berbers were crushed in a great battle at Tabarka and she, their leader, was pursued and killed at a well that from that date was to be known as Bîr al-Kâhina.

The country had been one of the chosen lands of Christianity but for all that it was not an exclusively urban phenomenon, the faith did not survive the Arab conquest. Christian communities had preserved their identities and were to continue to do so in Syria, Lebanon, Egypt and Spain, but here, they disappeared before the advance of Islam. Adopted with fervor by the Berbers, Islam was often to lead them to martyrdom. The impact of the conquest, together with Islam's tolerance towards the converted, led to mass conversion and often a return to the faith of the fathers as soon as the Arab horsemen had departed.

Sidi 'Uqba had founded Kairouan with the express purpose of combating apostasy. Its prestige as a great center of learning still lay in the future, but at this time it nonetheless played a strategic role as a military outpost and religious center. Preachers of conversion set out from here and it was a symbol for the converted.

Twenty years later Mûsâ ibn Nusayr carried the practice of conversion into the extreme Maghrib, to work for the moral conquest of the Berbers who, amalgamating with the victors, eventually became the most reliable material for subsequent conquests[6].

It was especially under 'Umar ibn 'Abd al-'Azîz, an extremely devout and religious caliph, that method was brought to the task of Islamization of Africa and crucial to his ends was the zeal of Ismâ'îl ibn 'Abd Allâh, who, with ten others, dedicated himself wholly to preaching. The consequence, and crowning achievement of Islamization, was Arabization, consisting not so much in the immigration of Arab groups as the adoption by the Berbers of a civilization that assimilated them to the immigrants. The most characteristic feature of this civilization was the Arab language; its diffusion in North Africa truly marked the start of a new era. This does not mean that Arabic supplanted the Berber tongue, as the Camitic idiom survived in outlying areas that were difficult to penetrate, but it certainly brought an end to Latin, the language of the towns, of administration and of the Church.

The policy of violence and rapacious taxation practiced by the Arabs in respect of the Berbers soon brought storm clouds to the horizon. The assassination of the governor of Tangiers in 740 was the signal for revolt, and the entire Maghrib rose up in arms. Its first leader, Maysara, was killed, but although the 'Umayyad caliph sent reinforcements, they proved inadequate to prevent the Berber troops under a new leader, Khaled ibn Hamid, from advancing on Shelif where they were met by an army composed of Arabs of pure race. In the ensuing battle, called the Battle of the Nobles, the Arab general and all the heroes in his company were massacred. Revolt became general, imbued for the first time with religious sentiment inspired by the Kharigite doctrine.

The means by which Kharigism penetrated the Maghrib and spread are shrouded in obscurity but there are no doubts at all that the principle of the absolute sovereignty of the people, whose consequent right it was to depose an unjust caliph or imam at any moment, reflected the aspirations of the Berber peoples. As had been the case with the *Shî'a* among the

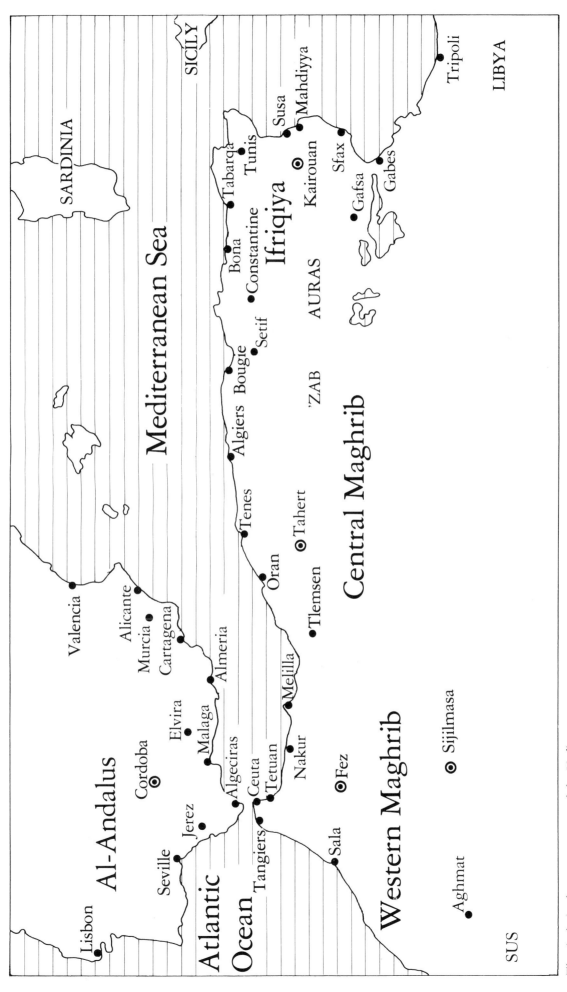

The Arabs in the western sector of the Mediterranean

Persians, adhesion to kharigism provided an outlet for opposition to growing despotism and state bureaucracy and for the desire for more egalitarian political and social structures.

By 750 almost the whole of North Africa was Kharigite, but by the mid-tenth century the majority was to return to Muslim orthodoxy and few communities would remain faithful to Kharigite principles. Although the new governor managed to crush Berber resistance in 742 at Asnâm in the vicinity of Kairouan, it was clear by this time that the fate of North Africa lay, from thence onward, in Berber rather than Arab hands.

The struggle was significant because it allowed Islam to put down firmer roots among the as yet unsubdued tribes, and Kharigism proved a convenient vehicle not only for the major diffusion of the new faith but also one by which a better understanding of the tenets of the faith was acquired, productive, moreover, of a number of Berber theologians, especially in Gabal Nafûsa and in the Tâhert region. Islamization emerged strengthened, while Kharigite presence acted as a stimulus for orthodox theology and indirectly contributed to the famous school of Kairouan that was to produce so many brillant minds in the tenth century.

The Maghrib in the Abbasid period

With the transfer of the caliphate from Damascus to Baghdad, a consequence of the Abbasid rise to power, Islam entered a new period in its history. The central area of the Abbasid empire from Mesopotamia to Syria was also the obligatory world trade route between the Mediterranean and the Indian Ocean, the crossroads of the great African, European and Asiatic continents. The salient features of the civilization of the Abbasid world up to the eleventh century were flourishing commercial activity, vivacity of urban life, and cultural development.

But there were also contradictory aspects: political and financial crises, social, religious and ethnic crises. The area of territory covered by the Abbasid empire vast by the standards of the time as much as by those of today, was a contributory factor in weakening the ties of dependence on the center and the bond of unity with it: in different ways, autonomy beckoned to the two extremities.

To the east, the empire, bordering on the steppes, lay vulnerable to the hordes of nomad invaders; from these regions there came the Turkish populations, slowly to be assimilated to Islam and, later, the Mongols, who were to give what had by that time become an empire in decline its final death blow by destroying Baghdad and murdering the caliph in 1258.

In the West, the call for autonomy was determined more by such factors as local ethnic distinctions, the belligerent encounter with the Christian world, the specific mode of adoption of Islam and the provenance of its various governors. Here, autonomy soon became synonymous with separation, the most radical form of this being the constitution of the autonomous caliphates. But even in these extreme cases strong ties with the original fount of Islamic history lingered on, variously expressed through nostalgia, feelings of inferiority or even by the proud declaration of personal successes. Despite political and schismatic divisions Islam continued to be a great unifying entity, a perennial source of common nourishment, and of relevant experience, and a criterion to measure up to.

This tension between personal identity and aspirations on the one hand and, on the other, unity of the Islamic community with its obedience to the caliphate, is the distinguishing mark of the history of Western Islam, especially in North Africa where the start of the Abbasid period coincided with a movement towards a new balance of political power.

The emirs sent by Baghdad were unable to ensure obedience to the Abbasids even in the eastern sector of the Maghrib where, in 880, an Arab governor of Mzab, Ibrâhîm ibn al-Aghlab had been installed as governor of Ifrîqiya by Harûn al-Rashîd. A form of independent dynasty developed, mindful of Abbasid sovereignty but not always fully subservient to it. The dynasty is of historical importance chiefly for the conflict with the Shi'ites that brought about its downfall and for the overseas enterprises that led to the conquest of Syria.

The center of its unstable dominion was Kairouan where, under strong Eastern influence, Maghriban architecture originated. There are no surviving palaces to represent it, its existence is only perpetuated by the great sanctuaries of the town and by those of Tunis. From these and from the fortified monasteries that rose up along the coast, and from objects of domestic art that have come down to us we may gain an understanding of what the civilization of that time was. The complexity of styles in the Great Mosque of Kairouan points to numerous sources of influence: the plan is of the basilican type while the courtyard conforms to the Arab model; the square minaret is certainly of Syrian provenance, while the form and roofing of the arches are eloquent of contacts with Egypt; the structure of the domes comes from Mesopotamia, and we owe the carved decorations to the Berbers.

But Kairouan was not only a model of Muslim urban life in North Africa, it was also an important center of scholarship. Under the Aghlabids intellectual life flourished in the fields of theology and jurisprudence, but the first productions of Maghriban poetry also began to appear. The spiritual atmosphere was one of religious devotion and men of religion were regarded with respect and admiration in a society that was experiencing a period of asceticism. *Ribat* were built everywhere to give shelter to men in prayer and in battle array and the number of schools multiplied to house disciples coming from the East and from Spain. In this context questions of religion inform every aspect of the daily lives of an entire people, not just a class of intellectuals.

Of the four juridical schools formed by the *Ahl al-sunna*, the «Followers of Tradition» or Sunnaites, two were influential in Ifrîqiya, the Hanafite and the Mâlikite. The earlier of the two, the more flexible, valorizing reasoning by analogy (*qiyâs*), was founded by the Iranian Abû Hanîfa. Mâlikism, founded by Mâlik ibn Anas, an Arab from Medina, was brought to Ifrîqiya by the future leader of the invading forces in Sicily, Asad ibn al-Furât. Advocating a strictly literal interpretation of the Scriptures and hostile to any more rational interpretation, this, of the two, became the dominant form.

From the start of the tenth century to the middle of the eleventh the Maghrib had to adjust to continual political changes, the first of these derived from the rise to power of the Fatimid dynasty in Ifrîqiya.

The Fatimids made lengthy preparations for their conquest of the Maghrib. At the end of the ninth century reconnaissance work was carried out by Abû Allâh al-Shî'î, sent as a preacher of the Shi'ite faith and to pave the way for the Mahdî. As a missionary (*da'i*) he converted his hosts, the Kutama, to a unifying religious ideal and, at his instigation, they set out to conquer Ifrîqiya. The Fatimid scout entered Kairouan in 909 and established himself in the Raqqâda palace. In Syria, 'Ubaid Allâh took the title of Mahdî and left to join his *da'i*. As al-Mahdî he ceremoniously entered Kairouan in 910, assuming the title of amîr al-mu'minîn, Lord of the Faithful. From al-Mahdiya, the new capital where he established his residence, he governed a state that was to maintain its hold over the Eastern Mediterranean for centuries.

It was not the Maghrib in itself that interested the new dynasty; confident of eventually conquering the East, what it looked for was acknowledgment of its new status by the Muslim world in its entirety. The zenith of Fatimid domination was reached with Al-Mu'izz, whose rule began in 953. Subsequent to the conquest of the extreme Maghrib as far as Fez, Ceuta and Tangiers, the cherished ambitions of the dynasty were crowned with success when Egypt fell to them, an easy prey, in 969. Four years later the Fatimid capital was transferred to Egypt where, in the vicinity of al-Fustât, building began on a military colony to be used also as a residence, and on the Great Mosque of al-Azhar. The residence took the name of al-Qâhira al-Mu'izziya (The Victorious Town of al-Mu'izz). The whole of North Africa from this residence — Cairo — to the Atlantic coast was now united under a single rule.

Government of North Africa in Fatimid name was entrusted to Bologuin, a Berber, the son of Ziri, a faithful supporter and member of the Sanhâga tribe. But the bonds of vassalage proved irksome, especially when Bologuin's son, al-Mansûr, inherited the Zirid kingdom. His struggle to shake off the Fatimid yoke left the extreme Maghrib in the hands of his adversaries, the Zenata, allies of the 'Umayyad caliph. The Fatimids were no longer powerful enough to send an army of their own to intervene, but nonetheless found the way to take their revenge on this disloyal vassal. On the instigation of the vizier of the Fatimid caliph a certain number of bedouin tribes encamped in the Nile Valley, in enforced isolation as punishment for the numerous plundering exploits they had been guilty of, were encouraged to migrate to North Africa. These groups, the Banû Hilal and the Banû Sulaim, set out for Cirenaica in 442/1050-1051 and the following year penetrated Ifrîqiya where they defeated the Zirid troops at Gabal Haydarân and laid waste Kairouan. The Zirids sought refuge in al-Mahdîya but their resistence proved vain, leaving the entire country open to devastation.

The Hilalian invasion, by increasing the Arab-Berber ethnic component that still populates much of North Africa today, helped to liberate the Maghrib from its subjection to the East and to the Fatimid caliphate of Cairo; but the consequences of a second nomadic invasion a few years later were to be very different.

In this case the nomads were Berbers who had lived in the regions of the Western Sahara for many centuries and who were known to the peoples of the north as the *al-mulaththamun*, the Veiled Men. Later they were to receive the name of *al-murâbitûn*, Almoravids, from the *ribât* of Lower Senegal where these Saharan camel drivers received a military and religious training that transformed them into fighters for the faith. The cause of their migration may be attributed with certainty to religious zeal.

The Maghriban 'Abd Allâh ibn Yâsîn, had persuaded the chieftains of the local tribes to found a military convent (*ribât*) on an island in the Senegal river where, under his leadership,

30

life might be conducted in accordance with the strictest rules of Mâlikism. The virtue and discipline practiced in the *ribât* soon drew to it over a thousand of the faithful, all resolved to impose strict observance on unbelievers and tepid Muslims by force of arms. After the initial successes, Yâsîn left his followers in the hands of one of his first converts, Yahyâ ibn 'Umar, of the Lamtuna tribe, later to be replaced by his brother, Abû Bakr ibn 'Umar.

On the death in combat of ibn Yâsîn in 1059, absolute power fell to Abû Bakr, under the watchful eyes of the *fuqahâ*, the jurisconsults specialized in Mâlikite law, who held a place in the emir's council and accompanied him wherever he went, ready for consultation on every occasion and to give a juridical opinion, *fatwa*, that was often to be binding.

With the continued growth of the community, Abû Bakr decided to found a new capital to the north of the High Atlas. Building began on this town, Marrakesh, in 462/1070. But in January 1071 Abû Bakr, called away to deal with insubordination in the south, left power in the hands of his cousin, Yûsuf ibn Tashfîn, who began to consider Morocco as his own from that moment.

Ibn Tâshfîn made his authority felt throughout the extreme Maghrib at once. Fez was captured in 467/1075, followed by Tlemsen; he advanced as far as Algiers, without, however, venturing into the Kabilia Mountains. As we shall see in the following chapter, a request by the Muslims of Spain for aid in unifying Islamic possessions there led him to annex the territories one after another, an act that changed the course of Almoravid history.

It is true that Andalusian comfort together with a purely formal religious life, void of true content and reduced to interminable canonical and juridical discussions, had caused Almoravid military and spiritual vigor to decline. They no longer had the strength to resist the movement gaining impetus among the Almohads in a valley of the High Atlas.

In c. 512/1118, a Berber from Sûs, Muhammed ibn 'Abd Allâh ibn Tûmart, returned from the East after traveling for years, like many others, in search of the Truth. He seems to have dedicated himself chiefly to studying the theology of al-Ash'ari, the founder of orthodox scholasticism (*kalâm*), but he had acquired a knowledge of the doctrines of al-Ghazâlî and was convinced that Maghriban life was not what it should be. The moral laxity of Marrakesh scandalized him so much when he was there that the sight of the emir's sister riding unveiled on horseback through the town, accompanied by her women, caused him to throw her down. Islam imposes this censorial duty on every believer: whosoever witnesses a practice condemned by religion is obliged to intervene personally to bring it to an end. If too weak for direct action, verbal condemnation must be resorted to and if prevented from this, condemnation must be expressed in the heart. For al-Ghazâlî, the suppression of shameful acts is the corner stone of Islam.

Ibn Tûmart met the skill of the Almoravid *fuqahâ* in finding scholastic answers to every juridical subtlety, by upholding the original sources of the faith, the Koran and the prophetic Tradition of Medina. In 518/1124, in the heart of the High Atlas, he founded a community of like believers who took the name of *al-muwahiddûn* «Those who proclaim the Oneness of God» or Almohads. In opposition to what he called the anthropomorphism of the Almoravid theologians he declared himself the defender of a concept called *tawhîd*, unitarianism.

This was the theology already preached by al-Ghazâlî in the East; but whereas the great master at forty years of age, coming to the conviction that intellectualism could not lead to the Truth, had abandoned his teaching at the Madrasa Nizâmiya in Baghdad to take up the staff of the dervish pilgrim and preach the love of God wherever his wanderings might lead him, Ibn Tûmart was prepared to enforce the triumph of Truth. Having gained recognition for himself as the Mahdî come to restore order to the world, he attacked Marrakesh in 524/1130, but was repulsed. When he died shortly after, he was succeeded by his disciple, 'Abd al-Mu'mîn, a potter from the village of Tagra who was to be the true founder of the temporal power of the Almohad dynasty.

It was in the Maghrib that 'Abd al-Mu'mîn first appropriated the title that belonged by tradition solely to the Eastern caliphs *amir al-mu'minîn*, Commander of the Faithful. In a few short years he made himself master of the mountainous and Saharan regions of Morocco. With the defeat of the last Almoravid sovereign, Tâshfîn ibn 'Alî, he soon became overlord of all Almoravid territories and in 545/1150 received a delegation of Andalusian notables eager to be free of the Almoravid and ready to recognize him as sovereign. Two years later the conquest of Ifrîqiya began, and was concluded in 1161. 'Abd al-Mu'mîn was making preparations to cross over into Spain when he died in the fortress of Ribât al-Eath in 1163. His successor was his son, Abû Ya'qûb Yûsuf who, having established peace in Ifrîqiya, took his army to Spain and died there from wounds sustained in the siege of Santarem.

The Almohads made enormous efforts to meet the challenge of the Reconquest and regain the Iberian peninsula for Islam but their great conquests slowly transformed the character of their empire. The religious fervor that had brought them so many victories revealed a tendency to conservatism and formalization. Al-Mansûr's son, a timid and solitary figure who came to power in 1199, lacked the strength needed to face up to such important changes as were taking place. The Banû Ghâniya tribe, representing an upsurge of the Almoravid clan, was making frequent incursions into Ifrîqiya; the Almohad troops had met with defeat at Christian hands in 1212 at Las Navas di Tolosa; discouraged by these events the ruler abdicated in favor of his sixteen-year-old son, Yûsuf al-Mustansir, who by reason of age was unequal to the task of restoring order in the all-too-vast domains of his ancestors where civil war was soon to break out. His successors continued to rule in Morocco while even Seville, the capital of Muslim Spain, succumbed to the Christians; but in 1269 their own capital, Marrakesh, was taken by the Banû Marin, Berbers of the Zenata family. The fruits remained however, of a civilization that had shown itself capable of bearing the torch of Truth once it had been handed to them by the Arabs of the East. Poets, historians, theologians and philosophers once thronged to the court of Marrakesh. Every honor was accorded to Ibn Tufail and Ibn Rushd (Averroes). The stature of what Islamic civilization made from this blending of the pure Arab tongue, the grace of Andalusia and the austerity of the Berbers is beyond question.

It also produced great works of art, although there are few surviving examples of these. The remains of Tîmnâl, of Rabât, and the minaret and prayer hall of the Qutûbiya of Marrakesh, are in no way inferior to the finest creations of the East. The harmony and robust beauty of this art claim our attention. It is an art in which all response to the living world is translated in terms of decoration. And this is a tribute to the syncretic capacity of this unique power that brought unity to the entire Muslim West.

Notes

[1] B. Lewis, *The Arabs in History*, London 1950.
[2] F.M. Abel, *Histoire de la Palestine depuis la conquête d'Alexandrie jusqu'à l'invasion arabe*, Paris 1952, 2 vol.; H. Lammens, *La Syrie, précis historique*, Beirut 1921, 2 vol.; M.J. De Goeje, *Memoires sur la conquête de la Syrie*, Leiden 1866.
[3] F. Gabrieli, *Gli Arabi*, Florence 1954, 59-61.
[4] Ph. Hitti, *Storia degli Arabi*, Florence 1966, 173-174.
[5] A.J. Butler, *The Arab Conquest of Egypt*, Oxford 1902; G. Wiet, *Précis de l'histoire d'Egypte*, Cairo 1932.
[6] Ibn 'Idhârî, *al-Bayân al-mughrib fi akhbâr al-Maghrib*, ed. R. Dozy, Leiden 1848-'51; Fr.tr. by E. Fagnan, Algiers 1901-'04, I, 35-36.

CHAPTER TWO
ISLAM ON EUROPEAN SOIL: POLITICAL ISSUES AND MILITARY CAMPAIGNS

The Conquest of Spain

On the death of Wittiza in 710, the opposition party in the Visigothic Kingdom of Spain elected duke Roderic, the governor of Baetica residing at Cordoba, as their king. It was in the course of his reign that the Arabs turned their attention to Spain and crossed the straits in 711.

Among the causes of the invasion all Arab historians point to the episode of «Count Julian,» exarch of Septem (Ceuta), the last Byzantine possession in Africa after the fall of Carthaginensis. The exarch had thrown in his lot with the party of Akhila, Wittiza's son, whom Roderic had entirely dispossessed. The story is told by Ibn al-Athîr: «It was the custom among the rulers of Spain to send their offspring of either sex to the town of Toledo solely for the purpose of waiting on the king who resided there; when they grew up the king accorded each of them a dowry and they intermarried. During the reign of Roderic a daughter of Julian, governor of Algeciras, Ceuta and other places, came to the court where, finding her attractive, the king raped her. When the news of this violence reached her father it so enraged him that he sent word to Mûsâ ibn Nusayr, governor of Ifrîqiya in the name of al-Walîd ibn 'Abd al-Malik, offering his allegiance in exchange for aid. Mûsâ agreed to this proposal and no sooner had Julian received satisfactory assurances in respect of his own welfare and that of his kin, than he opened up his territories to the newcomer, furnished him with a description of Spain and pledged him to invade. This took place at the end of the year 90 (November 708). Mûsâ sent reports of his conquests to al-Walîd, pointing out what God offered in consequence of Julian's proposals. The caliph replied: 'Take a few troops to reconnoiter the country without exposing the Muslims to the terrors of the sea'[1]. Mûsâ's assurance that this was not a sea, merely a channel the other side of which was perfectly visible convinced the caliph to allow a number of detachments to be sent to attempt the enterprise». The first Muslim landing therefore took place in the month of Ramadan in the year 91 (July 710) with four hundred infantrymen and a hundred horsemen, led by a Berber officer named Tarif ibn Malluk.

After carrying out raids along the coast, Tarif returned to Africa well provided with booty

37

and slaves. Pleased with the success of the expedition and following Julian's advice once more, Mûsâ decided on invasion. Command was entrusted to one of his freedmen, Tarik, governor of Tangiers and Mûsâ's lieutenant general in the Maghrib al-Aqsa.

With Carteya on the Guadarranque estuary taken and Count Julian defending a fortified base set up facing the «Green Isle» (al-Gazîra al-khadra'), where Algeciras would later stand, the Muslim army together with reinforcements newly arrived from Africa then defeated Bencius, a cousin of Roderic. The king who meanwhile had been fighting the Franks and the Basques in the north of Spain, assembled a large army, certainly more powerful than that of the Muslims, and clashed with the enemy on the shores of Lake Janda, linked to the sea by the river Barbate, between Medina Sidonia and Vejer de la Frontera in the province of Cadiz. Akhila's partizans, led by Bishop Oppa and Sisebert, betrayed Roderic in the conviction that the Muslims, satisfied with the rich spoils that fell to them, would withdraw. Muslim victory was proclaimed on the twentieth day of the month of ramadan in the year 92 (19 July 711). The last Visigothic king disappeared, and the battle decided the fate of Spain. The Arabs advanced on Seville, took Ecija and laid siege to Cordoba. The town surrendered two months later when the population spontaneously opened the gates of the town and warmly welcomed the victors.

But it was chiefly the Jews, victims of ill-treatment in the last decades of Visigothic rule, who offered the invaders wholehearted support from this moment onwards.

Tarik, following the advice of Julian, but disobeying orders from his superior, sent detachments to Granada, Malaga and Tudmir while he himself advanced on Jaen and Toledo. Finding the Visigothic capital abandoned by its inhabitants, who had taken refuge beyond the mountains, he left it in the hands of the Jews while he proceeded in the direction of Guadalajara, crossing the Sierra of Guadarrama to carry out raids in Galicia as far as the town of Astorga.

Mûsâ, irritated by the behaviour of Tarik and jealous of the successes gained in such a short time by a mere *mawla*, left his son 'Abd Allâh to govern in his place at Kairouan and embarked for Spain in the month of ramadan of 93 (June 712). He was in command of a large army, made up this time of Arabs, many of whom were of noble lineage. He followed a different route from that of Tarik, capturing Medina-Sidonia, the fortresses of Carmona and Alcalà and, after many months of siege, Seville. Merida capitulated to him on the last day of ramadan in 94 (June 713) and he then sent messengers to Damascus to inform the caliph of his successes. After the conquest of Saragossa, where a mosque cathedral was founded, both Tarik and Mûsâ received their orders to leave Spain and proceed to Syria. They set out in the summer of 95/714, leaving 'Abd al-Azîz as governor of Spain.

'Abd al-Azîz, a son of Mûsâ, complied with his father's orders and completed the conquest of the peninsula, only to be accused of abuse of power after two short years of office and assassinated by officers acting on behalf of the caliph. He is believed by some historians to have married Roderic's widow, the princess Ailo, who converted to Islam and took the name of Umm'Asim.

Arab governors replaced one another with incredible rapidity and once nominated no hesitation over a course of action might be permitted, the conquest had to be consolidated, revolts that occasionally broke out among the vanquished had to be suppressed and occupation attempted of places lying beyond the Pyrenees in Frankish territory. After al-Hurr, who transferred the capital from Seville to Cordoba, the subsequent period was marked by contrasts between the Arab regents governing in the name of the caliph of Damascus and the Berbers who, for all that they had been the main strategists of the conquest, were the object of discrimination, obliged to pay a tax that by rights should only have been applied to non-Muslims.

As we have seen, there were strained relations between Arabs and Berbers even in the Maghrib. There were immediate repercussions to the great Berber revolt of 740 on African soil, on the other side of the strait; here, it gained ground first in the northern regions and then swiftly spread south to take its toll of the Arabs congregated in Cordoban territory.

The Spanish revolt was to be put down by the general of the Syrian army who had taken refuge in the town of Ceuta together with the vanguard of his troops. Balg ibn Bishr al-Kushairi obtained permission to cross the straits from the Cordoban government and after suppressing all Berber opposition in the peninsula inaugurated a regime of harsh repressive measures.

The peninsula in the early years of the history of Muslim Spain was also torn by rivalries among the Arabs themselves: Yemenites and Mudarates, Kalbites and Qaisids or Syrians and Medinese. Belligerency seemed placated by the victory of the Kalbite emir Abû-1-Khattâr by which the Syrians gained control of the southern regions between Murcia and the Algarve, but hostility flared up once more and the Kalbites were defeated by their enemies in the battle of Guadalete in 127/745 that led to the proclamation of Thuwâba as emir. Two years later, Yûsuf Ibn 'Abd Rahmân al-Fihri was nominated governor, the last *wali* of Spain prior to the arrival of the 'Umayyads.

According to both Arab and Christian chroniclers, the Visigothic Kingdom held out only in the Asturias at Oviedo where, in the chain of mountains known as the Picos de Europa, and in the Covadonga valley, Roderic's successor, Pelayo, put up such tenacious resistence as to enter legend.

Another pocket of resistence to the Arab invasion was formed in the north of Aragon under the leadership of Garcia Ximenez who took possession of the town of Ainsa. Another small principate allied to Aragon was created in Navarre under the leadership of Iñigo Arista. However, the Reconquest effectively began when Pelayo's son-in-law, Alfonso I the Catholic, Duke of Cantabria, took advantage of the Muslim rivalries to raid Galicia and win it back from Islam together with the north of Portugal and the southern slopes of the Cantabrian Cordilleras, thereby opening up the Duero Valley to the Christian armies. When he died in 758 the Christians had recovered the Asturias, Santander, Burgos, Leon and Galicia. A kind of no-man's-land, the Marches, lay between the two domains, vulnerable to raids from either faction.

Such was the situation that 'Abd al-Rahmân ibn Mu'âwiya found on his arrival in the Iberian peninsula, having survived the wholesale massacre of the 'Ummayad family ordered by the founder of the 'Abbasid dynasty. He was born to a Berber slavewoman in 113/731 at Damascus and had managed to save his life only by swimming across the Euphrates, together with his sister and his four year-old son Sulaymân. After some years of roaming he was allowed to settle among his mother's people, the Nafza Berbers. It was in this period that he began to take Spain into consideration and in 754 sent his freedman Badr to the Syrians of Damascus and Qinnasrîn with the news that Elvira and Jaen were still faithful to the 'Umayyads. Spain was still torn between the Qaisids and the Kalbites, the moment looked favourable. With the support of 'Ubaid Allâh and Ibn Khâlid, leaders of the Damascene Syrians, of Yûsuf ibn Bukht, leader of the Qinnasrîn Syrians and of the Yemenite faction at war with the Qaisids, 'Abd al-Rahmân ad-Dâkhil (the Immigrant) landed at Almuñecar in the month of rabi'I of 138 (August 755) to be greeted by the mass desertion of al-Fihri's troops eager to join with the prince whose cause won even Berber support. After entering Seville in mid-March 756, to the enthusiasm of the population, he advanced on Cordoba and decided on Maisara on the Guadalquivir, at the gates of the town, as the scene of the battle. Al-Fihri saved his life by fleeing. On Friday 14 March, a feast day and the anniversary of the battle of Marg Râhit by which the 'Umayyads had come to power in the East, 'Abd al-Rahmân was proclaimed emir of al-Andalus in the Mosque of Cordoba.

He opened the frontiers to all the surviving 'Umayyads that might wish to take refuge in the peninsula and set himself to establishing peace in the state. The system of administration he adopted was that of the governors who had preceded him, with the introduction of such minor modifications as might adapt it to the new reality he planned to bring about: an independent Spanish Muslim state, all political ties to the 'Abbasid caliphate severed and close relations established with the Arab-Berber West.

The country, following the 'Umayyad system in Syria, was divided into districts (*kûwar*), each of which was under the jurisdiction of a governor (*wali* or *a'mil*) who was expected to reside in the main town (*ka'ida*). This form of administration lasted until the end of the caliphate.

Al-Rahmân recruited a standing army of professional soldiers, formed mainly of North African Berbers, whose ranks were swelled by large numbers of non-Muslim soldiers. He never adopted other titles than those of *malik* (king) and *amir* (emir), followed by the mention *ibn al-khala'if* (Son of the Caliphs), and ruled his state with firmness, intelligence and the occasional touch of despotism, such as would be characteristic centuries later of the fifteenth century princes in dealing with their feudatories. Under his rule, Cordoba became a great Muslim capital and building was begun on the Great Mosque in 169/785. The former governors' residence of the Goths was replaced by a new palace built between the Guadalquivir and the mosque. Here he set up court, abandoning al-Rusafa, a great residence on the banks of a stream some three kilometers from the capital, nostalgically named after a summer residence of the caliph Hishâm sited between Palmyra and the Euphrates. A great

On the preceding page: Gate in the north front of the caliphal Castle of Gormaz (Soria), tenth century. On this page: the hill from which the castle dominates the plain and two views of the still well-conserved walls. On the following page: two gates in the south front, the one on the left with a horseshoe arch.

Facing: The Great Square, the walls and a view of the ruined Alcazar at the eastern extremity of the Castle of Gormaz. Above: The north front of the castle. On the following pages, respectively: Alcala la Real (Haen), the De la Mota Castle (fourteenth century); Las Navas de Tolosa, the highlands on which the Almohad army fought the troops of Alfonso VIII of Castile in 1212; Consuegra, the castle ruins and the windmills typical of the Mancha in the highlands.

Above and facing: Cordoba, the Alcazar (reign of Alfonso XI, fourteenth century). Detail of the battlements and the walls. Cordoba, the Calahorra Tower, an Arab fortress restored in the fourteenth century. Below: remains of Arab mills on the Guadalquivir. On the following page: Malaga, the Gibalfaro Fortress (reign of Yusuf I, fourteenth century).

statesman, accustomed to having his wishes carried out, he succeeded in overcoming his opponents, crushing rebellion and making his frontiers safe from Christian aggression. A man of culture, skilled orator and poet of talent, his death in the month of rabi' II in 172/788, evoked general sorrow and praise.

He was succeeded by his son Hishâm I, a figure of erudition in the religious sciences and a lover of letters, who took the holy war into the Asturias and among the Franks in victorious summer campaigns (sa'ifa). Under his rule Muslim Spain officially adopted the Mâlikite doctrine, thus strengthening the ties with the East, especially in respect of the disciplines allied to Islamic studies. This led to the formation in the peninsula of a religious and intellectual aristocracy consisting of Mâlikite jurists and theologians enabled by the protection of the ruler to bring their influence to bear on state affairs. We owe it to Mâlikism that Spain would always be on the side of orthodoxy, always ready to fight against and firmly repress even minimal dissent and to suppress any controversial attitude that might arise.

His son and successor, al-Hakam I, facing a recurrence of internal strife, tried to use the same harsh repressive methods that his father had often resorted to. At Toledo he crushed the more turbulent elements in the notorious «day of the ditch» when the chief exponents of town life all lost their lives. He used equal severity to stamp out opposition at Cordoba where the center of dissidence was the suburb of Arrabal del Sur on the left bank of the Guadalquivir: in 818 in the course of particularly ferocious reprisals the entire population of the district was expelled and many thousands of families set out on the road to exile. A number of these later took Crete from the Byzantines and set up an independent principality.

On his death, his son, 'Abd al-Rahmân II, inherited a discontented kingdom but a united one, a kingdom in which the eternal internecine warfare between the clans had been placated by the promotion of a policy of intermarriage. His rule coincided with the emergence of the first signs of the intellectual primacy that al-Andalus was to exercise over the Muslim West. Al-Hakam's legacies were a well-organized system of administration, thriving economy and a prosperous financial situation. These years, known as ayam al-'arus, the period of Perfect Agreement between State and Sovereign, represent a period of renewal in which observance of Syrian tradition is accompanied by a receptiveness towards the new currents of thought issuing from the 'Abbasid court.

Having gained the support of both his people and the fakhîh, 'Abd al-Rahmân personally led victorious campaigns against the Christians of the Asturias, Galicia, north Portugal and the territories beyond the Pyrenees, where he reached the outskirts of Narbonne. His chief merit however, is that he kept a firm hold on the evolution of a small state that had come into being to the north of the Ebro, a state that with its capital Pamplona was already in all but name what would later become the kingdom of Navarre.

In 844, the Spanish coasts were raided by Scandinavian pirates, known to the Arabs as al-urdumaniyun or, more frequently, magûs (idolaters). They descended the coasts of Galicia and, repulsed, attacked Lisbon, reached the mouth of the Guadalquivir, took the port of Cadiz and mercilessly plundered Seville. On this occasion the entire country gave proof of absolute fidelity to its emir who regained the occupied towns and showed no quarter to the infidels.

Henceforward the government of Cordoba began to broaden its political horizons to encompass the seas and established a great shipyard at Seville. This enabled it, only four years later, to send three hundred ships to quell disturbances on the islands of Majorca and Minorca. The Norsemen would return, but they were never again to land and plunder.

More serious difficulties arose for the 'Umayyad government from their Muslim subjects, for social and religious motives.

In 879 rebellion broke out in the south of Spain, led by 'Umar ibn Hafsûn who, from his fortified citadel of Bobastro, proclaimed himself Defender of the Spanish People and opened up negotiations with the 'Abbasid caliph and with Ibn al-Aghlab, emir of Ifrîqiya. The power of the state was further undermined by revolts among the Berbers who were reverting to a system of tribal rule and unrest among the mercenary troops that formed the pretorian guard. The reactions of the emir 'Abd Allâh were desperate but he finally prevailed and reestablished his dominion over the towns he had lost.

When he died his throne was inherited by his namesake, Abû 1-Mutarrif 'Abd al-Rahmân, whose reign was to mark the golden age of Muslim Spain. Coming to power in the year 300 of the Hejira, he brought tenacity and intelligence to the reestablishment of central authority and the reunification of the provinces. In a few short years everything was changed. Having brought the Arab aristocracy to heel by depriving it of its leaders he then turned his energies to dealing with 'Umar ibn Hafsûn who, having converted to Christianity in the intervening lapse of time, had transformed his rebellion into a religious war and lost Muslim support in consequence. Al-Rahmân, going from victory to victory, laid siege to Bobastro and conquered the stronghold in 928. In the course of the battle ibn Hafsûn's line became extinct. With peace reigning in Andalusia once more al-Rahmân made a united state of Muslim Spain, crushing nascent Fatimid interference and reestablishing the security of his northern frontiers by a series of dazzling victories over the Christians of Ordoño II of Leon and of Sancho, king of Navarre.

At the end of 316 (the beginning of 929) he made the most significant gesture of his political career, a gesture heretofore avoided by his predecessors, by adopting the title of *khalifa*, Caliph, and of *amîr al-mu'minîn*, Commander of the Faithful, the prerogative until that moment of those who ruled over the rest of the empire from Baghdad. In addition he assumed the honorific appellation of *an-Nâsir li-din Allâh*, «He who fights victoriously for the religion of Allah.» By this means he asserted his spiritual and temporal authority at one fell swoop and his name resounded in prayer throughout Spain.

The figure of caliph become supreme judge, infallible arbiter and absolute sovereign, was to be the corner stone of the State; an everwidening gulf was to separate him from his subjects who would no longer see their prince passing among them at annual festivities. He was to become a mysterious, distant figure occasionally to be glimpsed surrounded by ceremonial pomp; he would rule unchallenged from the Alcazar, the destiny of the nation solely in his hands.

Cordoba became the political and cultural capital of the West, receiving ambassadors from every European nation. The sharp intelligence of 'Abd al-Rahmân III involved him in fostering the development of agriculture, commerce, industry, the arts and the sciences, without overlooking the slightest detail in his efforts to create a political reality that would foreshadow

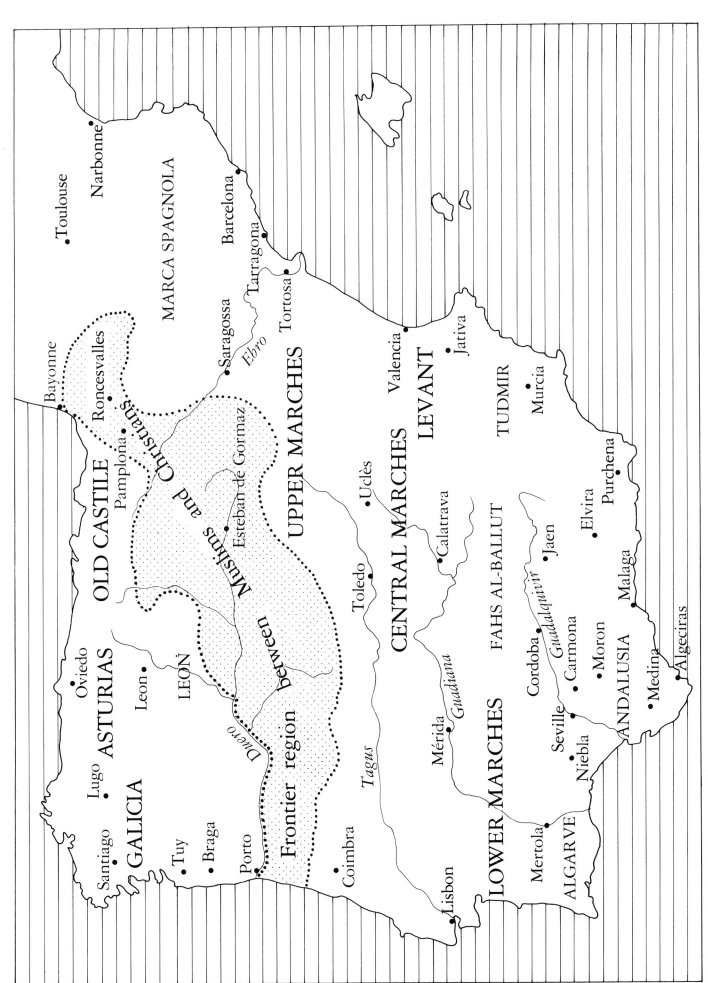

Muslim and Christian Spain in the ninth century.

the great national monarchies of Europe where the palace was the center of power and public life.

«The greatest danger for a State in which the reins of power are held by one pair of hands is that such a man might be a mediocre individual, subject to the influence of his favorites. Instead, where the ruler is a man of character, capable of imposing unity of direction on his government, of establishing political continuity, of uniting maturity of conception and undeviating purpose in execution, where this man is capable of handling the instruments of government available to him, the army, diplomacy and administration, then the empire can expect nothing but good from a sovereign who decides for himself.»[2]

Even the Basileus, Constantine Porphyrogenitus, sent missions from Byzantium to gain this man's friendship and when he died his son and successor, al-Hakam II al-Mustansir billâh «He who seeks the victorious aid of Allah,» preserved the prestige that had been created by his father's rule.

The first symptoms of decadence appeared at the death of al-Mustansir when power passed to his eleven-year-old son. The regency was held by his mother, Aurora, a Christian slave known to the Arabs as Subh Ga'far, and by al-Mansûr. The latter, then known as Ibn Abî Amir, member of the ancient and noble Yemenite family, the Banû Abî Amir, was to be the effective ruler of al-Andalus for more than twenty years. He won immediate recognition as the paladin of Islam in the peninsula by reviving the holy war, to which he devoted himself with enthusiasm and success, defeating and humiliating the kings of Leon, Castile and Navarre. Forty-two campaigns against the Christians earned him the title of *al-Mansûr*, the Victorious. This was the Almanzor of Christian chronicles and of the *Romancero*, who burnt down the sanctuary at Santiago de Compostela, goal of pilgrims from every part of the Christian world, triumphantly to return to Cordoba, his prisoners bearing the church doors and bells.

From his residence of Madinat az-Zahra', the Resplendent City, he governed the State as a dictator, while the caliph's position was reduced to a purely religious one. As with all palace rulers he too succeeded in founding a dynasty. When he died at Medinaceli during his last campaign against the Rioja territory in 392/1002 he was succeeded by his son, who had displayed prowess as a general and gained so many victories over the Christians as to earn him the title of *al-Muzaffar*, the Triumpher.

On his death at the early age of thirty-five, during a winter campaign against Sancho Garcia, the reign was inherited by his son 'Abd al-Rahmân, known as Sanchuelo, who also managed to have himself nominated heir to the caliph Hishâm II. This act made him all the more unpopular with *fuqaha'* and populace alike, already ill-disposed towards him because of his infidel origin, his mother having been a Christian princess. The third and last of the Amirids was executed, while the caliph abdicated in favour of a relative, Muhammed ibn Hishâm ibn 'Abd al-Gabbar, who took the name of al-Mahdî, the Well-Lead.

This was the beginning of dramatic times that were to lead to the fall of the caliphate. Dark moments of struggle and anarchy ensued in which the warring protagonists were Arabs, Berbers and Slavs, one time slaves now often in high office. After a bitter siege the capital of the caliphate surrendered to Berber troops in 1013 and was mercilessly plundered. Some years later the Slav faction was instrumental in enthroning the last of the 'Umayyads, al-Hishâm III al-Mu'tadd, but he was overthrown by the people in 1031. The viziers proclaimed the abolition of the caliphate and the institution of government by a council of state.

A poet, lamenting the fate of Cordoba wrote:

> Weep for the splendour of Cordoba, on whom
> misfortune has fallen.
> Fate placed trust in her, but soon
> required her recompense.
> She attained the zenith of her beauty,
> in ease and amenity, but observe her plight,
> scarcely two happy souls
> may be found there.
> Say goodbye to her, and go in peace,
> if you have decided to leave.[3]

The people, thrown back on their own resources, mourned the past and looked fearfully into the future. Muslim Spain was sundered. The Berbers shared out the south, the Slavs the east, and what remained was distributed among the small number of families that, by pure chance, had eluded the blows inflicted on the aristocracy by 'Abd al-Rahmân III. This was the age of the mulûk at-tawâ'if, the Reyes de Taifas.

Muslim Raids

The Pyrenean chain had not formed the northern frontier of Gothic power which reached into the Lower Languedoc and into Roussillon; beyond, to the north-east lay the ancient Septimania, so named for its seven main towns: Narbonne, Nîmes, Agde, Beziers, Lodève, Carcassonne and Mauleon.

These Gallic territories were systematically crossed by expeditions organized by the Arab governors of Spain from the earliest times of the conquest[4] in a period in which, with the Merovingian monarchy in its death-throes, they were unable to fend for themselves.

Of the numerous raids, inevitably leading to devastation and plundering, the Christians best recall that of 'Abd al-Rahmân 'Abd Allâh al-Gahâfiqî. His army, stationed at Pamplona, crossed the Pyrenees in the summer of 113/732 by the Roncesvalles pass and, reaching Aquitaine annihilated the army of the duke Eudo at Garonne as they advanced north. But between Poitiers and Tours the Arab hordes met up with the Austrasian troops that Charles had been bringing to the aid of Eudo, in the vicinity of the Roman road linking Chatelleraud to Poitiers, *in suburbio Pictavensi.*[5]

The Arabs were calamitously defeated and 'Abd al-Rahmân killed. The battle took place in the month of sha'bân of 114/October 732; the place was ever after referred to by the Arabs as Balat al-shuhada', the Martyrs' Road.

The importance of this episode is often exaggerated by Western historians who see in this battle the end of Arab expansion in the West. It was not an event of world importance on which the fate of Western civilization depended, simply an armed raid bent on looting and plundering. In Muslim chronicles it stands as an episode associated with defeat during a raid, without consequence for future operations.

Nonetheless, in a few short years, the obstinate resistance of Charles Martel and later, of his son Pepin the Short, succeeded in ridding the Septimania of Arab domination for ever. Toponymy has lent uncertain credit to theories by which a number of Muslim campaigners later renounced Islam and settled in the regions that had in former times been the scene of raids, chiefly in the Auvergne and in the Provençal Alps.

In the decades that followed, Charlemagne's relations with the Muslims were marked by cordiality towards Baghdad and constant hostility towards the 'Umayyad emir of Cordoba. In 157/774, Sulaymân ibn Yazqân al-Kalbî al-'Arabî, governor of Barcelona and Gerona, joining forces against the emir with the governor of Saragossa, Ausayn ibn Yahyâ al-Ansarî, enlisted Charlemagne's aid and invited him to Andalusia.

Charlemagne accepted and at the Pyrenean frontier his army split up, one group crossing the mountains to the east, the other, led by the emperor, following the old Roman road through the Roncesvalles pass. After besieging and defeating Pamplona, in Basque territory, it linked up with al-'Arabi and laid siege to Saragossa. News of a Saxon revolt at home forced Charlemagne to abandon the field in the month of shawwâl 161/July 778. On the return journey, at the Roncesvalles pass to the north-east of Pamplona, the Basques, reinforced by Muslim rebels, lay in wait for him. Many of the best Frankish warriors fell here, in an episode that would later enter legend through the *chansons de geste* of the Middle Ages.

On his return home, Charlemagne created the kingdom of Aquitaine that, together with the four ecclesiastic provinces of Bourges, Bordeaux, Auch and Narbonne was to have the task of keeping permanent watch on the activities of the Muslim rulers on the Pyrenean frontiers. The defeat changed his policy towards Muslim Spain. Now aware of the strength and preparation of his adversary and forced to recognize his own limits in respect of these, he made overtures of friendship that, by and large, met with little success.

Clashes between Franks and Spanish Muslims diminished with time. The small Christian kingdoms of northern Spain had gained strength and there was no longer call for Frankish aid. The Andalusian rebels preferred to enlist aid from the Pyrenean border regions in consequence of the fact that with the death of Charlemagne, his kingdom, divided between his successors, no longer possessed its former strength. Instead, diplomatic relations flourished and ambassadors were exchanged between the emirs and, later, the caliphs of Cordoba, the Frankish kings and the German emperors.

Moreover Christians now journeyed to Andalusia in search of science and learning. In 960, Gerbert, later to become pope under the name of Sylvester II, went to Spain to study physical sciences and mathematics. From the romances of chivalry we learn that Charlemagne as a child had been sent to Spain to be educated by the Muslims.[6]

The period under examination therefore reveals the existence not only of diplomatic exchanges and political contacts but also a real desire for knowledge, confirmed by the Arab writers of the classical period who, beyond their familiarity with the territories of the great Islamic empire, are also well informed about other countries with which the Muslim world

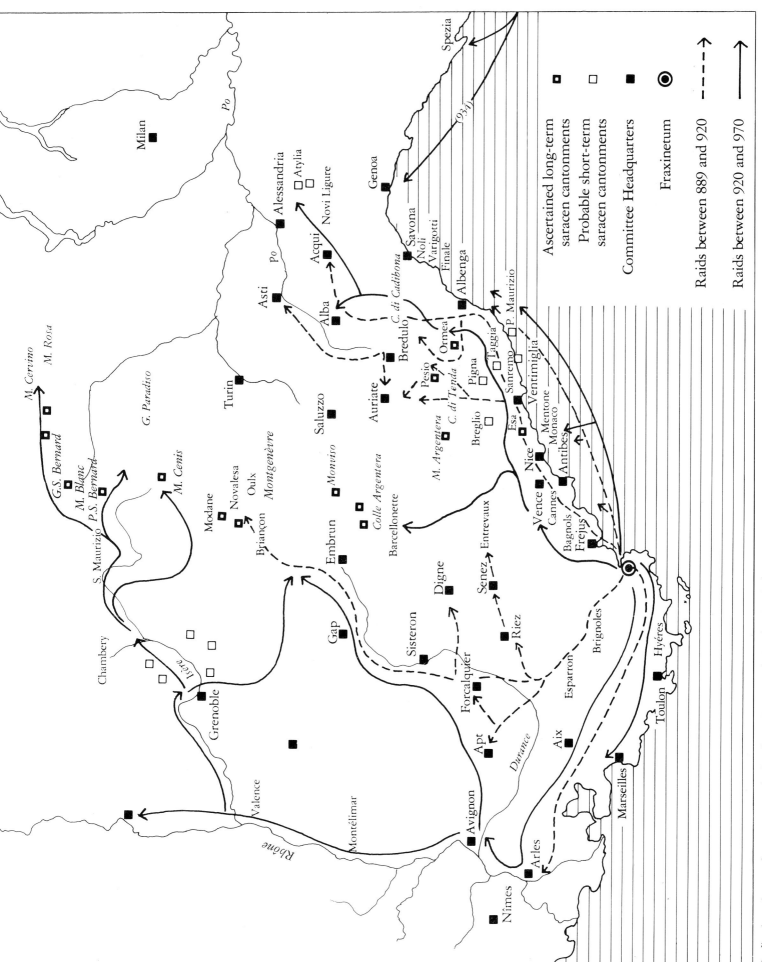

Muslim invasions and cantonments in Southern France and North-West Italy.

Milan

M. Rosa
M. Cervino
G.S. Bernard
M. Blanc
P.S. Bernard
S. Maurizio
M. Cenis

Chambery

Grenoble

Valence
Rhône
Montélimar

Nîmes

Arles
Avignon

Marseilles

Toulon
Hyères

Esparron
Brignoles
Aix
Apt
Forcalquier
Riez
Senez
Entrevaux
Digne
Sisteron
Gap
Embrun
Barcellonette
Colle Argentera
Briançon
Montgenèvre
Oulx
Novalesa
Modane

Turin
Saluzzo
Monviso
M. Argentera

Po
Asti
Alessandria
Atylia
Novi Ligure
Acqui
Alba
Bredulo
Auriate
Pesio
Ormea
C. di Cadibona

Genoa
Savona
Noli
Varigotti
Finale
Albenga

P. Maurizio
Taggia
Sanremo
Ventimiglia
Esa
Mentone
Monaco
Antibes
Cannes
Nice
Vence
Bagnols
Fréjus
Breglio
Pigna
C. di Tenda

Spezia

(934)

Po

G. Paradiso

Isère

Durance

□ Ascertained long-term
saracen cantonments

□ Probable short-term
saracen cantonments

■ Committee Headquarters

◉ Fraxinetum

--- Raids between 889 and 920

— Raids between 920 and 970

was in contact. Europe was certainly a zone of great interest and even though it was the land of infidels against whom every Muslim should fight for victory, it furnished the markets of the empire with such highly desirable and much admired goods as weapons, furs and slaves. It was for these motives that the old continent, in the ninth and tenth centuries, entered the orbit of interests of the Arab geographers.

The term *al-Ifrang*, Franks, was used by Muslim chroniclers to refer to many European peoples. For the Arabs of Spain the term indicated all Christian peoples, although the use of *Rûm*, Romans, was also very common. To refer to the regions under Carolingian domination the term *al-ard al-kabîrah* was used, the Great Land.[7]

An interesting trace of Arabism survives in the lands of the Franks. This is the Arab inscription in Kufic script decorating one of the doors of Puy cathedral.[8] It is carved on eight wooden panels, some of which are indecipherable, the work of Gauzfred or Godfrey, a twelfth century Christian artist who almost certainly only understood the decorative potential of the Arab language. He must certainly have had the original inscription to work from, probably brought from Andalusia, perhaps from Madînat az-Zahra'. The phrase, repeated several times and varying in decorative treatment, might signify «There is no God but Allah.»

Muslim belligerency also threatened from the sea in the eighth century. It spelled danger for Provence and the Ligurian coasts. The first half of the century brought the sack of the districts around Nice and plundering raids in the area of Fréjus and in the Rhone valley. By the second half of the century, notwithstanding the castles and fortresses that had proliferated, the menace was on the upsurge.

In 889 Muslim ships from al-Andalus landed at a point on the French coasts known as Gabal al-qilâl. Arab geographers[9] report that the place was uninhabited, the coastline splendid and good fertile land lay behind. Effectively, between 891 and 894, Andalusian pirates, in what still remain obscure circumstances, did take possession of a natural stronghold on the gulf of Saint Tropez and create a bridgehead, Fraxinetum, present-day Garde-Freinet. This was the start of a series of raids that lack of reliable documentation prevents us from analyzing systematically.

The town of Fréjus itself was razed to the ground. Then other centers between Fréjus and Albenga came under attack. Once confident of the coast, the Muslims crossed the Maritime Alps and swarmed up the Bevera and Nervia valleys to reach the hill of Tenda. They devastated Ventimiglia, the village of Sant'Ampelio on Cape Bordighera, Villa Matuciana (San Remo), Taggia and the surrounding district. In a short space of time the Muslims had pushed on as far as the upper course of the Durance and the entire region of Forcalquier was in their hands.

By the early years of the tenth century they had reached the Alps. They set fire to the monastery of Novalesa and destroyed that of Oulx, between Susa and Briançon.[10] Other columns carried destruction to Piedmont, to Pedona, Chiusa, Morozzo and Bredulo. Saracen raids in Piedmont also came from the sea. Acqui was sacked in 905 by the same raiders who later reached Tortona and built fortifications there. The abbey of Giusvalla was razed to the ground and the countryside around Asti brutally plundered.

The first reactions of the Christian populace were timid. For all the valuable aid provided

On the preceding page: Miramas-le-Vieux (Bouches du Rhône), ruins of a defense-works. Above: Le Puy (Haute-Loire), wooden portal of the cathedral with Kufic inscription. The other illustrations show the castle ruins at Grimaud (Var), a reminder of the town's past as a Saracen stronghold.

On the preceding page: Noli (Savona), the ruins of the thirteenth-century castle, a reminder of the times of Saracen raids.
Above: Bergeggi island (Savona), the site of a defense-works.

Varigotti (Savona), the Mediterranean seen from the banks of one of the numerous watchtowers from which warning would be given of Saracen approach. On the following page: the remains of one such tower crowning the slope.

by the Byzantine fleet, an expedition against Freinet in 931 was unsuccessful.

In the second quarter of the tenth century devastation was brought to the regions to the west of the abbey of S. Gervase at Fos in the Camargue. The first victim was the monastery of S. Victor, then the lands of Avignon.[11] By the decade 925-935 Muslim aggression was being felt in the central valley of the Rhone, in the area of Valence, Embrun and Grisivaudan. Muslims commanded the alpine passes and in 940 ca., pilgrims were still prevented from entering the valleys of the Dura, the Stura and Chisone.

In 935 the Byzantine fleet sailing in Corsican waters was severely defeated by a flotilla of Egyptian provenance returning from the sack of Genoa.

Saracen marauders penetrated beyond the frontiers of Burgundy into the German lands, especially into Raetia where the lands of the bishopric of Coire were laid waste. The whole of Switzerland was constantly subjected to raids.

Modest results were obtained by an expedition undertaken in 942 by Ugo, King of Italy, and the emperor Romano Lecapeno. Only in 973 when William, Count of Arles, later Marquis of Provence, persuaded the major feudatories to form a vast alliance, was any seriously organized attempt made to evict the Saracens. The years between 975 and 980 saw the definitive fall of Fraxinetum.

Ruins of ancient cylindrical towers may still be seen today scattered along the Ligurian coast and throughout the valleys on the interior. They were built as defense works or look-out posts either by the Saracens or by the Christians, in imitation of Arab models. In their vicinity there are often ruins of castles and fortifications that may be attributed to the Saracens.

The ruins to be found in the district of Fraxinetum however, are those that may be more confidently attributed to the Saracens. Imposing vestiges of walls, often in a state of total disrepair, are to be found in the mountains behind the gulf of Saint Tropez. There is a hill cut by ancient ditches near to Nôtre Dame of Miramas,[12] great ruined walls, the remains of the Moors' main fortifications, dominate the village of La Garde-Freinet; nearer to the sea stands the Grimaldi tower at Grimaud, named after the famous Giballino to whom the victory of Christianity owes so much; the remains of the castles of Pontévès, Revest, Saint Tropez and La Moure at Gassin may all well be of Saracenic origin since they were originally within the sphere of influence of Fraxinetum. In the ancient county of Fréjus there is no dearth of towers and forts scattered over the highlands. This is also true of Vidauban in the valley of La Napoule and of Antibes, where there stand two famous towers traditionally known as the «Saracenic Towers;» vestiges of the Saracens are also to be seen at Saint-Hospice, where the harbor was probably originally built by the Moors, at Villeneuve, Carros and Gattières. In the same zone the ruins of a castle at the village of Eze dominate the highlands of the principality of Monaco. Near Menton stand the ruins of a tenth century castle, at Sainte Agnès.

At San Remo, on the Italian coast, there is a round tower, probably built on the ruins of an earlier one dating from the period when the town was sacked; vestiges are also to be found at San Giorgio nearby Taggia, Porto Maurizio, Ceriale, Finale Ligure, Varigotti, Noli and on the island facing Bergeggi.

There are more abundant remains in the alpine zone: vestiges of fortifications at Oyace, Bossel and Montmayeur; a Saracen tower known as the Pilone del Moro (the Moor's Pillar) stands on the Colle del Borgo nearby Pesio. There was probably a chain of look out posts crossing the valley from Veynes to Oze, Saint-Aubind and Savournon, made up of round towers laid out on high rising land, their fires clearly visible by night, their smoke by day.[13] So-called «Saracen Towers» are to be found at Vevey in the Swiss Alps, walls at L'Avenche. There is a *Tour des Sarracins* on the outskirts of Montagny, ruins of fortifications at Saint-Lion and the castle at Lauzet above Monêtier-les-Bains. Other similar vestiges are to be seen throughout the regions of Marseilles, Aix, Arles, Toulon, Apt, Gap and Digne.

Alongside the defense works there survive traces of civil commitment in the form of mines, irrigation channels and silos. Tombs are of dubious identity, but eighth century Western coins have been found in various places in the Alps, certainly brought in from other Muslim territories for purposes of commercial exchange.

Muslim chronicles ignore these episodes and indeed the whole question of piracy, as do Byzantine chronicles for all the intervention of their fleets. This was not a holy war, such enterprises were not official, although the complicity of the Cordoban state lay behind them.

At the center of the Mediterranean roads and weakened by dissension between its Byzantine governors and the center of the empire, Sardinia was especially vulnerable to pirate raids. According to the historian Ibn al-Athîr the Muslims first attacked Sardinia in the year 92/711, causing great bloodshed and committing such serious abuses that their ships were overturned by a storm on the return journey.[14]

The raids continued and led to the creation of such securely established bases that the expedition against Rome set out from the island. However these were pirate raids that never led to settlement on such a scale as to leave traces of Muslim presence on the island.

Just as the strategies involved in the conquest and consolidation of power over occupied territory had accepted the Pyrenees as a demarcation line, so too, after the conquest of the island of Sicily, the Strait of Messina seemed to mark the border line between dar al-Islam and dar al-Harb, the seat of Islam and infidel territory. Penetration of the Italian peninsula, chiefly in the south, took the form of raids that were often suggestive of piracy although attempts were made to establish more permanent settlements. In fact, the Arab settlement at Garigliano, while lasting from 800 to 915, was little more than a base for raids.

The duration of such centers of stable Islamization as Bari and Taranto, for all the support of the emir of Kairouan, was a mere decade or two while Italy as a whole experienced Arab presence as a piratical scourge. These latter incursions were not protected by a dynasty nor were they mediated and planned; they may perhaps have had the support of the Muslim agglomerate at Fraxinetum and that of captains of fortune with their eyries in Corsica and Sardinia. The pirates came from everywhere, not only from Aghlabid Sicily but also from the Maghrib, the emirate of Crete, Spain and, occasionally, Syria.

The episode that shocked Christianity and made the Western conscience aware of the need for defence, was certainly the assault on Rome. «In the month of August, writes Prudenzio, bishop of Troyes, the Saracens and the Moors attacking Rome sacked the basilica of the Blessed Peter, Prince of the Apostles, and carried off, together with the altar above his tomb, all the ornaments and treasures. A number of the emperor Lothario's dukes were cut to pieces.»[15]

Rome
•
Ostia
•

Montecassino
•
Gaeta
•
Capua
•
Naples
•
Salerno
•
Amalfi
•

Benevento
•
Venosa
•

Canosa
•
Bari
•

APULIA

Brindisi
•
Taranto
•
Lecce
•
Otranto
•

Matera
•

Cassano
•

Cosenza
•

CALABRIA

Gerace
•
Messina
•
Reggio
•

Palermo
•
Cefalù
•
Troina
•
Taormina
•

Marsala
•
Mazara
•

Castrogiovanni
•
Girgenti
•

Catania
•

Syracuse
•

Noto
•

Areas affected by Saracen raids in Central and Southern Italy.

On the instigation of the emperor Ludwig, the Pope and the Basileus, an anti-Muslim league was formed to fight the common enemy. It bore fruit in the shape of the naval victory of Ostia, to which Cesario, son of the duke of Naples contributed, laying aside for the occasion his traditional policy of alliance with the Arabs. Later, when the rivalry between the Lombards Radelchi and Siconolfo had been placated by the creation of the two principalities of Benevento and Salerno, the struggle was revived on three separate occasions: in 851-853, in 857-858 and in 866-871.

Only the third campaign gave appreciable results, and this was due to the support of the Eastern emperor who sent two fleets in aid. The enterprise, leading to no more than the reconquest of Bari, was pursued no further because it encountered the hostility of the local dynasties who presumed so far as to hold Ludwig captive at Benevento, together with Sadwân, the emir of Bari defeated some months earlier. The Muslims, defeated once more in Calabria by Nicephorus Phocas, also disappeared for some years from Campania as a result of clashes between Arabs and Berbers in Sicily. The Byzantines strengthened their hold over Apulia and Calabria at the expense of the Lombards.

It was at this point that papal authority took over from imperial policy in the south. John VIII excommunicated the coastal towns of Naples, Gaeta and Amalfi for forming alliances with the Arabs for commercial motives. This same period coincided with the demolition of the abbeys of S. Vincent at Volturno (881), Montecassino (803), Farfa (897) and S. Clement at Casauria (916).

But in such difficult times even the efforts of papal policy ultimately left the people unprotected in the face of the enemy. Consequently they prepared to fend for themselves: castles and towers began to appear everywhere. In 902 another grave incursion was inflicted on the South. This was led by Ibrahim ibn Ahmad who, after the fall of Taormina and Messina, had crossed the Strait and marched up through Calabria to Cosenza without encountering opposition. The town, unwilling to surrender, had put up bastions and made ready to fight to the last man when the Arab leader, having laid waste the surrounding district, died of a contagious disease.

The situation here differed from that of Spain; the invaders of South Italy were not animated by ambitions of permanent conquest, they were merely autonomous bands, often divided among themselves by reason of religious and political dissidence.

Ships set sail from the seaboard town of al-Madhiyya for the Calabrian coasts, to found the short-lived mosque of Reggio in 952. Approaching the year 1000, Muslim troops appeared once more on the horizon at Bari but were obliged to withdraw by the doge, Pietro Orseolo. These were the last sparks from a great fire that was dying out.

One must not conclude that Saracenic domination of South Italy, by reason of its unstable and provisional character was to vanish without leaving traces of itself, without modifying in some way the civilization and history of those lands. Saracen presence was conducive to commercial development and, a sure sign of prosperity, in tenth-century Italy the dînar and the gold bezant were recognized currency.

The coastal towns being the first brunt of the wave of conquest, could not sit back and wait for aid from the Lombard and Byzantine rulers but were forced to take autonomous measures, learn to negotiate with countries overseas, learn the true meaning of religious tolerance.

Relations between East and West in these centuries of the Early Middle Ages were not confined to wars and exploits of plundering from both sides; more constructive relations in the form of economic and cultural exchange did exist.

Wars did not exclude exchanges, and this confounds Pirenne's bold thesis by which severance of Mediterranean unity after the Arab invasions is envisaged as a factor destined to destroy the equilibrium of the Christian world.

On the contrary, from the tenth century relations proceeded, especially in the economic field. Men, goods, and the various national currencies circulated in greater liberty than they do today. The Mediterranean was still the bond uniting Eastern and Western Europe, even before the crusades.

For all the dangers, the sea and land routes were never closed and the Mediterranean basin retained its function as a fairway of exchange. It conveyed not only goods but also men. In a period, moreover, in which the West was exhausted and impoverished by barbarian invasions and internal conflicts, geographers, ambassadors, pilgrims and scholars, bearers of spiritual over and above material wealth, had much to learn from the East.

The Muslims in Sicily

Sicily had already experienced Muslim incursions in the mid-seventh century during the period of Arab expansion in the Mediterranean basin. The first of these took place in 652 under the caliphate of 'Uthmân. The enterprise was carried out by the commander of his choice, Mu'âwiya ibn Hudaig, leading a fleet that must have sailed from Pentapolis, which had become an important naval base in North Africa. Slaves and church treasures were profitable wares on the Eastern markets and raids, although meeting with Byzantine resistance, became more frequent especially during the reigns of Hassân and Mûsâ when the occupation of the small island of Pantelleria created a useful stepping stone between Africa and Sicily. In 740 the governor of Africa, 'Ubaid Allâh ibn al-Habhâb, laid siege to Syracuse but the assault was called off on the payment of tribute money. During the second half of the eighth century, with North Africa in a state of anarchy, Sicily was rarely troubled by raids. Only after the creation of the powerful Aghlabid state were expeditions resumed.

An attack in 815 involved both Civitavecchia and Nice but after this date the Muslims appeared on the island only in 827. Their conquest of the island began when the Aghlabid sovereign of Kairouan answered a call for help from Euphemius, Byzantine commander of the fleet, rebelling against his governor Photeinos. This is how Ibn al-Athîr tells the story: «In the year two hundred and twelve (2 April 827-21 March 828) Qiâdat Allâh assembled an army and shipped it to the island of Sicily. He gave command of this expedition to 'Asad ibn al-Furât, *qâdî* of Kairouan, a disciple of Malîk and author of the 'Asadîah, a treatise of law according to the Malikite school. When this army arrived in Sicily it took possession of a great part of the island. The motive of the enterprise is as follows. The king of the Rûm in Constantinople had set a patrician by the name of Constantine over Sicily in the year two hundred and eleven (13 April 826-1 April 827). When Constantine was installed on the island he gave command of his army to a rûmi named Fîmî (Euphemius), a man of purpose and a courageous one.

This latter raided Africa (on his own initiative); he took possession of the markets along the coast, looted them, and stayed away for some time. The king of the Rûm then wrote to Constantine, ordering him to capture Euphemius, captain of the army, and punish him (for a crime he was charged with).

Hearing of this, Euphemius put the case to his men, who confirmed their allegiance and continued support of his cause. Upon which, on return to Sicily with his ships, he invaded the town of Syracuse. Constantine marched against him but was defeated in battle and took refuge within the walls of Catania. Euphemius counterattacked but the governor's troops fled, leaving the governor himself to be taken prisoner and executed while Euphemius was acclaimed as king. Euphemius subsequently placed a region of the island under the jurisdiction of a man named Balâtah, who broke faith and rebelled against him. Balâtah was supported in this by his cousin, Michele, the governor of Palermo. Together, they quickly assembled a great army, made war on Euphemius and defeated him; Balâtah then took possession of Syracuse. Euphemius and his supporters set sail for Africa, where he sent envoys to the emir Ziâdat Allâh to solicit his aid and offer him rule of the island of Sicily.

Ziâdat Allâh set out with an army in the month of rabî' I of the year two hundred and twelve (31 May-29 June 827). When they reached the town of Mazara in Sicily the Muslims attacked the enemy of Euphemius, Balâtah.»[16]

The latter fled to Sicily where he died and the Arabs laid siege to Syracuse. During this siege Asad ibn al-Furât himself died of the plague. Despite their efforts the situation of the besiegers was placed in jeopardy by the arrival of the patrician Theodorus who took command of the Byzantine troops and counterattacked with decision. Defeat seemed imminent when unexpected aid in the form of co-religionists from Spain arrived in 830. Theodorus was defeated by al-Asbagh, the new commander of the Muslim troops, and Palermo, conquered in 831, became the capital of the new province. Only in 843 did Messina fall to the Aghlabid prince, Abû 1-Aghlab Ibrâhim, and the fortress of Castrogiovanni held out for years before it was taken by the prince's successor, 'Abbâs ibn al-Fadl. The emblem of Byzantine civilization and of Hellenism in the West, Syracuse, was attacked by the Muslims of Ga'far and wiped out in 878. In 902, with the destruction of Taormina and the subjugation of the district of Etna, the conquest of Sicily was complete and Ibrâhîm II died having brought the holy war to terra firma. The island would remain in the hands of the Aghlabid dynasty until this fell in 910. Then Fatimid domination began and Sicily became a province of the empire that the Egyptian dynasty had built for itself in Africa. The revolt led by Ahmad ibn Qurhub, who replaced the name of the Fatimid caliph with that of the 'Abbasid caliph in ritual prayer, was easily suppressed.

In 948, rule of Sicily passed by proxy from the Fatimids to the Arab family of the Banû Kalb and the Kalbite emirate, whose first representative was al-Hasan ibn 'Alî al-Kalbî, transformed itself into a hereditary power under the aegis of a brilliant dynasty.

The island attained prosperity under the rule of al-Kalbî, adviser to the Fatimid al-Mansûr, and it was in this period too that Arab culture was assimilated by the population. Agriculture and commerce flourished anew and there was an upsurge of conversions, not induced by coercion but arising spontaneously from contacts with devout men and from admiration for the superior civilization of the rulers. The prosperity and refinements of the East and the cultural life of Baghdad, Cordoba and Cairo were reflected at the court of Palermo but with the reign of Yûsuf, son of al-Hasan, and later with Ga'far, these splendours were dimmed. Civil war broke out, the beginning of the end for the dynasty and for Sicilian Islam. The island's inhabitants, burdened by new taxes, rose up against the emir Ahmad and solicited the aid of the Byzantines, while Berber troops led by the emir's brother landed in support of the rebels. This struggle, in which the general interests of the party were subordinate to the desire for personal advantage, was transformed into a conflict between the Arab aristocracy and the population of converts to Islam, the former assembled at Syracuse, the latter at Girgenti and Castrogiovanni. In 1061, the Arab ibn ath-Thimna, defeated by the opposing faction, called on the Normans to invade. Only in 1092 however «Roger reigned over the entire island; in which he settled the Rûm and the Franks alongside the Muslims, depriving all the inhabitants of the use of bath houses, shops, mills and bake-houses... When his son Roger succeeded to him, he followed the customs of the Muslim kings (introducing to his court) the offices of *gânib* (aide-de-camp), *hâgib* (chamberlain), *silâhî* (equerries), *gândâr* (body-guards) and others such. In this way he made a departure from Frankish usages because such roles were unfamiliar to them.

Roger also instituted a Diwân al-mazâlim (Court of Vindication) where victims of abuses might lodge their complaints and (the king) do justice by them, even though it should be against his own son. Roger held the Muslims in esteem, was free in his ways with them, defended them against the Franks, and in consequence they loved him. He created a great army and took possession of the islands lying between al-Mahdîah and Sicily, the islands of Malta, Pantelleria, Djerba and the Kerkennas. He extended (his domain) to the coast of Africa (where) he carried out what we shall relate next, if God be willing.»[17]

The decline of the Kalbite dynasty, the rise of small independent emirates and Byzantine intrigues paved the way for the invasion of Sicily by Count Roger, son of Tancred d'Hauteville. In a century marked by a general revival of Christian activity when mere defense of their coastlines no longer sufficed, when Christians were in hot pursuit of the Muslim fleets, indeed, provoking them, presuming so far as to land in Africa and set fire to the countryside and the arsenals, in times such as these, between 1075 and 1087, Sicily was conquered by the Normans. Having gained the island, their ambitions soon turned to invading the coasts of Africa. The admiral, George of Antioch, a Byzantine who had entered the service of King Roger, conquered the island of Djerba, facing Gabes, in 1134; shortly after, the Sicilians invaded the island of Kerkenna, facing Sfax, at the other extremity of the gulf.

Tripoli was taken in 1146; Gigelli, to the east of Bougie, was invaded and sacked in the same year.[18]

In 1148 Mahdia, Sousse, Gabes and Sfax were all taken and plundered. With the exceptions of Tunis and Kairouan, all the towns of the eastern Maghrib from Tripolitania to Numidia were paying tribute to Roger II.

The turn of the year 1000 was marked by changing attitudes in the mentality of the populations on both shores of the Mediterranean. There arose a greater urgency in affirming the authenticity of religious beliefs and in eliminating falls, betrayals and deviations from the course of history. It affected both Muslim and Christian worlds, formerly characterized by a fluidity of encounter, albeit with moments of crisis, and while this instance of reform might have expressed itself in other ways, it settled for a gunboat diplomacy that would henceforth lead to frontal clashes and to the holy war.

It was in Western Islam that this new spirit first became a movement, initially conquering a territory by force of arms, then imposing religious reform there: as we saw in the previous chapter, the Almoravids were already moving away from the southwestern Saharan regions at the dawn of the eleventh century and would cross the strait in 1086. In the Christian world this martial spirit was expressed in the growing popularity of the crusades and in Spain it gave momentum to the Reconquest.

The crusades involved the central area of the Mediterranean basin, Egypt and Syria were particularly hard hit by them; but there existed other outlets for relations between Muslims and Christians and these, thanks also to the merchants of the Italian towns, continued to flourish.

Spain was split up between the numerous reyes de Taifas. The Hammudites were, though only in name, the leaders of the Berber party, claiming rights over all the Arab territory in the peninsula but possessing in reality only a few towns, among them, Malaga, Granada and Ronda. The Aftasids, reigning at Badajoz, were also Berbers.

The outstanding men in the opposition party were Khairân, ruler of Almeria, Zuhair, who succeeded to him, and Mugahîd, ruler of the Balearics and of Denia, a pirate famed for his expeditions against the Sardinian and Italian coasts and also for the esteem he enjoyed among men of letters. 'Abd al-Azîz, a nephew of the celebrated al-Mansûr, was proclaimed King of Valencia. The noble Arab family of the Banû Hûd rose to power at Saragossa. Lastly, ignoring the large number of tiny states, there was the kingdom of Toledo, ruled by the Banû n-Nûn, an ancient Berber family that had taken part in the conquest of Spain with Tariq.

The most influential families at Cordoba entrusted administration to a widely respected man, Ibn Gawahar, who carried out his duties as consul of the republic justly and wisely but without restoring political preeminence to the town. That leading role, thenceforward, belonged to Seville where, after the expulsion of the Berbers, the inhabitants had entrusted power to the Banû 'Abbâd family, a member of which, coming to the throne in 102, was to achieve renown under the name of al-Mu'tadid.[20]

The sovereign of Seville was a cultivated man, a poet and patron of letters, not insensible to sybaritic pleasures nor indeed to power. He fought against the Berbers of Carmona and Niebla, attacked the tiny state of Silves at the cape that still bears his name today and made war on al-Qâsim, the ruler of Algeciras. There was little tranquility even in the rest of Spain: towards 1055, having resolved their disagreements, a change of attitude was noticeable among the Christian kings.

In this epoch Ferdinand, king of Castile and Leon, directing all his energies against the Arabs, deprived them of their castles and fortresses and advanced on Alcala. The kings of Saragossa, Badajoz and Toledo were obliged to declare themselves his vassals and submit to the payment of tribute money. The following year Coimbra surrendered to Ferdinand and all the Muslims living between the Duero and the Mondego were ordered to leave the region. Then the Christian king attacked Valencia and the castle of Barbastro, the most important fortress in the northeast, destined to be the scene of ignominious slaughter: the soldiers, who surrendered after the signing of a treaty by which their lives should have been spared, were all massacred, and with them, the civilians, who were put to the sword. Only death was to free the Muslims of this terrible adversary, at Leon, in 1065. Shortly afterwards death also claimed al-Mu'tadid, who was succeeded by his son, al-Mu'tamid.

The new sovereign's literary discernment and poetic talents soon earned him the admiration of all Arab Spain; he lived a life of splendour, often walking on the Silver Meadows along the banks of the Guadalquivir. His court «was a place where guests stayed on, a meeting place for poets; all hopes were centered here.»[21] But times were to change, and fortune with them. Storm clouds gathered over the ephemeral delights of the Andalusian court and disquiet spread: «O people of al-Andalus, spur on your horses, it is a mistake to remain.» The verses of the Poets' sura resound: «Poets are followed by none save erring men. Behold how aimlessly they rove in every valley, preaching what they never practice.»[22]

Alfonso VI, king of Castile, Leon, Galicia and Navarre, was now determined to conquer the entire peninsula, financed by the money and treasures received in tribute from the reyes de Taifas. The first town to fall was Toledo, which the Christian king entered in 1085; then it was the turn of Valencia. Saragossa was beseiged. At the other end of Spain, his captain, Garcia Jimenez, entrenched in the castle of Aledo not far from Lorca, carried out incessant raids on the kingdom of Almeria. Faced with the arrogance and pride of Alfonso the unprotected Muslims had but two choices open to them: either surrender to the Christian king or emigrate en masse. «There is an enemy among us who never leaves us; / How can one survive with a serpent in the pannier?» sang a poet.[23]

But someone still held out hopes, recalling his co-religionists in Africa, the Almoravids, who had played a leading role in the history of Islam. Al-Mu'tamid turned to Yûsuf ibn Tashfîn for aid.[24] Aware that he was courting danger, he declared: «I prefer to be a camel-driver in Africa rather than a swineherd in Castile.»[25] Agreement was soon reached at Ceuta and at the end of June more than a hundred ships transported an army to Algeciras.

According to Ibn al-Qardabûs, Alfonso, having assembled all the forces available to him, wrote to Yûsuf offering a peace-treaty, but the amîr al-muslimîn replied in verse: «I have no other cards but swords and lances, no other ambassadors but my numerous army.»[26] In the meantime the Muslims had set up camp on the outskirts of Badajoz without crossing the Guadiana; the Christian troops were assembled in the Zallâqa plain, present-day Sagrajas. The battle was opened by the Christians on Friday 12 of the month of ragâb in the year 479 (23 October 1086) and the great army of Alfonso was routed before sunset.[27] The king narrowly escaped with his life and five hundred horsemen. Yûsuf, who had intended to continue his march north, was dissuaded by the news that his eldest son had died at Ceuta. Before leaving he summoned all the Andalusian sovereigns and exhorted them to put aside their mutual hostility and unite against the enemy; the Christians won, he argued, because of their numbers. But he was fully aware that the differences between then would never be overcome.

No Andalusian prince any longer paid tribute to the Christians but the Castilians barricaded in the fortress of Aledo continued their harassment of the tiny principates in the Levant.

Al-Mu'tamid, grasping the danger of the situation, went in person to solicit Almoravid intervention once more. The ruling classes feared the Almoravids but the people and the ministers of the faith were behind him. In the summer of 1090, the reyes de Taifas were all subjected to the authority of Yûsuf who, having brought all the Andalusian lands under his command and interrupted the course of the Reconquest, set sail for Africa once more, determined that his generals should concern themselves with the task of dethroning princes who, in preference to reaching peace and unity with one another, had made alliances with Alfonso, the common enemy. The Almoravid army besieged and captured Cordoba and Tarifa and then laid siege to Seville, which turned to the Christian kings for aid. A large army sent to Andalusia under the command of Alvarez Fañez met with crushing defeat at Almodovar.[28] Seville surrendered in September 1091, and in its wake, Almeria, Murcia, Denia and Jativa. Badajoz and Valencia, which had been conquered by the Cid Campeador only eight months earlier, followed suit. All Muslim Spain was reunited under the command of the sovereign of Marrakesh. 'Ali, Yûsuf's son, pursuing paternal policy, delivered a crucial blow to Castile by attacking the great fortress of Uclés, capital of the Santaver district. The numerous contingents of Christian troops sent to the area were defeated in 1108. The Infante was killed in action in the course of this battle.

The lives of non-Muslims became increasingly difficult. Heavy taxes were imposed on the Jews,[29] popular feeling turned hostile to the Mozarabs, settled in large numbers in the province of Granada, because they were frequently found to be in conspiracy with the Christian sovereigns. For this reason many of them were deported to Africa. But the Muslims were content: order had finally been established in the interior and they were protected from the enemy from without.

During the thirty-six years of 'Ali's reign Andalusian influence in the Maghrib rapidly increased. One of his creations was that of the Christian Militia, a body of brave mercenaries animated by a spirit of adventure and by great loyalty towards their prince. One of this number, the celebrated Rodrigo Diaz de Vivar, the Cid Campeador, has already been named here, but he was not alone. There was, for example, the Catalan, Reverter, a staunch paladin of the Almoravids, who died in combat against the Almohads. A Christian sanctuary dedicated to S. Eulalia existed at Marrakesh.

But in 1121 the Almohad revolt broke out in the Maghrib and the withdrawal of defence troops from Andalusia was turned to immediate advantage by the Christians. In 1125 Alfonso of Aragon devastated Andalusia; in 1133 Alfonso of Castile brought fire and bloodshed to the regions of Cordoba, Carmona, Seville and Jerez, returning five years later to devastate the outlying districts of Jaen, Baeza and Andujar. In 1143 Cordoba and Seville were victims once more. The following year the whole of Andalusia was sacked from Calatrava to Almeria.

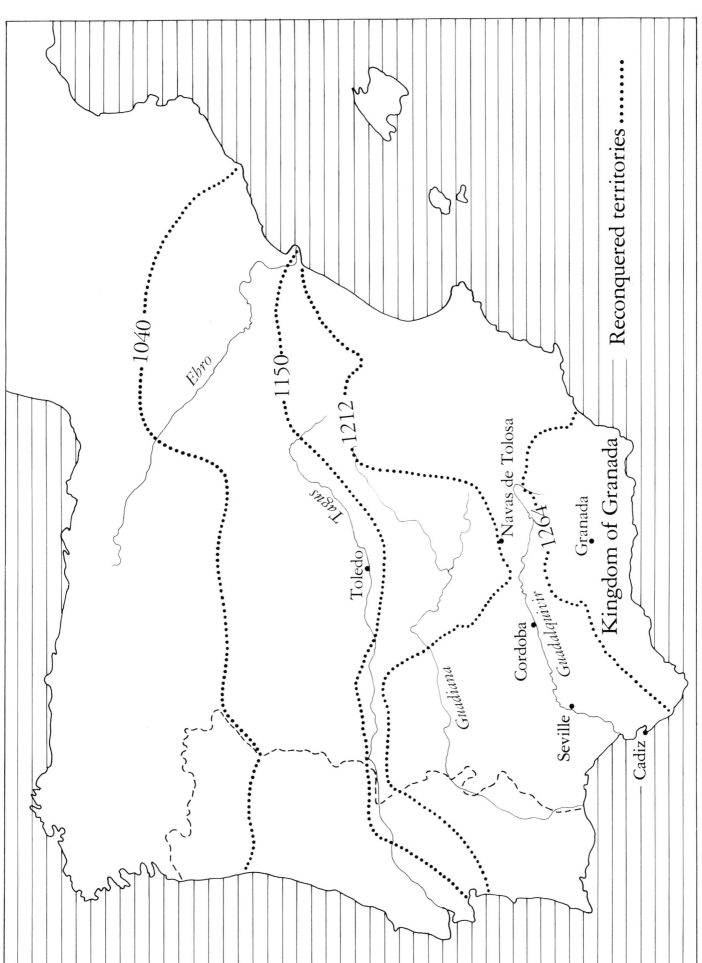

1040

Ebro

1150

1212

Tagus

Toledo

Navas de Tolosa

1264

Guadiana

Cordoba

Granada

Guadalquivir

Seville

Kingdom of Granada

Cadiz

Reconquered territories ....

The progress of Christian reconquest from the eleventh through thirteenth centuries.

In the meantime, Marrakesh had become the capital of the Almohad caliph[30], the amîr al-mu'minîn, who now sent to Spain an army that in five years restored law and order everywhere. He gained the respect of the king of Leon and Castile by his victory at Alarcos[31], compared by Arab chroniclers to that of Zallâqa though judged to be even more efficacious because al-Mansûr had proved capable of exploiting his success by penetrating Christian territory and occupying Guadalferza, Malagon, Calatrava and Caracuel. The victory of Alarcos and the subsequent two great summer expeditions demonstrated that the Berbers, under the white standards of the Almohad caliph, were fully capable of bringing the expansionistic ambitions of the Castilians to a halt. After the death of al-Mansûr in 1199, Spain, at the dawn of the thirteenth century, under the rule of an-Nâsir, enjoyed years of peace.

In 1210 Innocent III issued a papal bull whereby the Spanish bishops were required to invite the kings to prepare for war; indulgences were offered to those of them who should take part in the first campaign. An-Nâsir, with peace now reigning within his immense empire, assembled his troops at Tarifa in May 1211. A few days later he set up camp at the gates of Seville, the new capital, and from there advanced on the fortress of Salvatierra, the stronghold serving the knights of Calatrava as a base for their harassing raids. Alfonso VIII of Castile, first calling on the bishop of Segovia to preach the crusade, then opened the campaign in May 1212, after the arrival of reinforcements led by the archbishop of Narbonne. The battle took place at Las Navas de Tolosa, and ended with the overwhelming defeat of the Almohads[32].

Unity in the Maghrib was splintering into myriad factions that would soon lead the great empire into a state of anarchy and thence to an end. The defeat of subsequent military expeditions brought the cycle of great African invasions to a close.

In the years following the Christian victory of Las Navas, an Arab chieftain of the Jaen region, Muhammad ibn Yûsuf Nasr of the Banû 1-Ahmar family, built a kingdom for himself in the southeastern area of Andalusia where, in 1238, Granada became his capital. He proclaimed himself to be a descendant of a companion of the Prophet, Sa'd ibn 'Ubâda. The Nasrid kingdom, surrounded by Muslim towns surrendering one after another to the might of the Reconquest, remained the last strip of Muslim territory in the Iberian peninsula, enabled to survive only by acceptance of Christian vassalage.

The political life of the kingdom of Granada in the two and a half centuries that were to follow was marked by alternating phases of struggle against Castile, alliances with the other Christian sovereigns and requests for aid from the princes of the Maghrib. It was under the reigns of Yûsuf I (1333-1354) and Muhammed V (1354-1359) that the power and splendid civilization of the Nasrids reached its zenith.

In the first half of the fifteenth century Castile took the offensive once more and only the ardor and dedication of civilians and troops alike saved the kingdom from a difficult situation. This was so grave in 1464 that the sultan called on the Mameluke, Khushqadam, to intervene[33]. The answer to this plea is not recorded.

Shortly after, in 1469, Ferdinand, heir to the crown of Aragon, married Isabella of Castile, sister of Henry IV. While Granada was corroded by internal strife, Spain achieved unity. Towns and fortresses, including Alhama, considered to be impregnable, were rapidly defeated.

The Muslims summoned up the strength to inflict defeat on the Christians in the battle of ash-Sharqiyya, between Malaga and Velez-Malaga, but the following year, with the fall of Alora and Ronda, Granada was totally isolated. War was transformed into a state of siege, to which the Christians brought massive numbers of troops. In less than a month first Serrania then Vega fell to enemy hands. The Muslims sensed that the end was near at hand. Malaga, commanded by Ahmad al-Tagrî, and under continuous fire from Castilian cannons, held out for two months but was forced by hunger to surrender in August of 1487. When Baza fell, the Nasrids sought the aid of their traditional allies, the sovereigns of Fez and Tlemsen, but their intervention was blocked by a diplomatic initiative taken by Ferdinand.

At this point, the scholar Ibn al-Azras, traveled to Egypt to implore the aid of the sultan, Azraq Sayf al-Dîn Qâ'it Bây,[34] who negotiated, through the mediation of the clergy of Jerusalem, with the king of Naples to obtain his intervention at the Spanish court.[35] Despite the arrival in Spain of two Franciscans of the Holy Sepulcher, Ferdinand and Isabella replied that their decision was irrevocable. The last fortress of the kingdom surrendered to Gonsalvo of Cordoba at the end of 1489 while the Granadines continued to fight with all the strength that was left to them. In the night between the first and second of January of 1492, a number of Christian commanders entered the town and received the keys of the Alhambra from its last sovereign Boabdil. On the day of Epiphany,[36] the Catholic rulers made their entrance and the Reconquest was concluded.

Notes

[1]   Ibn al-Athîrr, *Annales du Maghreb et de l'Espagne*, Fr.tr. by E. Fagna, Algiers 1898, 41-42, Arab text 444.

[2]   C. Diehl- G. Marçais, *Le monde oriental de 395 à 1081*, Paris 1945, 494-495.

[3]   C. Sanchez Albornoz, *La España musulmana*, Madrid 1978, I, 527.

[4]   Ibn Haiyân, in Al-Maqqarî, *Analectes sur l'histoire et la littérature des Arabes d'Espagne*, ed. R. Dozy -G. Dugat-L. Krehl-W. Wright, Leiden 1855-'61, I, 173.

[5]   *Chronicon Moissacense*, in *Akhbâr Magmu'a*, ed. Lafuente y Alcantara, Madrid 1867, 166.

[6]   J.T. Reinaud, *Muslim Colonies in France, Northern Italy and Switzerland*, Eng.tr. H. Kh. Sherwânî, London 1964, 224.

[7]   Al-Maqqarî, *Nafh at-tîb...*, ed. 'Abd Allâh Hamid, Cairo 1941, I, 126, 128; Ibn al-Khatîb, *A'mâl al-A'lâm*, ed. E. Lévi-Provençal, Beirut 1956, 67, 219.

[8]   G. Marçais, *Sur l'inscription arabe de la Cathédrale de Puy*, in *Mélanges d'histoire et d'archéologie de l'occident mussulman*, Algiers 1957, I. 205-210.

[9]   M. Amari, *Biblioteca arabo-sicula*, Turin-Rome 1880, I, 7-9.

[10] *Chronicon Novalicense*, in B. Luppi, *I Saraceni in Provenza, in Liguria e nelle Alpi occidentali*, Bordighera 1952, 224.

[11] R. Poupardin, *Le royaume de Provence sous les Carolingiens*, Paris 1901, 243-273.

[12] M. Reinaud, *Les Invasions des Sarrazins en France, en Savoie-Piémont et dans le Suisse*, Paris 1836, 161-162.

[13] Martignier-Crousaz, *Dictionnaire du Canton du Vaud*, Lausanne 1867, 46.

[14] P. Martini, *Storia delle invasioni degli arabi e delle piraterie dei barbareschi in Sardegna*, Cagliari 1861, 53-55; Ibn al-Athîr, *Annales...*, 51.

[15] *Annales Bertiniani*, in M.G.H.SS. in usum scholarum, ed. G. Waitz, Hanover 1883.

[16] Ibn Al-Athîr, in M. Amari, *Biblioteca Arabo-sicula*, Turin-Rome 1880, I, 364-365.

[17] Ibn Al-Athîr, in M. Amari, *Biblioteca...*, I, 449-450.

[18] Al-Idrîsî, *Description de l'Afrique et de l'Espagne*, ed. and Fr.tr. by R. Dozy-J. De Goeje, Leiden 1866, 245-246.

[19] Ibn 'Idhârî, *al-Bayân al-mughrib fi akhbâr al-Maghrib*, ed. R. Dozy, Leiden 1848-1851; Fr.tr. by E. Fagnan, Algiers 1901-.04, V. III ed. E. Lévi-Provençal, Paris 1930, 194-196.

[20] 'Abd Al-Wâh'd Al-Marrâkushi, *al-Mu'gib fî talkhîs ta'rîkh al-Maghrib*, ed. R. Dozy, *The History of the Almohades*, Leiden 1845, 42-43; Fr.tr. E. Fagnan, *Histoire des Almohades*, Algiers 1893.

21 Ibn Al-Khatîb, al-Ihâta fî akhbâr Gharnâta, Cairo 1319, II, 74.

22 The Koran, XXVI, p. 204; Eng.tr. by N.J. Dawood; Penguin Books 1956.

23 Al-Maqqarî, *Analectes...*, II, 672. The poet is Ibn al-Ghassal.

24 Al-Maqqarî, *Analectes...*, II, 674.

25 Al-Maqqarî, *Analectes...*, II, 678.

26 A.H. Miranda, *Las grandes batallas de la Reconquista durante las invasiones africanas (Almoravides, Almohades y Benimerines)*, Madrid 1956, 38.

27 'Abd Al-Wâhid Al-Marrâkushî, *al-Mu'gib...*, 93-94. Ibn Khaldun, *Kitâb al-'Ibar wa dîwân al-mubtada' wa-l-khabar fî ayyâm al-'Arab wa-l-'Agam wa-l-Barbar wa man 'asarahum min dhawî as-sultanâ al-akhbar*, vol. 7, Bûlâq 1284, VI, 186-189. *Histoires des Berbères*, ed. De Slane, Paris 1847-'51, vol. 2; Fr.tr. by De Slane, Paris 1852-'56, vol. 4, II, 78-79; Ibn Abî Zar', *Rawd al-Qirtâs*, ed. and Lat.tr. by Tornberg, Uppsala 1843-1846, I, 93 ss; Ibn Al-Khatîb, *al-Hulal al-mawshiyya fî dhikr al-akhbar al-marrakushiyya*, Tunis 1329, 43.

28 *Annales Toledanos*, II 404.

29 Al-Idrîsî, *Description de l'Afrique et de l'Espagne*, ed. R. Dozy-M. De Goeje, Leiden 1866, 205.

30 'Abd Al-Wâhid Al-Marrâkushî, *al-Mu'gib...*, 145-146.

31 Ibn Abî Zar, *Rawd...*, 140.

32 A.H. Miranda, *Las grandes batallas...*, 253-272.

33 R. Arié, *L'Espagne musulmane au temps des Nasrides (1232-1492)*, Paris 1973, 146.

34 Al-Maqqarî, *Analectes...*, I, 941-942.

35 A. Zakî, *Mémoires sur les relations entre l'Égypte et l'Espagne pendant l'occupation musulmane* in *Homenaje a Cordera*, Saragossa 1904, 476-477.

36 M. Gaspar y Remiro, *Documentos àrabes de la corte nazari de Granada o primeros pactos entre los Reyes Catòlicos y Boabdil sobre la entrega de Granada*, «Revista de Archivos, Bibliotecas y Museos», 1910, 415-422; Mª Del Carmen Pescador del Hoyo, *Como fué la toma de Granada a la luz de un documento inédito*, «Al-Andalus», (1955), 283-344.

CHAPTER THREE

MUSLIM SPAIN

The Geography of al-Andalus

The term al-Andalus appears for the first time in 98/716, shortly after the conquest. Its use was introduced by Arab writers to refer to Muslim Spain as opposed to Hispania, the nomenclature applied by Latin chroniclers to the Iberian peninsula. Certain authors, such as Ibn Sa'îd, trace the origin of the term back to the name Andalus, son of Tûbal, son of Yâfet, son of Nûh, who was the first settler; others, like Ibn Hayyân and Ibn Khaldûn, derive it from the form al-Andalîsh, Vandals, the people that gave the name of Vandalicia to the Roman Baetica.[1]

Until the fourth century of the hegira, the tenth century A.D., al-Andalus was an Islamic province little known to the peoples of the East. Only with the restoration of the 'Umayyad caliphate did its geographic attributes fall into perspective.

Ibn Hawqal had the good fortune to visit Spain personally in the reign of 'Abd al-Rahmân III. It was the tenth century, the golden age of Andalusian learning. This is how he speaks of it in his *Surat al-ard*: «Spain is one of the finest peninsulas. Its position is important because of everything that is to be found there, most of which I shall describe. I reached Spain at the beginning of the year 337 when Abû-Mutarrif al-Rahmân was on the throne. It would take a month to walk the length of the country and twenty days or more its breadth. There are stretches of wild land but most of it is well cultivated and densely populated. One meets with running water, woods, fruit trees and freshwater rivers everywhere...»[2]

For a coordinated picture of Spain we must look to the Cordoban chronicler of Eastern origin, Ahmad ar-Razî (d. 344/955), in the introduction to his great history of al-Andalus.

«The land of al-Andalus constitutes, to the west, the extremity of the fourth terrestrial region. The knowledgeable consider that there are excellent stretches of land suitable for cultivation there, very good, fertile soil. It is generously irrigated by numerous streams and rivers and by springs of fresh water. There are very few poisonous reptiles. The climate has no extremes, the temperature and force of winds are well regulated; spring, autumn, winter and summer follow a harmonious course and the temperature keeps to mean values throughout: a season never overlaps another or cuts it short.

Fruit ripens continuously in almost every season of the year, so much so that it is always available, one never notices any shortage; nearer the coast and along the sea shores it ripens early but the harvest comes later in the Marches and on the mountains where the climate is particularly cold. In such circumstances fruit is picked throughout the year and the country is never without.

Certain features of al-Andalus contribute to the excellence of her flora that, for certain aspects, may be compared to that of India, a country notable for her production of essential plants; one such is the *mahlab* plum, one of the most important spices, considered to produce the best soda, and which only grows in India and in Spain.

Al-Andalus has fortified towns, impregnable castles, well-guarded fortresses and magnificent palaces. It has sea and land, both plains and mountainous regions.

Its form is triangular. Al-Andalus is made up of two zones, distinguished by such factors as determine the movement of the winds, the rainfall and the course of the rivers: a western and an eastern zone. Western Spain is the zone in which the rivers flow into the Atlantic, whose rains are regulated by the west winds. This zone starts in the east with the territory that runs from the north in the direction of the Santaver region and at Agrîta, nearby Toledo, turns toward the Algarve on the one hand and, on the other, toward a point on the Mediterranean coast situated nearby Cartagena in the territory of Lorca.

With regard to eastern Spain, known as al-Andalus al-aqsâ (extreme Spain), its waterways flow out to the east and the rains are regulated by the east winds. It is bordered on one side by the Gascons' mountain and follows the Ebro valley to the Santaver region, to the north and west of which lies the Atlantic, to the south, the Arabian Sea that becomes the Middle Sea, lapping the shores of Syria: this is the sea that also goes by the name of Tyrrhene, meaning 'the sea that crosses the circumference of the earth.' It is also known as the Great Sea.»[3]

The great fresco of al-Idrîsî was written two centuries later. His great-grandfather belonged to the great Hammudite family that reigned over the principate of Malaga until the town was annexed to the kingdom of Granada in 1057. The writer's grandfather then took refuge at Ceuta where al-Idrîsî was born in 493/1100, when the town was ruled by the Almoravids.

Here, with scientific precision, is how he describes his homeland: «No region of the territory of al-Andalus comes within the limits of the third terrestial region, whereas the fourth overlaps the southern coastline and takes in Cordoba, Seville, Murcia and Valencia; it then continues across the sea to Sicily, including the other islands off its shores, with the sun behind one. The fifth runs through Toledo, Saragossa and surrounding districts, touching on Aragon at whose southernmost extremity stands the town of Barcelona, to proceed towards Rome and her subject states and divide the Gulf of Venice in two parts, then taking in Constantinople and her regions, with the planet called Venus behind one. The sixth region touches the northern coast of al-Andalus, washed by the waters of the surrounding sea, and includes part of Castile and of Portugal, the greater part of the Franks' country, Georgia and the Slavs' region as well as that of the Russians, leaving the planet called Mercury behind one. The seventh region comprises the sea to the north of al-Andalus, the island called England and the others surrounding it, together with the remainder of the Franks' country, of the

Slavs', of Georgia and of Berjân. According to al-Bajhakî the seventh and last region, leaving the moon behind one, encompasses the island of Tûlî, the two islands of al-Agbâl (Norway), an-Nisâ and many other Russian regions...»[4]

«It is there that the land of al-Andalus is to be found, known in the Greek tongue as Ishbâniyâ and also bearing the name of Gazîra because its triangular shape narrows on the eastern side, so much that there is barely a five days' walk between the Mediterranean and the Ocean that border it. The broadest span of the peninsula can be crossed in about seventeen days: this is the western side, where the inhabited part of the land ends, bounded by the Tenebrous Sea. No one knows what lies beyond this sea... But returning to our description of Spain and her provinces... Let us say then that Spain forms a triangle. It is in fact surrounded on three sides by sea, that is to say the Mediterranean to the south, the Ocean to the west, and to the north what is known as the English sea (these are a Christian people). In length it stretches from the Corvo church, which overlooks the Ocean, to the mountain called the Temple of Venus, for a distance of about 1,770 km, and in breadth, from the church of S. James sited on a promontory overlooking the English Sea, across to Almeria, a town sited on the Mediterranean shores, for a distance of 965 km. The Spanish peninsula is divided into two parts for its entire breadth by a chain of mountains called ash-shârrât, at the center of which stands Toledo.»[5]

In the fourteenth century one of the last great figures of Andalusian Islam, the vizier of Granada, Lisân ad-Dîn ibn al-Khatîh, sang the praises of his homeland as follows: «Almighty God has granted that this land of ours should be distinguished from others by gentle hills and fertile plains, by her good, healthy food, by the great number of useful animals, the quantity of fruits, abundance of water, comfortable dwellings, handsome clothes, fine pottery and utensils of all kinds, splendid weapons, pure and healthy air and the proper manner in which the seasons of the year follow one another. He has also endowed her inhabitants with genius for the sciences and the arts of domestic life, with quick wits, lively intellect, courage, an ardent love for everything that is beautiful together with many other excellent qualities that are not to be found all together in the peoples of any other country.»[6]

Compared to Syria for her gentle climate and pure air, to the Yemen for her constant temperature, to India for her penetrating scents and to Aden for her coastal riches, Muslim Spain will always be extolled by poets in admiring and enthusiastic tones. One cannot but quote the following lines by one of them, Ibn Khafâga, the poet of Alcira:

> O inhabitants of Spain, what happiness there lies for you
> in these waters, these shades, these rivers and these trees!
> If it is not here, the Garden of Happiness does not exist,
> and were the choice mine, it is here that I should choose.[7]

Victors and Vanquished

For all that they had played no part in its creation, the new rulers of Sicily after the Muslim conquest turned the ethnic and moral unity of the country to their own advantage in the establishment of an entirely new political and social order, that of Islam. In compliance with the laws and constancy of observance of Islam, Muslim Spain never made a distinction between the temporal and the spiritual; by making her emirs and caliphs Lords and Defenders of the Faith her aim was to oppose firm resistance to the particularism that had afflicted the Visigothic kingdom. Following the principle that all believers are equal she offered her subjects the Islam of orthodoxy, an Islam purged of all heresy and obedient to a single juridical school, the Mâlikite, in order to discourage individualism and anarchy.

While the Christian kingdoms of the north became increasingly susceptible to the influences of the Christian civilization beyond the Pyrenees, influences that were to create the vital lymph of the future Spain, Muslim thought, absorbed in Islam and the great civilization from which it had sprung, was impervious both to these and to the Isidorian culture that strove to survive among the Christians of al-Andalus.

Nonbelievers, who belonged to the category known as *ahl at-kitâb* or *ahl adh-dhimma*, the category subject to the payment of tributes, were better organized here than in any other part of the Muslim world.

Their circumstances at the time of the conquest were regulated by a pact drawn up by Mûsâ ibn Nusair and the Visigothic prince Theodomir, who obtained very favourable conditions. The victors committed themselves to respecting the defeated without challenging their authority, interfering in their religious rites or burning their churches. In exchange, the Christians were to show loyalty towards the victors, pay them an annual tribute and respect the agreements.

The victors allowed the defeated to observe their own laws and to keep their judges. The serfs stayed on the land, with the obligation to give the Muslim proprietor four-fifths of the harvests;[8] those who lived off land belonging to the State and who had had the fifth part of their lands confiscated at the moment of conquest had to give up only one third of their crops. In general, the Christians retained most of their property, over which they exercised the right of transfer. They were subject to a state poll tax (*gizya*) calculated on the basis of social status and income but certain categories such as women, children, monks, the sick, beggars and slaves were exempted from this. Owners had to pay the *kharâg*, a tax on production that usually amounted to 20% and this, unlike the poll tax, was not lifted on conversion to Islamism.

Andalusian society was already composite at the moment of conquest.[9] In the tenth century, the most flourishing epoch of the 'Umayyad dominion, it would have been possible to single out Arabs, *muwallad*, Slavs, Berbers, Negroes, Jews and Mozarabs. Notwithstanding such diversity of ethnic elements, the culture was Arab and Arab alone.

The Arabs — who came from very different countries, from Higiaz, Yemen, Iraq, Syria, Egypt and Ifrîqiya, and were given to maintaining distinctions between the *balâdîgûn*, the firstcomers, and the *sha'mîyûn*, the Syrians who came with Balg — had brought with them to Spain the ancient rivalry between Qaisids and Kalbites. The most influential of the former, who declared themselves to be descended from 'Adnân, the Kuraishites, stood highest in the social hierarchy, particularly when the 'Umayyads took power. The second and more numerous group, that of the Yemenites, comprised all those who were in some way associated with the descendants of the *ansâr* and Defenders of the Prophet; they established themselves chiefly in the Levant, the Algarve and the Toledan region. The dynasties that ruled in the various towns after the fall of the caliphate belonged to this group. Shortly before the arrival on the scene of 'Abd al-Rahmân ad-Dâkhil, the Syrian *gund* of Balg settled in the southern part of the peninsula, at Granada, Malaga, Algeciras, at Seville, Niebla, Jaen and Murcia, following a system of military circumscriptions that was to be maintained for the entire duration of the 'Umayyad dynasty and form the basis for future land ownership. But the Arabs, despising agricultural life, settled in the main towns and left the tillage of their lands to the *muwalladun* masses.

Under 'Umayyad rule the rivalry between the groups waned, finally to disappear in the *mulûk at-tawâ'if* era. By that time, the Arab population found itself enriched by merchants, craftsmen, artists, poets and men of letters who, together with their families, had moved here from every part of the empire bringing with them their language, the classical Arabic consecrated by the Koran, the offical idiom of the man of state, the minister and the secretary, the essential instrument of eloquent verbal expression.

The Berbers, the people who truly engineered the conquest, were the first to reach Spain. They formed the effective fighting force of the Muslim army that defeated Roderic and then advanced north over the Pyrenees. Widescale immigration from North African territories, particularly from Morocco, became a constant of the times and lasted until the Almohad conquest. It received every encouragement from the caliphs, who needed mercenaries in their struggles against the Arab aristocracy and later against the Slavs.

Scattered over a vast zone between southwest Portugal and the fertile Ebro valley, the Miknâsa, Zanâta, and later the Sinhâga tribes, formed, together with the *muwalladun*, the greater part of the population. They chose to live in the mountains, where they could breed animals and practise horticulture, the mountains such as those of Carmona, the Serrania at Ronda and Malaga, the Sierra Nevada, and at Medina-Sidonia in the Sierra of Almaden. The southern and western regions of the Iberian peninsula, with the exclusion of the geographical area of the plains, were largely Berber territories.

Even in the towns, especially the capital, a large Berber minority might often be found. At Cordoba, for many years, they were mostly clients of the 'Umayyad princes and, once urbanized, entirely forgot their African origins. Very often they were involved in humble trades, but not infrequently one of their number would achieve fame in the study of the religious sciences. Such a one was Yahya ibn Yahya al-Laithi, who, in the eighth century, was one of the chief instigators of the diffusion of the Mâlakite doctrine. Others held important posts in caliphal administration and in the military hierarchy, often rising to the rank of vizier and becoming totally assimilated into the Arab group.

At the fall of the caliphate the Berbers were to be found established in two principalities, those of Toledo and Badajoz, whose princes had long adopted Arab ways. The Du-n-Nûn of Toledo dedicated themselves chiefly to the study of the exact sciences, so much so that the town observatory was one of the most celebrated of the epoch. When their last prince, al-Qâdir was obliged to abandon his capital he took an astrolabe with him as a memento. Al-Muzaffar, of the Banû 1-Aftas of Badajoz, was a keen grammarian, a philologist and man of letters.

Assimilation into the Arab group only took place among the aristocracy however, as the common people and the soldiers kept up the every day use of their mother tongue. During the Reconquest most of them returned to Morocco and Algeria.

Although Arabs and Berbers were the main engineers of the conquest they were not alone in playing a political and cultural role in Muslim Spain. The greater part of the Muslim population was formed of Spanish Jews and Iberian Romans who had been converted to Islam. Arab chroniclers refer to them as *masâlima* and make a distinction between the former, *islâmî* or *isrâ'îlî* and the latter, *asâlima*. Their sons and descendants, the *muwalladun*, were indistinguishable from the older Muslim population and almost always adopted Arab names.

These were persons who had spontaneously adopted the faith of the conquerors without undergoing any form of coercion and they often enjoyed a respected social position, becoming so well integrated with Muslim society that, at times, they might disavow their origins. In the plains they took up animal husbandry and farming, on the coast, fishing and seaboard activities, in the towns they became craftsmen and traders. In this way they became a force to be reckoned with in the economy of the peninsula and it is thanks to them that Arab-Islamic culture achieved its preeminence in Andalusian society. They were also responsible for the development of the Romance language, a derivation of the Latin spoken until the arrival of the Arabs, albeit written in Arab letters and enriched with the contribution of many Arab words. The two tongues were used contemporaneously, particularly after the tenth century.

Rapidly Islamized, the *masâlima* and the *muwalladun* were to play a significant political and social role, much as did the Banû Angelino and Banû Sabarico of Seville in the times of 'Abd al-Rahmân II. They are representative of the homogeneous fusion of the Arab component with their subject peoples.

An aspect of tenth-century Spanish society, particularly of Cordoban society, which was to be a crucial factor of the political strife at the fall of the caliphate, was that of the *saqâliba*. Medieval Arab geographers used this term to refer to the peoples who inhabited the territory bordering on that of the Khazars, between Byzantium and Bulgaria. In Spain, however, it meant not only those who had been taken prisoner by the Germanic peoples during their conflicts with the Slavs but, in general, all the slaves of European origin that had been bought, not only on the shores of the Black Sea but also in France, Italy or Germany, to be used in the army, the palace or in the royal harem.

Transported to the peninsula initially by al-Hakam I, they soon grew in number and many rose from their servile circumstances to become *mawâlî*, holding positions of importance in the political world and in society as a result of their credit with the caliph and the great wealth they had acquired. During the reign of an-Nâsir they held key positions in administration and in the military hierarchy and, shunning contact with the rest of the population, constituted a close-knit association readily involved in all the country's major conspiracies, thus creating inauspicious disturbances for the central authorities. In the eleventh century a number of them made a bid for independence, at Tortosa and Valencia, while others managed to set up a powerful principality in the province of Denia, incorporating the Balearics, which they utilized as the point of departure for raids on the European coasts.

In this social melting pot that was Muslim Spain there was still one category in servile circumstances: the African slaves, known as *'abîd* or as *sudân* because they came from *bilâd as-Sudân*, the «negro country». They formed the bodyguard of the caliph, to whom they were so devoted that they were admitted to the ceremony of investiture.

On the fall of the 'Umayyad dynasty they threw in their lot with the Berbers who, however, prevented them from attaining posts of any importance in civil and military administration.

Black female slaves were perhaps more numerous in the peninsula than their menfolk. They were to be found in the harems, often as wives, as opposed to concubines, acquiring luster not infrequently for their excellent knowledge of philology and prosody; such a one was Ishrâq as-Suwaidâ', the slave of Abû l-Mutarrif ibn Galbûn at Valencia. The mulatto children of these unions were quite frequently to be met with among the Muslim aristocracy and bourgeoisie, as oblivious to racial prejudice in the Middle Ages as it is today. Arqâm, brother of al-Ma'mûm, was one of the most distinguished men of letters at the Toledan court of the Du-Nûn; Abû Muhammad ibn Hûd al-Gudâmî served al-Mutawakkil, the ruler of Badajoz, in the capacity of ambassador at Lisbon.

Christians and Jews in the Cordoban Caliphate

As we have seen, the pact stipulated at the conquest allowed the defeated complete freedom of choice either to embrace Islam or to continue to profess the religion of their fathers. There were no cases of coercion but, once converted to Islam, it was forbidden to leave the faith. One might remain a Christian subject of caliphal Spain but apostasy of Islam was punished by death.

There was freedom of worship but the Church was not free: strict controls and harsh restrictions were imposed on her. Councils might still be held but the right to convocate them was the prerogative of the Arab emirs.

Spanish Christians who did not convert to Islam yet continued to live on Muslim soil were called Mozarabs, from the Arabic *musta'riba*, although in eleventh-century Spanish literature the most commonly used appellative was *'ulûg*, signifying captive Christians. The most frequent term for Mozarab Christians and Christians of foreign countries was *'agam*, the exact opposite of *'arab*, used to refer to those who spoke in an obscure and incomprehensible tongue, barbarians.

Subjected to the regimen of the tolerated religious minority, the Christians nonetheless continued to live in circumstances of relative autonomy, allowed to pass on from one generation to the next the fundamental elements of their own culture, straitened though its circumstances were compared with the vigorous flourishing of Arab literature and culture.

This unstable equilibrium was jeopardized in the mid-ninth century when a vocation for martyrdom, nourished by the ancient Christian example of third century African and Spanish martyrs, spread among the Mozarabs, particularly at Cordoba.

The guiding spirit of the movement was Eulogius, member of a Cordoban family animated by fierce hostility towards the Muslims. At San Zoilo where he was ministrant he struck up friendship with Alvaro, a rich Cordoban patrician later to become his biographer, and was strongly influenced by Flora, daughter of a Christian mother, a woman extremely active in the ranks of militant Christianity. When another priest, Perfectus, was executed after the feast of ramadan in 850 for abusive and blasphemous conduct in respect of the Prophet, a group of Christians decided to face the supreme penalty in emulation. Then, a year later, a monk of

Tabanos stood before the *qâdî* with the resolute intention of blaspheming against the Prophet; conduct that led to his death and to those of a further eleven martyrs in less than twelve months. While the emir issued a decree prohibiting Christians from seeking martyrdom, others of the faith sought a pacific solution by collaborating with the central authority to restore peace to the community.

Recafred of Seville pressed for a Council to be summoned and in 852, despite the opposition of Saul, bishop of Cordoba, the bishops condemned voluntary martyrdom, which was assimilated to suicide and prohibited. Eulogius however persisted on his path towards martyrdom and was imprisoned, together with many others. Some years later he was decapitated by Muhammad I and the opposition to the Muslims was extinguished. After the episode of the Martyrs of Cordoba, the Mozarabs of the ninth and tenth century caliphate lived in harmony with all classes of Andalusian society and were deeply influenced by Arab culture.

The Christian communities of Muslim Spain chose their own administrators, only the formal approval of the caliph was called for. Their governor, on the other hand, holding the title of *qûmis*, was nominated by the central authority and might be Arab or Spaniard. Certain of them, like Servando of Cordoba and Toddo of Coimbra, were celebrated men. At Cordoba, the Mozarabs were represented before the caliph by a defensor, a town magistrate. Taxes were collected by the exceptor, a revenue officer. The Christians took their disputes to a court of first instance to be heard before the *qâdî l-nasârâ* or *qâdî l-'agam*, the Latin censor, who applied the Visigothic law of Liber Judicum, later called the Fuero Juzgo.

The most important Christian communities of Muslim Spain were to be found at Seville, Cordoba and, primarily, at Toledo, which had retained its preeminence as the religious metropolis of the peninsula and was the seat of residence of the Metropolitan (the *matrân*). Churches (*kanâ'is*) were quite numerous. In the capital there was a basilica in the weavers' district and another, not far away, in the parchment makers' district. In Campiña, among others, there were two churches, dedicated to S. Martin of Tours and to S. Eulalia.

The clergy, under their bishops, held regular religious services in the churches, Al-Maqqarî provides us with a most unusual description of one, quoting a passage from the Matmah of Ibn Hâkân: «In one of the Cordoban churches, adorned with myrtle branches and overflowing with happiness and the joy of family reunion, 'Amir ibn Shuhaid passed the night. He was moved by the sound of the bells when the sparkling wine suddenly shone like a lamp and at that moment the priest, elegantly dressed in splendid sashes, appeared among the worshippers of the Messiah (*Masîh*). Joy was abandoned, all pleasure was pushed aside. Ibn Shuhaid stayed on among them drinking wine as though he were drinking from ruby lips; the liquid gave off the most delicious scent to him, like words answered by the softest kiss.»[10]

Around the main towns there were monasteries (*dair* pl. *adiâr*) still inhabited by monks (*râhib* pl. *ruhban*), like that of Armilât (Guadimellato), on the road from Cordoba to Toledo.

Until the fall of the caliphate the Christians of al-Andalus had three flourishing metropolitan provinces; these were episcopal seats with jurisdiction over numerous dioceses. Toledo presided over the bishoprics that stretched as far as Osma and Palencia and, in the Levant, as far as Valencia, Denia and Elche; Lusitania, with a seat at Merida, covered territory that extended to Salamanca and Coira, as far as south Portugal, from Coimbra to Ocsonoba;

Baetica, with its seat at Seville, had jurisdiction over the Andalusian bishops who resided at Medina-Sidonia, Niebla, Cordoba, Elvira, Malaga and Ecija. The other ecclesiastical provinces of Spain, those of Tarragona and Braga, were, by the tenth century, detached from the territories of Islam.

We know only the Arabic name of the archbishop of Toledo, 'Ubaid Allâh ibn Qâsim, who died in 956, but there is more information available to outline the figure of an ecclesiastic of al-Andalus of the caliphal epoch: Rabi ibn Zaid, baptized as Recemundo and author of the celebrated *Kitâb al-Anwâ'* or Liber anoe, popularly known as the «Cordoban Calendar» and later translated into Latin. Recemundo was entrusted by 'Abd al-Rahmân III with important diplomatic missions to the lands of the Holy Roman Empire, to Constantinople and Syria; moreover, he was an honored guest at the court of al-Hakam II.

Within the community, the Mozarabs lived in separate districts, even though daily contact with the Arabs led them to adopt Arab names, Arab costume, and occasionally to keep a harem. A mere fifty years after the conquest Christian adoption of Arab culture was already well under way; so much so that Alvaro of Cordoba, the friend and companion of Eulogius in the tenth century could write: «My fellow Christians are fond of reading Arab poems and novels; they study the writings of Arab theologians and philosophers not to challenge them but to gain a grounding in elegant Arab diction. Where does one find a person today who knows how to read the Latin commentaries on our sacred texts? Who studies the Gospels, the Prophets and the Apostles? Alas! All the young Christians of recognized talent know only the Arab language and its literature; they create immense libraries at great expense and openly proclaim that this literature is admirable. Try to speak to them of Christian books: they will tell you that that are not worthy of their attention. The Christians have forgotten their tongue; it would be hard to find one in a thousand capable of putting together a decent letter in Latin to a friend. But when it is a question of writing in Arabic, one finds innumerable persons who express themselves with the greatest elegance in this tongue, and you will note that from the artistic aspect they compose better poems than those of the Arabs themselves.»[11]

Alvaro was in a position to judge, because he himself spoke both Arabic and Hebrew perfectly. John Hispalense, the Muslims' Sa'îd al-Matrân, who died in c. 840, wrote a commentary on the Bible in Arabic after translating the Book itself into this language. Documents in Toledo cathedral archives provide confirmation that the Mozarabs used Arabic for their own public and private documents until the beginning of the fourteenth century.

Proof of the close relations between Christians and Muslims are certain poems expressing, at times, a delicacy of sentiment that seems to herald the themes that were to be dear to the trouvères. Abû 'Abd Allâh ibn al-Haddâd, one of the Almerian court poets, sings of his love for a young Christian girl of Guadix, Gamila, addressed as Nuwaira:

> Perchance in the Name of Jesus you will grant peace
> to my sick heart!
> Beauty has given you the power of life and death over me,
> has led me to ardent love of the monk's and the ascetic's cross.
> Here I stand, subjected in your name to harsh trials, while
> there is no radiant end to the torments you inflict on me.

I find no solace in oblivion because you hold me captive,
tightly enmeshed in the tentacles (of your heart).
I have by now shed many tears of blood, yet
you show no pity for he who weeps.
Do you know perchance what your eyes have decided for mine?
Do you know perchance the fire kindled in my heart
by the subtle radiance (that shines on your face)?
You have concealed from my eyes this, your radiance,
that shines more brightly than the sun;
The slender branches and the sandy hills
evoke your flanks;
In the flower-bed I discover your cheeks, in its scent
your scent.
Nuwaira, though you flee from me, I instead love you,
I love you.
Your eyes reveal that I am one of your victims.[12]

The People of the Book, *ahl al-kitâb*, included the Jews among their number. Living chiefly in the urban agglomerates and enjoying freedom of movement and the tolerance of the new conquerors, they were far more appreciative than the Christians of the benefits that accrued from their subject status.

Already persecuted after the conversion of Constantine, defined by the first Christian emperors as secta nefaria, the Jewish people had seen the idea of racial inferiority codified in the Codex Theodosianus, their celebration of the paschal lamb forbidden and their rights to worship interfered with by Justinian. Such conditions of life were certainly worse in Visigothic Spain, where they formed a significant part of the population. After the tolerance of the Aryan rulers the situation changed rapidly in the seventh century when the Councils of Toledo intensified discrimination by imposing conversion or exile. These measures led to the characteristic phenomenon in Spain of crypto-Judaism. The Muslim conquest of the country marked the start of a new epoch in the European history of the Jews.

When Tariq crossed the straits the Jewish component in general welcomed the conquerors warmly, so warmly that the Arabs often entrusted them with the custody of the vanquished towns. Their circumstances rapidly changed and many Jews came to hold influential positions to which they brought a political, cultural and intellectual commitment that was a source of stimulus for the Muslims themselves. Many towns had a predominantly Jewish population, like Granada, long known as the «town of the Jews,» Lucena, between Cordoba and Malaga, and Tarragona. Speaking of Lucena where there was an important Academy thriving in the twelfth century, al-Idrîsî says: «The suburbs are inhabited by Muslims and Jews; the mosque cathedral is to be found here, not, however, surrounded by walls. Instead, the town itself has stout fortifications and is girdled by a deep moat and canals that keep it well supplied with water. The Jews live in the innermost part of the town and prevent the Muslims from entering. They are richer here than in any country living under Muslim domination and maintain guards to defend themselves from their rivals.»[13] In the tenth century the most important Jewish community was that of Cordoba, chiefly made up of slave-traders.

The rabbins, who also had a profound knowledge of Arab literature, created a famed talmudic school in the caliphal capital and this, in the times of 'Abd al-Rahmân III, was the scene of the Jewish revival under the auspices of Hasdai Ibn Shaprut, physician at the caliphal court, perspicacious diplomat and minister for foreign trade. The protection he offered and the enlightened direction of Moses Ibn Hanoth, chief rabbi of the Jewish community of Cordoba, caused a splendid theological and philological school to blossom, at the hands of Dunash Ibn Labrat and Menahem B. Saruk. With the re-establishment of fruitful relations with the Jews of the East, Jewish literature, though often following Arab models, took on great importance. Samuel Ibn Nagdela, known as The Prince, vizier to the king of Granada at the start of the eleventh century, was renowned for the extreme perfection of his Arabic style.

At the fall of the caliphate the Jews offered their services to the small kingdoms as advisers, administrators and physicians. They were well received everywhere: at Saragossa, by the Hûdite rulers, where they created an influential community; at Badajoz, by al-Mutawakkil; at Seville, where al-Mu'tamid received at his court the astrologer Isaac ibn Albalia, the chief rabbi of the town; at Denia too, as well as at Valencia, Tudela, Almeria and Huesca. A community of many thousands of Jews settled in Toledo.

With the arrival of the Almoravids the Spanish Jews avoided conversion by paying heavy tributes, but even under these new overlords Jewish physicians were to be found at the court of 'Alî, son of Yûsuf ibn Tashfîn, and Cordoba continued to be an important cultural center and the residence of the poet Joseph b. Jacob Ibn Sahlo and the philosopher Joseph Ibn Zaddick. The end of this prosperity came with the Almohads, who forbade the practise of the Jewish faith, closed the synagogues and introduced obligatory conversion to Islam. Many Jews emigrated, others accepted Islam while continuing to profess their true faith in secret; they were often involved in conspiracies against the authorities, such a one led to the expulsion of the Almohads from Granada. It was this last town, together with its dependencies, Malaga and Almeria, that was to be the chosen territory of the Jews during and after the period of the *mulûk at-tawâ'if*.

The cultural commitment of the Jews continued up to the epoch of the Reconquest, with translations from Arabic, the study of the sciences, especially of medicine and astronomy, without ever losing touch with the culture of the Arabs whose tongue had become the common means of expression.

Ibn Gabirol, the Abû Ayyûb Sulaymân Ibn Yahyâ of the Muslims and the Avicebron of the Scholastics, used Arabic to write both his *Fons Vitae*, influenced by the philosophy of Ibn Masarra, and in writing his minor works. One of his contemporaries, Bahia ben Pacuda, wrote the *Duties of the Heart* in Arabic, a work that owes much to the mystic and moral doctrine of al-Ghazzâlì. Moses Ezra, the unfortunate Granadine poet, exalted joy, love, and the pleasures of life as much as any Arab.

Rising above them all however is the figure of the philosopher who was to surpass his predecessors, Ibn Maymûn, the Latin Maimonides.

Notwithstanding all the diversity of local traditions, belonging to the great web of the empire set the seal of unity even on Andalusian society in that observance of the religious norms of Islam created a similarity in patterns of behavior. The family formed a jealously guarded microcosm, defended against all forms of outside intervention. The law gave a man the right to four legitimate wives in addition to an unspecified number of slave concubines; but only the more prosperous might avail themselves of this circumstance, not the average citizen. The husband was the unchallenged master and everyone respected his authority. The household of a wealthy man might be recognized by the number of women it contained, by the white slaves and black ones, by the eunuchs and the presence of the major-domo. These households, not only among the aristocracy but also in the lower social ranks, discouraged too-frequent contact with the outside world. The well-off woman, wearing the veil as an emblem of distinction and modesty, as prescribed in numerous passages of the Koran, lived in the harem. The word, meaning *sacred place*, signifies that part of the household, reserved to women and children, to which access was severely forbidden to all males outside the family itself. Eunuchs took charge of this sector of the household, not merely as custodians, for many of them became confidants entrusted with important affairs connected with the family life.

The women spent their lives between the silence of the chambers and the cool of the gardens, absorbed in the organization of daily life, distributing tasks among their servants and planning the education of their children. A part of their time was devoted to care for their persons and there might be the occasional visit of women friends or saleswomen; precious occasions, eagerly arranged for the exchange of opinions or gossip. Such gatherings were very often enlivened by music, by singers and dancers. The musicians had to be blind to be admitted to the harem. Moments idly spent watching the time of day go by and listening to the sounds of nature were not infrequent: «The setting sun's rays had grown long on the surface of the earth: the gentle rain you would have thought to be silver powder sprinkled over a carpet of golden leather.»[14]

In addition: «It is a cloud approaching like a bank of darkness, swaying like an injured man. / The force of the east wind scatters its pearls and behold, the cloud lights up beacons for the wind.»[15] Thoughts often turn to love: «The east wind comes to me, laden with the perfume of love.»[16]

The intellectual level could not have been very high, but from the eleventh and twelfth centuries, with the arrival of the Almoravids, there was a reappraisal of the status of women, not only in the family but throughout the entire social structure. A number of them embraced the liberal professions and devoted themselves to law, poetry and medicine.

In this epoch it became customary to mingle with the men after prayer and, at Seville, they sometimes organized parties on the river. These were customs confined to the lower walks of society. Ibn al-Khatîb, who was present when the royal court of Yûsuf I arrived at Granada in 1354, declares that the streets were crowded with women and confesses that his admiration was torn between the gleaming weapons and the splendor of eyes, the red of the Nasrid standards and the colour of cheeks.

Family life in Andalusian society was marked by the ritual ceremonies accompanying birth, marriage and death, ceremonies that differed in no way from those in every other Muslim country. The new born, welcomed with joy, especially when male, were named when they were seven days old. From the tenth century, a fashion set in Baghdad led to girls receiving descriptive names such as Shams (Sun), Bahar (Narcissus), Banafsag (Violet), Hugaima (Little Star). From the age of nine girls wore the veil and dressed like women, albeit continuing their childish pastimes.

Towards their seventh year male children were circumcised, in accordance with ancient Semitic tradition observed also by the Jews. The ceremony was the occasion of great celebrations. At five years of age children of both sexes learned ritual ablution and began to recite the prayer their grandparents taught them together with interminable and fascinating tales inspired by Islamic history.

Any family that was not indigent tried to provide its children with a good education. Means permitting, a private tutor would be employed; elsewhere, sons might be sent to a state school (*maktab*) where parents paid for the first principles to be taught by a *mu'allim*, under the guidance of the town *muhtasib*. Teaching was based on the Koran; the pupils were taught to recite the sacred text correctly and harmoniously, with a proper observance of pauses and intonation, a form of instruction that indirectly left its imprint on their manner of holding everyday conversation. The principles of grammar and syntax were learned by heart. Subsequently, certain of them would be sent to learn a trade while others continued their studies at the mosque school where the curriculum included the rudiments of Mâlikite law and letters. The curriculum was established by tradition. Ibn Hazm, in his classification of the sciences, confessed that it would be preferable for the pupil to be taught the Koran after he had learned to read and write; only then should philology, poetry and liberal studies be introduced. A passion for learning was widespread and rather than abandon the science it was not unusual for pupils to face extreme hardship to be able to pay for their studies.

In the mid-eleventh century Yûsuf I founded a *madrasa* at Granada that was soon to become renowned throughout the Muslim world.

For all this attachment to reason, the sentiments were no less esteemed. Love was certainly one of the dominant passions of the Muslims of al-Andalus. There was nothing stereotyped in the manner in which it was represented and womankind was evoked with grace.

«Between you and me if you so wish there shall be something lasting, a secret that will always remain concealed when the secrets of others have been divulged.

Know then that if you give my beart to hear what others cannot, I shall bear it. Be haughty, I shall support it; waver, I shall be forbearing; proud, I shall humble myself before you; reluctant, I shall make bold; speak and I shall listen; command and I shall obey you.»[17]

Elsewhere, the sublimity of love is evoked: «I would that my heart were laid open with some blade that I might take you in and enclose you within my breast.

There you should remain, unable to wander, until the Day of Resurrection and of the Last Judgement.

You should live in my heart until the end of life and, when that I might die, you would reside in the deepest shade of the Tomb.»[18]

The religious respect for woman often takes on the hue of platonic love, almost portending the troubadour's song of courtly love: «The union of souls is a thousand times finer than that of our bodies.»[19]

Ideal love becomes reciprocal renunciation in which desire is perpetuated.

The last act of life is marked by great simplicity. The awareness of the ephemerality of existence and the vanity of worldly possessions is intense. «I have withdrawn from the world saying: Better far from you for I would not be deceived about the truth. In a corner of my house I have a garden where I may confide my secrets to my trusty companion, one of my books. He taught me the histories of another age and only within him is the truth written and jealously preserved. Death is my goal and they shall bury me without knowing who I am.»[20]

Pomp and circumstance was prohibited at funeral ceremonies. The deceased was taken to his last resting place wrapped in a winding sheet and buried in the earth with his face turned towards Mecca. The only funerary monument might be an epigraph bearing the name of the deceased, some passage from the Koran and, occasionally, a reminder to the onlooker to pray to God in favor of the dead person. As in the East, the color of mourning was white. Later, the Almohads adopted blue, although Jerome Münzer, visiting Granada at the end of the fifteenth century, noted that women following the funeral procession were dressed in white.

The people of al-Andalus, like all Muslims in the Middle Ages, were very attentive to their personal appearance. We can see from miniatures that the men all wore beards, a sign of distinction and social standing. In the epoch of Ziryâb, a broad silk garment with wide sleeves, the *gubba*, worn by men and women alike, had been introduced in Spain. By 'Umayyad times the *burnûs*, a hooded woollen cloak, was used outdoors. The same type of apparel for both sexes was common and men distinguished themselves from women by what was worn on the head: a linen hat (*kufiya*) or a felt skullcap for the male and flowing veils for the female.

At the Alhambra, the paintings in the Kings' Chamber and the figures animating the scenes in the Partal provide us with valuable documentation for the study of Andalusian Muslim apparel. Such was the skill of the craftsmen that the jewels they created were eagerly sought after by women of all classes.

Since the body was respected and cared for, medical science, a field in which the Jews excelled, was held in high esteem. There are, however, no documents of early date confirming the existence in Muslim Spain of public institutions set up for the care of the sick.

Infirmaries made their appearance in the West as an Eastern importation in the Almoravid period after Ibn Ya'qûb had founded the *maristân* of Marrakesh and that of Fez in the twelfth century. A sick person in these establishments received such assistance as might be necessary after recovery to tide him over until he was fit to work again.

At the Nasrid court, physicians not infrequently treated needy patients free of charge and would also dip into their purses to provide additional aid. Only in 1365 did the first *maristân* appear in al-Andalus. Built at Granada by Muhammad V, architecturally speaking it was the fruit of an enchanting and exquisite art that envisaged the adornment of even a place of suffering with flowers and plants, fountains, and carpets covering floors and walls.

The Andalusian house, like that of other Muslim countries, showed no external signs of the family's circumstances; it displayed a high wall in which a small door had been cut, together with even smaller windows shielded by wooden gratings. Behind this facade the sparsely furnished rooms all gave on to an interior courtyard, generally rectangular in shape.

Furnishings would consist of long divans around the walls, low, round tables at which meals were taken, shelves to support cooking utensils and a dais covered with cushions on which the owner of the house received visitors. Cupboards, in the true sense of the word, did not exist. Clothes were stored in large wooden chests. Flanking the entrances to rooms in the wealthier houses one might find niches carved in the walls, containing refreshing drinks for the guests. There is an example in the Hall of the Two Sisters and in the pavilion of the Generalife at the Alhambra. Candles or terracotta oil lamps provided lighting although the houses of the wealthy were furnished with bronze chandeliers. Heating was provided by charcoal-burning braziers. These would be placed at the centre of the rooms, and might be made of stone or marble, metal or terracotta. Mats covered the floors of the poor, rugs, those of the rich. In the wealthier households the walls might be adorned with wall hangings of fine wool or silk.

Respect for the two main festivities of the Islamic calendar called for worthy celebrations. The two dates were the Feast of the Sacrifices (*'id al-adhâ*) and the Feast of the Breaking of Fast (*'id al-fitr*). The latter marked the end of the month of fasting, ramadan, coinciding with the appearance of the new moon in the month of shawwal. The annual slaughter of the ram took place on the tenth day of the month of dhu-l-Ligga.

These were occasions for group prayer, for the exchanging of gifts and for parties to which flowers, songs and dances lent further vivacity. Here just as in the East, a third canonical feast was observed, this was the ashûra, falling on the tenth day of the month of muharran and observed by ritual fasting. Celebrations for the anniversary of the Nativity of the Prophet (*al-mawlid al-nabawî*), the twelfth day of rabi', were introduced at a much later date. Two seasonal festive occasions of ancient date were also observed. These had Persian names, nayrûz, the first day of the Iranian year, coinciding with the spring equinox, and mahragân, falling on the 24 June and celebrated by the lighting of great bonfires.

The Andalusian aristocracy was addicted to horse racing, combat between animals, and *tabla*, a game in which horsemen hurled their lances at a wooden target. The people were given to ruder pastimes such as combat with cudgels, a practice severely condemned by the *muhtasib*. The games of chess and checkers were held in high esteem although prohibited as a distraction from the observance of religious obligations.

Chronicles of the times throw light on street life. Peddlers, countrymen came to town to sell their produce, jugglers, acrobats, astrologers, soothsayers, much despised by Ibn Khaldûn, sellers of ointments and story-tellers. The presence of the singers of *zagal* was tolerated because they often exhorted onlookers to take part in the holy war or urged the faithful to undertake pilgrimages. But from the ninth century, singing, music and the dance became art forms with a status, often considered the most important feature of a reception or a party even when the Mâlikite doctrine condemned the use of musical instruments. «The profession of musician must be prohibited. Where interdiction is not possible, musicians must at least be debarred from going into the country-side without the authorization of the *qâdî* who will make provision for them to be accompanied by a sufficient number of police officials charged with the responsability for preventing the festive occasion from degenerating into disorderly behavior.»[21]

The economy was flourishing and diversified, with a sharp distinction existing between town and countryside. All Arab geographers agree in presenting Muslim Spain as a garden, a country of trees and well-watered crops. It suffices to travel in the south of the peninsula to find that one shares this opinion. But the economic prosperity of al-Andalus was not based solely on agriculture. The mines were worked well; they supplied the greater part of the requirements of the metallurgical industry, together with the raw materials for goldsmithery and whatever was needed for the development of the applied arts. The weaving industry was well organized, producing textiles of every kind, fabrics that were appreciated for their quality and workmanship in every Muslim country. Ibn Hawqal speaks significantly of this: «There is more than one textile factory in Spain whose products are exported to Egypt and from there as far away as the borders of Khorasan and to other places.... In al-Andalus woollen goods of excellent quality are produced as well as costly velvet cloths of ermine... With the wool and other fibers that can be dyed they make textiles of extraordinary quality, thanks to the tints obtained from the plants that grow in that country... No one, in any part of the world, can equal the craftsmen of Spain in the production of felts, prepared exclusively for the sultan... The cloaks made at Pechina are exported to Egypt, to Mecca, to the Yemen and elsewhere. Linen clothes are made up for the sultan and his people that are comparable to the finest fabrics of Dabîq.»[22]

The craftsmen often brought their craft to such perfection that real masterpieces were produced, works that enter the domain of art. Merchants and craftsmen were organized and divided into groups, although it is difficult to say whether they came under some form of State control, as in Byzantium, or whether their associations were spontaneous, as was the case in Europe in the late Middle Ages.

In every town of any importance there did exist, however, an official responsible for exchange and commerce who carried out his duties under the control of the *qâdî*. This official, in later times, was given the name of *muhtasib*, that is to say the person responsible for the *hisba*, whose concerns were the promotion of good and the repression of evil in all questions of public morality, rules of behaviour for followers of different faiths and observance of Koranic and religious prescriptions. The *hisba* covered life in both its secular and religious aspects, it ranged over morality, social values and the rules governing the world of work in general and commerce in particular.

It can be seen that religion was the basic component of not only state structure but that of Muslim society as a whole, as much in al-Andalus as in the East. Muslim Spain was the only country in Islam in which the *fuqahâ*, the men of religion, openly participated in governmental decisions and held a place alongside the sovereigns to assure themselves of their rulers' legitimacy and that the state was being governed in accordance with divine law.

They were a group of men who enjoyed the confidence and respect of the population. Those in power always sought their support as a means of gaining prestige. In every epoch of her history Muslim Spain was marked by her severe and undeviating respect for orthodoxy; this was reflected in every aspect of family and social life, whose origins to a large extent stemmed from it.

The life of every Muslim, not just the Andalusian, was regulated by the faith in even the simplest details of day-to-day existence. Every category brought zeal and conviction to the observance of religion, by which the sentiment of belonging to the much greater society of Believers was fortified.

In the years immediately following the conquest Spain was still considered almost as a land of exile. In the following verse, ad-Dâkhil expresses the sentiments aroused in him, his fortunate circumstances notwithstanding, by the sight of a palm, a poignant reminder of his native land:

Alas! palm of my heart, how you resemble me!
How great is your solitude in the grief of absence
Like me you suffer the heartache of a life
Lived far from family and kin,
At the earth's extremities.[23]

The *gund*, brought to the peninsula by Balg, and the other Syrians driven there by life's vicissitudes, jealously preserved the customs of their forbears. Moreover, Islamic sentiments ran deep, the bonds could not be broken, strong though the fears of Abbasid reconquest might be. Exchanges between Islamic East and Muslim West were fostered by the commitment to pilgrimage that drew the Andalusians towards the centers of Eastern culture, impelled not by faith alone but also be the desire for knowledge or, more simply, by the spirit of adventure. The reputation of al-Andalus in the East rose in the tenth century after al-Hishâm officially adopted the Mâlikite doctrine and gathered about him a religious and intellectual body of jurists and theologians dedicated to the constant defense of orthodoxy and the development of the sciences allied to religion.

Ninth-century Cordoba had already acquired a populous colony of Egyptians, Syrians and Iraqi that had become established on Andalusian soil and was fully integrated in local society. Towards the middle of the century, during the reign of Abd al-Rahmân II, Ziryâb introduced the Andalusian aristocracy to the refinements of the flourishing civilization of Baghdad.

Abû l-Hasan ibn Nâfi, known as Ziryâb because of the dark color of his skin, was born in Mesopotamia and had been a freedman of the caliph al-Mahdî. He soon attracted attention as a pupil of the famous musician and court poet Ishâq al-Mawsîlî. After performing before Harûn al-Rashîd, fearing the jealousy of his master he left the East and sought exile in al-Andalus. He arrived in 822 and remained until his death in 857. Ziryâb was received with great honor by the Umayyad emir and at Cordoba he created a school in which Andalusian music acquired a physiognomy of its own. We are indebted to him for many technical innovations such as the five-corded lute and the bone plectrum to replace the wooden one, but music was not his only interest, for he was well informed in matters of astronomy and geography, and it was through his mediation that the Cordobans were introduced to the elaborate cuisine of Baghdad and the code of manners that reigned there.

The growing receptivity of Spanish Islam to Abbasid influence is amply confirmed in surviving documents; the case of Ziryâb, though well-known, is but one instance of it. 'Abd al-Rahmân II sent 'Abbâs ibn Nasîh to Mesopotamia to buy and to have copied the scientific works that the Greeks and Persians had transmitted to the Arabs. By this time everything that came from Baghdad was received with enthusiasm; new horizons in the fields of science and literature were opening up for Andalusian culture. Meanwhile, in the East, Ibn Nâsil made the acquaintance of Abû Nuwâs; in Cairo, al-Mutanabbî encountered Abû l-Walîd ibn 'Abbâd who, returning from the pilgrimage, declaimed for him a number of verses of the Cordoban Ibn 'Abd Rabbih, the earliest of the Andalusian authors to gain an established reputation in the Arab literature of the West.

The caliph al-Mustansir attracted scholarly Muslims to his court from every Islamic country; such men as the celebrated philologist Abû 'Alî al-Qâlî, a native of Armenia, and the Iraqi poet, al-Muhannad. His ambassadors traveled throughout the Arab world to buy manuscripts, offering a huge sum to the famous Abû l-Farag al-Isfahani for a copy of his *Book of Songs*. Al-Mustansir endowed the Cordoban Alcazar with a very well furnished library, employing bands of *warraq*, professional scribes, to copy out existing works. One of his successors, Ibn Abî 'Amir, received the Iraqi Sa'id at Cordoba. Princely sums were exchanged for Eastern slave girls, skilled musicians and singers such as the Medinese Fadl, 'Ilm and Qalam.

But relations also thrived with the West and with Byzantium. Long before the arrival of ambassadors, merchants came from the Christian world to buy luxury goods, cloths, gold and silver coins, silk, sugar, wool, citrus fruits and bananas. The West bought its paper from Muslim Spain right up to the thirteenth century. But above all the Christian nations provided the Muslim world with Slav slaves. The trade was chiefly in the hands of Jewish merchants who bought everywhere, in Lombardy as much as in the great markets of Lyons, Verdun and Venice.

At Lisbon, Alcacer de Sal, Almeria, Saragossa, Toledo, Malaga and Seville, merchants from the various parts of the Christian world encountered Muslims for the exchange of wares. An exchange that provided the occasion for the transmission, in an entirely unilateral direction, of customs, ideas, forms of thought and of art; in this way Christianity drew on the Islamic world for such material as would contribute to her rebuilding. These contacts increased during the reign of an-Nâsir, a period in which the entire Western world paid homage to the powerful ruler of al-Andalus.

In the summer of 338/949, a Byzantine delegation disembarked at Pechina and was received with elaborate ceremony at the court of Cordoba. In the same year ambassadors of an-Nâsir were received at the Byzantine capital. Liutprando of Cremona records a meeting with them in his *Antapodosis*. Byzantine master craftsmen were called in for the building of Madînat az-Zahra', to instruct the Cordobans in new constructional techniques and methods of decoration, particularly in the field of mosaic work. To this purpose the prelate Rabi' ibn Zaid was sent to Byzantium in 955, returning with numerous workmen and works of art.

The successor of an-Nâsir, al Hakam II, renewed these relations by sending a deputation to Nicephorus Phocas charged with the task of obtaining for Spain a specialist in the preparation of mosaic (*fusaifisa*) who would supervise the decorative work planned for the extensions to the Great Mosque of Cordoba. Many diplomatic missions from Christian countries arrived in Cordoba until 974. March 972 saw the arrival of the legates of John Zimisce, June 974, a mission from Otto II.

The society of Muslim Spain was to be influenced by Byzantine civilization, not by that of Western Europe and unlike 'Abbasid Iraq, the influence would penetrate beyond the field of art. Byzantium continued to be the beacon of the Christian world; the heir to the great scientific and philosophic patrimony of the Hellenistic East. During the ninth and tenth centuries only the court of Baghdad could rival her splendors. Among the manuscripts her ambassadors brought with them to Spain was a Greek copy of the botanical treatise of Dioscorides and an example of the work of Orosius, the great Latin historian of the fifth century. The Byzantine emperors viewed the splendid civilization of al-Andalus with wonder and admiration, Cordoba was the only capital of the Western world to enjoy a prestige that placed it on equal footing with Constantinople.

The reports of the diplomatic missions exchanged between East and West speak of the caliphal court of Cordoba as the scene of solemn official ceremonies, a fusion of the magnificent and the symbolic; a court dominated by a refined simplicity, exacted by the sovereign as a mark of the vanity of all worldly things and of total submission to the will and the power of God, before whom even the authority of the monarch is obeisant.

Lacking any precise documentation, it is difficult to provide a plausible picture of court life. The unassuming ways of ad-Dâkhil, the ruler given to mingling with his poorer subjects and those furthest from the throne were rapidly replaced by the sentiment of the unapproachable caliph who would show himself to his subjects with increasing rarity, and who would retire into almost claustral seclusion, an unassailable symbol of absolute power and infallibility dominating every aspect of life.

At the Great Mosque of Cordoba the *maqsûra*, providing the sovereign with a measure of security against eventual attempts on his life and effectively screening him off from the indiscreet gaze of the faithful, was completed in 250 H.

During the reign of 'Abd al-Rahmân II, al-Andalus increasingly drew on the East for its systems of administration and social organization, which came to resemble those prevailing at the court of Baghdad. The autocratic caliph, temporal and political leader of the community with the right of life and death over his subjects, presiding over the solemn prayer on Fridays, coining money in his own name, who had assumed the title of Commander of the Faithful and would regulate everything in accordance with his own wishes, differed in no way from the 'Abbasid caliph, his enemy. Just as at Baghdad the Andalusian sovereign held audience seated on a throne, holding in his hand the symbol of power, the curved scepter, wearing a ring inscribed with the royal seal and the prince's motto, symbols also embroidered on the standards and the cloths woven in the court *tirâz*. In the purest Eastern tradition the enthronement of the monarch in ninth and tenth century Cordoba was preceded by a solemn oath-taking ceremony, the *bai'a*, taken by the *khassa* in the great reception hall.

Al-Maqqarî leaves us a precise description of this ceremony: «The most high ranking *fatâ* took up their places in hierarchical order, from right to left, along the entire length of the corridor where al-Hakam stood: they wore white tunics in sign of mourning, their swords belted over these; on the terrace, at some distance, stood the slave bodyguards, dressed in gleaming coats of mail and armed with swords encrusted with precious gems; beyond them, beneath the arches of the entrance hall, stood the leaders of the eunuch slaves, dressed in white and with sword in hand, then the eunuch slaves themselves, in order of importance, bearing bows and carrying quivers on their shoulders. After the rows of eunuch slaves, but always drawn up according to rank, came the slave guards armed from head to foot in splendid fashion. At the extreme end of the hall, extending to the ranks of the palace guards, was a sheer wall of foot soldiers dressed in suits of armour covered with white cloaks, gleaming helmets on their heads and shields and shining weapons in their hands. The main door of the palace (*bâb as-sudda*) was guarded by the custodians and their subordinates. Beyond the door, as far as the porch gate (*bâb al-aqbû'*) *'abîd* horsemen were lined up and, stretching away towards the gates of the town, the mercenary horsemen, the various categories of *gund*, the slave soldiers and the archers.»[24]

When the sovereign was in residence in the capital, he left the Alcazar only to go hunting or to move to his suburban villas. In the palace itself, particularly from the tenth century onwards when, under al-Nâsir, court life was to be given its rigid and definitive form, the caliph would have daily contacts with people belonging to the various social classes: the aristocracy, the freedmen and the slaves.

The *khassa*, forming the Cordoban aristocracy, was made up of patricians of Arab origin and those who were more or less closely related to the caliph, people who were usually without public office; in addition to these there were the immigrants who had come to Spain in the ninth and tenth centuries in high hope of the caliph's favors. This group also included the high officials in central administration, of Arab or Slav origin, together with those who held more or less honorary office and who were rich enough to buy for themselves the right to be admitted to the most privileged category in the kingdom. There were three figures of particular importance in civil administration: the steward responsible for running the sovereign's household, the director of the chancellery and the head of the treasury. Above these, appointed by the caliph, was the *hâgib*, the highest court dignitary who had the right to officiate for the caliph, with full powers, during his absence. This title of *hâgib* was appropriated by the reyes de Taifas when the caliphate was dismembered, as proof of their authority to exercise power.

The term *ghilman* was used to refer to all slaves; those of higher rank were termed *fityân*. The eunuchs, almost all of foreign origin, were of particular importance; the mutilation they had undergone gave them free access to all rooms, including those of the harem. They often acquired great power; such was the case of the eunuch Abû l-Fath Nasr who played an important part in the military operations against the Normans in the territory of Seville.

The concubines might also play a determinant role, especially when they had the good fortune to give the emir a son; by this event they acquired the right to freedom after the death of their master. Names that have become famous are those of al-Baha', who gave her name to a mosque on the outskirts of al-Rusâfa; Mu'ammara, celebrated for the piety that led her to build a cemetery at her own expense in the capital; the beautiful Fakhr, Qalam, for whom the emir built a pavilion in the palace in which she took delight in directing singing and music making, and Subh, a figure of eminence in the epoch of al-Hakam II.

Besides those concerned with the caliph's special requirements other dignitaries lived in the palace. The *sâhib al-matbakh* (kitchen overseer), the *sâhib al-bunyân* (head of works), the *sâhib al-khail* (equerry), and the *sâhib al-burûd* (director of the post). The director of the *tirâz* had great standing, he was responsible for the royal factory where clothes were made for the caliph, clothes which might be given to court dignitaries in sign of particular benevolence and consideration. These dignitaries also, belonged to the *khassa* and were admitted to the solemn receptions held in occasion of canonical feasts, victory gained in a campaign or the arrival of important ambassadors.

In this throng of personages each had a specific duty, often more honorary than effective, that contributed to forming a system governed by rigid rules of etiquette. During the reign of an-Nâsir a kind of rich and powerful palatine aristocracy emerged, to play an important role in the life of caliphal Cordoba.

The capital was famed for its splendor among Arab geographers who called it Mother of Cities, Seat of Science, Refuge of the Sunna. A poet dedicated the following couplets to Cordoba:

> Do not speak to me of the court of Baghdad nor
> of its magnificence, nor boast of the various merits
> of Persia and China,
> Because there is no place like Cordoba anywhere
> on this earth, nor in the world men like the Banû Hamdîn.[25]

At its zenith, it was made up of twenty-one districts (*rabad*) that revolved on the Medina, the Great Mosque at its heart. Between the Guadalquivir and the Mosque rose the Alcazar, the caliphal residence, a city in itself and also the burial ground of the emirs and caliphs. The town was girdled by a series of palaces and villas (*munya*) where the sovereigns retired at their pleasure during the fine season.

The Saxon monk Hroswith, enchanted by the beauty of the spectacle that lay before his eyes, wrote: «Shining jewel of the world, new-born and magnificent city, proud of your strength, famed for your delights, splendid in your possession of every bounty.»[26]

Halfway through his reign, an-Nâsir felt the need to build a new residence a few kilometers from the capital on the last ramparts of the Sierra, *Gabal al-'Arûs*, the Mountain of the Bride. He called it Madînat az-Zahra', the City of az-Zahra', the name of his favourite. As we have said, artists and craftsmen from every part of the Muslim and Christian world took part in building this residence, the seat of the court in the second half of the tenth century.

When political unity was shattered and gave way to the domination of the reyes de Taifas, there was no consequent decline in the desire for learning. On the contrary, every town the seat of a dynasty became a lodestar for whoever was inclined to the study of science. Each court drew poets and men of letters, attracted by the patronage of the rulers. Once more as an echo of the East, the towns became miniature reflections of the great Baghdad.

Everyone in eleventh-century Muslim Spain knew how to compose verse; dexterity in manouvering the complex rules of poetic expression was, at times, worth the dignity of vizier, it always gained the esteem and friendship of the world. Neither political duties nor the toils of war would distract the Andalusians from their major commitment. The pole of attraction was now Seville, to whom Cordoba had yielded the palm. This is how Ibn Hisn describes it: I recall you, O Hims, with such passion that the tireless tormentor of lovers might die of envy!

> When the sun prepares to set, it resembles a bride,
> unchanging in her beauty;
> The river is your necklace, the mountain your crown
> above which the sun rises, like a hyacinth.[27]

The court of 'Abbadite Seville became the intellectual center of al-Andalus while the old capital languished. The novelty most worthy of consideration is certainly this popular involvement in the art of improvising good verse, a reflection of a love for poetry shared alike by prince and artisan, by minister and laborer in the field. But the poet, over dependent on the ruler for his livelihood, became the courtier and lost his way amid praises and commendations, all too ready to compose for every circumstance, a victory, a wedding, the solemn reception of a diplomatic mission. Every town had its glories: Mutawakkil of Badajoz was famed for his erudition, Ibn Razin for music, Ibn Tahir of Murcia for the elegance of his ornate prose, al-Muqtadir of Saragossa for science.

Religious concerns, the search for and the evidence of faith lost ground with the *mulûk at-tawâ'if*. The preference was for composing anthologies on spring flowers, the rhymes of the *zagal* were followed in a frenzied passion for beauty, and rising above all this was the figure of the emir of Seville who lived for poetry, offering the refuge of his court to all those who came to him from Sicily and the Maghrib.

The Spain of the reyes de Taifas proved capable of producing works that, even in respect of Eastern classicism, are original creations of men of culture, no whit inferior to the productions of Baghdad or Medina, even though the East for long held no great opinion of Western culture. In a letter to Ibn 'Abdûn, Ibn Abî-l-Khisâl says: «Is not the West, compared with other countries, a mere gloss between the lines?»[28] Al-Muzaffar ibn al-Aftas of Badajoz denied any Andalusian the right to compose poetry, declaring: «He whose poetry cannot rival that of al-Mutanabbî or al-Ma'arrî should be silent.»[29]

Admiration for the East proceeds by similes. Al-Higârî says: «Spain is the Iraq of the West, by reason of genealogy, for the delicacy of letters, the constant research applied to every branch of science and the ingenious variety that dominates prose and poetry.»[30]

Ibn Hazm himself, in his *Risâla* in praise of Spain, shows dissatisfaction and restlessness: «I am the sun that shines in the firmament of the sciences, but my defect is that I rise in the West.»[31]

The works that served as models for men of letters were all of Eastern provenance. Studies were based on the *Mu'allaqât*, the nine celebrated poems by Gâhiliyya, the *Hamâsa* of Abû Tammân, al-Mutanabbî, Abû-l-'Alâ al-Ma'arrî, Ibn Qutaiba, and the «Book of Songs» of al-Isfahânî.

But in the eleventh century the tide turned when the Cordoban al-Himyarî, vizier of Ibn 'Abbad at Seville, drew up a genuine manifesto in defense of the cultural values of al-Andalus: «Eastern poetry has monopolized our attention for so long that it has now lost its attraction for us; its jewels no longer seem so seductive. Moreover we need no longer concern ourselves with it, there is no further need, for by now the Andalusians have marvellous prose passages of their own, and poems of original beauty... The Easterners for all the care they show in composing verse, in writing up their history, aided by their long familiarity with Arabic, are yet unable to enhance their work by that appropriate application of simile to descriptive passages such as I observe, instead, in the compositions of my fellow countrymen.»[32]

In respect of tradition there is more collaboration on scientific and literary work among Andalusian scholars. The *Tafsîr* of Ibn 'Atîya and the *'Alfîya* of Ibn Mâlik are texts that had been used for scholastic instruction in the Maghrib for centuries. Elsewhere in the Muslim world the speculative sciences continued to be regarded as the handmaids of the traditional sciences, whilst in Spain there was a growing interest in man and in the development of all of his faculties. This was to become the most significant and characteristic aspect of the spiritual development of al-Andalus after the eleventh century.

After the arrival of the Almoravids, Ibn Bassâm writes: «The reality of what is comprehensible is more worthy of our attention than the futilities of prose and poetry.»[33] The new criteria of moral austerity and religious observance introduced by Ibn Tashfîn had brought a change of climate. The courts were deserted and silence fallen; the poets, finding no ready ear among the new rulers, were forced to seek refuge in the East and submit to singing the praises of those who had averted the foreign peril.

Beneath the astounded eyes of the population gathered on the banks of the Guadalquivir al-Mu'tamid was led out of Seville, to be taken into captivity at Aghmat in the Atlas regions, there to end his days, while the women who accompanied him were reduced to spinning cloth to earn a living. This was but the end of a way of life, not of the Muslim culture of Spain, which adjusted to the new circumstances.

More sparing of artifice, the forms and expressions by which nature was now evoked were well received; the structures of the *muwashshaha* and the *zagal* were given definitive form.

Under the Almohads, what remained of Muslim Spain reverted to a fruitful re-elaboration of tradition that proved eloquent of the inherent vitality of Islam, but after Las Navas, the towns fell one after the other and men of culture were forced to emigrate. Only Granada remained to sustain the fame of Muslim learning. The kingdom of the Banû l-Ahmar, the last strip of the Iberian peninsula to keep the flag of Islam flying, lay in the narrow coastal region from Gibraltar to Almeria, extending its reaches to the mountainous chain of the Serrania of Ronda and the Sierra of Elvira. The state distinguished itself for the vitality of its artistic and cultural life. Muhammad I had set up his residence in the former Zirid fortress of the Alhambra, standing on the left bank of the Darro. His successors transformed it and created the last refuge for the brilliant flowering of the Muslim culture of al-Andalus.

In the fourteenth century, Granada, a bulwark of Mâlikite orthodoxy, witnessed to a mystic fervour that took possession of its men of letters. A number of these *faqîh*, seduced by the beauty of this place in which «trees, rains, running water, gardens and orchards abounded,»[34] had been drawn here from such remote countries as Iran and India.

The Maghriban Ibn Battûta met with men from Samarcand, Konya, Tabriz and Khorasan during his stay at the Nasrid court in 751/1350; a stay that also gave him occasion to converse with Ibn al-Khatîb, a great historian who brought luster to the political life of the little state.

In the halls of the Alhambra and in the gardens of the Generalife intellectual life flourished: the sciences and philosophy, medicine and mathematics, were cultivated with passion and success in a world that produced outstanding figures, at a court that gave refuge to the great Ibn Khaldûn in his years of exile. The rulers were always attentive patrons of poetry, its themes, the re-evocation of the past, the splendors of the moment and the sorrowful fate of Andalusian Islam.

The poetic forms of Ibn al-Khatîb stem directly from the Andalusian environment; Ibn Zamrak, the last great Arab poet of Spain, attained perfection in the eulogy and the ornate poem. His verses, in ornamental letters, are to be found on the walls of the Court of the Myrtles, in the Hall of the Two Sisters, on the fountain in the Lions' Court, perpetuating Granadine ideals at the end of the fourteenth century.

A century later, the Egyptian 'Abd al-Bâsit entered the Alhambra to be received in princely fashion by the sultan Abû l-Hasan. It was an act of homage from the East, paying its last visit to Western Islam by now under siege from the renewed Christian forces to whom the union of Castile and Aragon had brought fresh energies. «There is no strength or protection but that of the Lord!»—the ancient words must have been on their lips, seeing the infidels so close to ultimate victory.

The town, for one last, brief moment, savors the splendors of its beauty: «Granada is a bride: the Sabiqa is her diadem, / the flowers, her jewels and raiment.»[35]

Notes

[1] Al-Maqqarî, *Nafh at-tîb fi gusn al-Andalus ar-ratîb wa dhikr wazîrihâ Lisân ad-Dîn Ibn al-Khatîb*, abridged ed. R. Dozy - G. Dugat - L. Krehl - W. Wright, Leiden 1855-'61, 2 vol. (complete ed. Bûlâq 1279 H./1862); partial Eng. tr. by P. De Gayangos, The Mohammedan Dynasties in Spain, London 1840-1843, I, 17.

[2] Ibn Hawqal, *Kitâb surat al-ard*, ed. J.H. Kramers, Leiden 1938, 108-109.

[3] Ahmad al-Râzî, cfr. E. Lévi-Provençal, *La description de l'Espagne de Râzî*, «Al-Andalus», 18 (1953), 51-108.

[4] Al-Idrîsî, in al-Maqqarî, *Nafh at-tîb...*, tr. P. De Gayangos, I, 19.

[5] Al-Idrîsî, *Description de l'Afrique et de l'Espagne*, Arab text and Fr. tr. by R. Dozy - J. De Goeje, Leiden 1866, 165, 173.

[6] Al-Maqqarî, *Analectes: Analectes sur l'histoire et la littérature des Arabes d'Espagne*, ed. R. Dozy, Leiden 1855-'61; Eng. tr. P. De Gayangos, I, 17-17.

[7] Ibn Khafâga, *Dîwân*, Cairo 1286 H., 72; cfr. al-Maqqarî, *Analectes...*, I, 451-452.

[8] R. Dozy, *Histoire des Musulmans d'Espagne jusqu'à la conquête de l'Andalousie par les Almoravides (711-1110)*, Leiden 1923, I, 276-277.

[9] Ibn Hazm, *Risâla*, in al-Maqqarî, *Analectes: Analectes sur l'histoire et la littérature des Arabes d'Espagne*, II, 105.

[10] Al-Maqqarî, *Analectes...*, I, 345.

[11] Alvaro, *Indiculus Luminosus*, in *España Sagrada*, XI, 274-275.

[12] Ibn Bassâm, *adh-Dhahîra fî mahâsin ahl al-gazîra*, Cairo 1942, I, t. 2, 215-216.

[13] Al-Idrîsî, Description..., 205.

[14] Ibn Billîta, in Ibn al-Abbâr, *al-Hullat as-siyarâ'*, extracts ed. R. Dozy, *Notices sur quelques manuscrits arabes*, Leiden 1847-1851, 192.

[15] Ibn Burd, in al-Maqqarî, *Analectes...*, II, 133.

[16] Ibn al-Labbâna, in al-Fath ibn Khâqân, *Qalâ'id al-'iqyân*, Bûlâq 1283 H., 256.

[17] Ibn Zaidûn, *Dîwân*, Cairo 1351 H., 279.

[18] Ibn Hazm, *Tawq al-humâma fi -l- ulfa wa-l-ullâf*, ed. Petrof, Leiden 1914, 58.

[19] Ibn Hazm, *Tawq al-hamâma...*, 92.

[20] Ibn Labbûn, in al-Maqqarî, *Analectes...*, II, 404-405.

[21] Ibn 'Abdûn, *Traité de Hisba: un document sur la vie urbaine et les corps de métier à Séville au début du XII siècle*, ed. E. Lévi-Provençal, «Journal Asiatique», 1934, 177-299; Fr. tr. by E. Lévi-Provençal, *Séville musulmane au début du XII siècle: Le Traité d'Ibn 'Abdûn*, Paris 1947, 120.

[22] Ibn Hawqal, *Kitâb al-masâlik al-mamâlik*, ed. J.H. Kramers, Leiden 1938, III, 113-114.

[23] Ibn 'Idhârî, *al-Bayân al-mughrib fî akhbâr al-Maghrib*, ed. R. Dozy, Leiden 1848-'51; Sp. tr. F. Fernandez Gonzales, *Historias de al-Andalus*, Granada 1860, I, 128.

[24] E. Lévi-Provençal, *L'Espagne musulmane au Xème siècle, Institutions et vie sociale*, Paris 1932, 58.

[25] Al-Maqqarî, *Analectes...*, Eng. tr. P. De Gayangos, I, 202.

[26] Schack-Valera, *Poesia y arte de los Arabes en España y Sicilia*, Seville 1881, I, 57.

[27] Ibn Hisn, in al-Maqqarî, *Analectes*, II, 181.

[28] 'Abd al-Wâhid al-Marrâkushî, *al-Mu'gib fî talkhîs ta'rîkh al-Maghrib*, ed. R. Dozy, Leiden 1881, 121.

[29] Ibn Al-Khatîb, *A'mâl al-alâm fiman buyi'a al-ihtilâm min mulûk al-islâm wa mâ yagurr dhalik min shugûn al-kalâm*, abridged ed. by E. Lévi-Provençal, Rabat 1934, 212.

[30] Al-Maqqarî, *Analectes...*, II, 107.

[31] Al-Maqqarî, *Analectes...*, II, 120.

[32] Al-Mimyarî, *al-Badî' fî wasf ar-rabî*, ed. H. Pérès, Rabat 1940, f.° 2 a-b.

[33] R. Dozy, *Scriptorum Arabum loci de Abbadidis*, Leiden 1846-'63, III, 43.

[34] Al'Umarî, *Masâlik al-absâr*, Fr. tr. by Gaudefroy-Demembynes, *L'Afrique moins l'Egypte*, Paris 1927, 224.

[35] Ibn Zamrak, Sp. tr. by E. Garcia-Gomez, *Cinco Poetas musulmanos*, Madrid 1944, 198.

CHAPTER FOUR
ART IN ISLAMIC
CIVILISATION

Islam is a religion that has produced a civilization and a culture in which the spiritual and the temporal are coalescent. Although God has given mankind a guide, strictly speaking there exists no other temporal authority but that of God himself. The right to exercise such power as stems from natural and divine laws is not given to man; it remains His prerogative.

The Koran alone is vested with legislative authority and it is in the Book and in the Sunna that the laws are to be found. God, the supreme lawgiver, has revealed His will and His laws to the Prophet. The caliph, vicar of the Prophet on earth, is not an absolute sovereign. He is not the lord of well-being on earth, nor does he possess any legislative power whatsoever in spiritual matters.

The life and art forms of the Muslim community, wholly consecrated to the purposes of religion, have been deeply influenced by the Koran. In the strict sense, Islamic art comprises architecture and ornamentation on the one hand and psalmodied recitation on the other. The subject and object of Islamic architecture is the mosque.

When the Prophet was forced to leave Mecca in 622, he and his most faithful *sahaba* (companions), among them Abû Bakr, moved to the tiny oasis of Yathrib where he bought a piece of land from two orphans, Sahl and Suhail. On this, using a technique that may have been of Abyssinian origin, he erected a building of sun-dried mud bricks. To the north he built a kind of great hall roofed with palm leaves and mud, the far wall of which faced towards Jerusalem. To the east he built two small rustic dwellings for Sawda and 'A'isha, the two brides taken by the Messenger of Allah after the death of his first wife Khadîgia. A shelter for the poor was put up on the southwest side. All the dwellings gave onto the courtyard. This was how, in the small township later to take the name of Madînat an-Nabî (Medina), the first very humble mosque came into being. Muhammad did nothing to improve on it because, he said, «The most unprofitable thing that eateth up the wealth of a Believer is Building.»[1]

The mosque did not conform to the pattern of Hebrew or Christian places of worship, the temple and the church, in that it was also used as an assembly hall in which the Prophet imparted religious instruction together with the rules governing the behavior of the community. An assembly hall in whose courtyard the nomads often put up their tents, for the mosque was open to all, it offered shelter to all, even to non-Muslims. At the dawn of Islam Muhammad avoided attributing to any worldly setting the sacred character that was the esclusive privilege of the Ka'aba. He used the term *masgid* when referring to his building. A term that indicates the place where God is venerated. It derives from the root S-D-G, to be on the ground, to prostrate oneself, to touch the ground with one's forehead. Much later many Muslim countries, especially those in North Africa, would show a preference for a different term, *Gâmi'*, from the root G-M, to gather together, together to withdraw into seclusion.

Initially the Prophet prayed towards Jerusalem, but when relations with the Jews of that city changed, he altered the direction and prayed towards the east, towards the Ka'aba at Mecca. At this time the minaret was unknown, prayer took place in the absence of the call to prayer. Only later did the Prophet give orders to the Abyssinian Bilâl to summon the faithful vocally from the highest rooftop in the vicinity.

The plan of a mosque is basically an enclosure (*sahn*), generally rectangular in shape, in which the *qibla* provides an indication of the orientation towards Mecca. At the center of the courtyard there is often one or more basins (*mîda*) containing water for ablutions, and occasionally fountains. The enclosure walls are usually flanked by a covered gallery (*mugâtta*) that, in coincidence with the *qibla*, takes on the scale and proportions of a hall (*liwân*). When the *liwân* ceiling is supported by columns, corridors known as *awriqa* (pl. of *riwâq*) are formed. It is not known when the practice of linking the columns by means of arches was first introduced. Round arches in imitation of the Byzantine style may be seen in the Qubbat as-Sakhra in Jerusalem, the first religious building worthy of the glory of Islam. Later, in the eleventh century, two new forms of arch appeared, the horseshoe arch (*manfîkh*) and the four-centred arch (*mahmûz*). The first of these was probably inspired by the Byzantine models prevalent in Syria, the second, a derivation from Persian tradition. At first, columns were copied from earlier monuments but later, square, rectangular and cruciform pillars appeared.

All the naves in a mosque lead to the *qibla* wall, inset with a niche, or *mihrâb*. This is not the focal point of the building, nor must it be confused with an altar. The level of the central nave is slightly raised in respect of the others and it is covered with one or more domes. The *gâma'* mosques, cathedral-mosques, are used chiefly for Friday prayer; they contain a pulpit, the *minbâr*, from which the preacher speaks to the faithful. The use of this furnishing, unlike the *mihrâb* that was introduced for the first time by the caliph 'Umar, was familiar to Muhammad, who received foreign visitors and addressed the mosque congregation seated on a modest chair of tamerisk wood, made for him by a Coptic or Byzantine artist. This soon became the symbol of political and religious power, neither a dais nor a pulpit but an authentic throne. Other furnishings may be found in very important mosques, a raised platform (*dakka*) from which the second and third call to prayer is made, a *qass*, or lectern, to hold the Koran, and large armchairs (*karâsî*, pl. of *kursî*) exclusively for the use of renowned professors or *hadîth* readers. The floor of the mosque is covered from wall to wall with carpets (*saggâda* pl. *sagâgî'd*). Lamps (*qindîl* pl. *qanâdil*) hanging from gold or silver chains were introduced in the Abbasid epoch to lighten the interior, while chandeliers (*tannûr*) made of semi-precious metals came in much later.

In mosques used by the sovereign there is a reserved area, generally partitioned off by a wooden screen. This afforded him major protection at the moment of prayer when he turned his back to the faithful. The *maqsûra*, introduced by Mu'âwiya, often isolated both the *mihrâb* and the *minbâr*. Moreover, since the presence of women in the mosque was not always accepted, this partitioned area was often reserved for their use. Each *maqsûra* was screened off by grilles, or *mashrabîya*. A mosque interior contains no other furnishings.

One of the distinctive features of the exterior of the mosque is the minaret, which the Arabs have three different names for: *midhana, saum'a* and *manâra*. It is usually built on the axis of the central nave on the opposite side of the courtyard to the prayer hall. Although there was a minaret as early as 705 in the mosque built by al-Walid at Medina, the origin of the structure is unknown.

To the visitor the mosque presents the appearance of a closed mass with very little outlook, frequently surrounded by thronged bazaars with their diverse wares, and access to the mosque doors on whatever side is gained by weaving one's way through the crowds. The mosque is indeed often so embedded in an agglomerate of dwellings that it is hard to identify.

This scheme does not produce different architectural styles in the true sense because there is a common line to all, but country, climate and builders' intentions do create variations in the type of mosque. When a large congregation has to be housed, it suffices to enlarge the courtyard and add to the number of naves in the *liwân*. This was the origin of the *'askarî* or military mosque, intended as a prayer hall for a marshalled army.

A different type of mosque again is that on the cruciform plan. Here, each of the four arms of the cross forms a *liwân* branching off a central courtyard. This is the *madrasa-mosque*, not only a place of worship but also, and primarily, a place for teaching.

The place and structure of the mosque with a central dome is very different from either of these. It was designed in the cold regions of Asia Minor to defend the faithful against the harsh climatic conditions in the winter and acquired special favor with the growing ascendancy of the sultanate and the consolidation of Ottoman power. The dome is to be found elsewhere in the mausoleum - mosque, built to commemorate figures who were particularly revered for their devotion and religious piety or for the significance of their achievements although it may also be used as a covering for simple funerary monuments that have not been elevated to the status of mosques. In this circumstance it is called a *qubba* or a *marbût*, essentially in the North African context, and a *shah-zâde* in Iran. When the deceased is venerated with particular intensity and devotion because he submitted to martyrdom the building bears the name of *mashad*. This is an exclusively Iranian usage.

There are no priests in the Muslim faith, no specially appointed persons to conduct worship. The prayer rite is led by the imam, a term signifying «he who guides», «he who precedes». In earlier times the head of the community, the caliph, was also the imam. Later, in the Abbasid age, the office was delegated to the governors of the various provinces, who in turn might call on the *sâhib ash-shurta* (chief of police) to stand in for them. This subsequently led to the nomination of a permanent official paid by the state. The caliph or the governor thenceforward performed the duty of imam only on special occasions, above all in the period of ramadan. The imam today is a reputable person chosen from among the faithful, one whose place may be taken by another of similar standing. He leads Friday prayer, delivers the *khutba* and keeps a watchful eye on the practices and morality of the area in which the mosque stands.

The summons to prayer, called, as the Prophet suggested, by the *mu'adhdhin*, is made three times: a summons to the mosque, the call on the Prophet himself, and the call announcing the commencement of the rite. Since the 'Umayyad period the *adhân*, the proclamation of the Oneness of God, has been made from the summit of the minaret.

Within the mosque other figures with special duties are to be found, the *qâss* and the *muftî*. The first term denotes the reciters of the Koran, who must be perfectly versed in the sacred text and the appropriate intonations to be used. The term *muftî*, on the other hand, means «he who expresses juridical opinions,» that is to say an official jurisconsult, one who takes up his place in the *maqsûra* to pronounce on the *fatwâ*, legal matters. In the Maghrib however, excluding Morocco, he is also the most influential religious figure, charged with the administrative affairs of the mosque and its maintenance.

In the early days of Islam the mosque was not only a sacred place but also a convenient space for public assembly to discuss anything and everything, public affairs, private interests and also war. Both Jews and Christians could enter, although regulations were later made more stringent, not only with regard to entrance of non-Muslims but also in relation to the faithful. It was laid down that footwear should be removed before entering the sacred enclosure and the presence of women was allowed on condition that they refrained from mixing with the men and did not allow their thoughts to stray during the canonical rite. For centuries the mosque had no prescribed opening hours; the faithful might enter at any hour of the day or night, and it offered shelter to travelers and to all those who might have need of it. But under the later Turkish conquest the sacred character of the building came to predominate.

Each day, little by little as the Word was revealed to him, the Prophet taught the Koran in the mosque. His assistants repeated his teachings until they had learned them by heart. Thus the mosque became a center for the transmission of thought,—a school. The building had no altars, no choirstalls, no shrines or paintings. This raises the question of the attitude of Islam towards imagery.

There is no interdiction of images, either paintings or statues, representing living beings, in the Koran. The only comment relevant to this concerns the pagan use of idols as cult objects. «Believers, wine and games of chance, idols and divining arrows, are abominations devised by Satan. Avoid them, so that you may prosper.»[2]

In the sixth sura Abraham reproves his father, Azar, for the veneration of idols: «Surely you and all your people are in palpable error.»[3] Nothing is to be found in the Koran that resembles the Biblical proscription «Thou shalt not make thee any graven image, or any likeness of any thing that is in heaven above, or that is in the earth beneath, or that is in the waters beneath the earth.»[4] This prohibition must have been familiar to Muhammad who knew the Jews and the Bible well, consequently, its absence from the Koran must be intentional. Indeed, as we know that the houses of Medina were generously adorned with paintings, it may be said that early Islam was not opposed to images, although it must be admitted that even in this period representations of living beings were not to be found in the mosques. The only exceptions that spring to mind are the mosaics in the Dome of the Rock in Jerusalem, in the mosque at Medina, and in the Great Mosque of Damascus. This is in keeping with the Tradition, the Sunna, the second source of the Law.

In the collection of *hadîth* one finds: The Angels will not enter a temple (*bayt*) in which there are images, bells or dogs.»[5] Since this statement is attributed to the Prophet it undoubtedly explains the absence of representations of living beings in the mosques. Another *hadîth* warns: «On Resurrection day the most terrible punishment will be inflicted on the painter who has imitated the beings created by God. He will then say: Give life to these creations.»[6]

To gain a better understanding of the prohibition it is helpful to read a text, written at some time between the fourth and the tenth centuries by Abû'Alî l-Fârisî, that says: «If the objection is raised that Tradition attributes the following words to the Prophet: 'Makers of images shall be punished on the Day of Judgment' and in certain versions, in addition to this, he is attributed with 'It will be said to them — Give life to what you have created —', the reply is that the words 'Makers of images shall be punished' applies to those who represent God in bodily form, and all additional comment belongs to the realm of personal interpretation for which there is no guarantee of authenticity. Seen in this way, the view of the *'ulama'*, as we have stated, goes unchallenged.»[7]

At a later date there will be a change of attitude. Tâg ad-Dîn as-Subkâ, a doctor of Law who died in Damascus in 1369, confirms this in the decree: «The painter must not represent the image of any living being, either on a wall, a ceiling, on any utensil whatsoever, or on the ground. Certain brethren have allowed the representation of images on the ground and on other analogous supports. This is contrary to the undisputed law, because the Prophet cursed painters in the following words: They shall know the greatest punishment on the Last Day of Judgment.»[8]

Initially the artists restricted themselves to representing architectural forms, flowers, landscapes and still lifes, obeying an aesthetic canon that was to become increasingly conceptual. The floral motif, which together with epigraphy and geometry is one of the essential components of Muslim art, differs from the flower of reality because of the stylized treatment it has undergone. The acanthus and the vine of the sculptors of Fez and Cordoba are not to be found in any garden or vineyard, the flowers and palms will not be dealt with in any botanical treatise. Form handled in this way is a creation of the spirit and art a product of the intellect. The painter is not concerned with a faithful rendering of a landscape or of a lion chasing a gazelle because he is transported by the art of the arabesque that the strict monotheism of Islam has suggested to him.

Al-raky and *al-khayt*, the two forms of the arabesque, the first seemingly the fruit of fantasy, the second, of geometrical research, do not derive from a whim. The Koran says: «To Allah belongs the east and the west. Whichever way you turn there is the face of Allah.»[9] In addition: «This is best for those who strive to please Allah; such men will surely prosper.»[10] Allah suggested the following short verse to the Prophet: «Coin for them a simile about this life. It is like the green herbs that flourish when watered by the rain, soon turning into stubble which the wind scatters abroad. Allah has power over all things.»[11]

The earth therefore implies mere empty appearances (XXVIII, 60; LVII, 20),[12] unlike the divine blessing, a thing of transiency.

The stylization of the arabesque speaks to us from the realm of fleeting intentions: «Let the life of this world not deceive you...»[13], because «This present life is like the golden robe with which the earth bedecks itself when watered by the rain. Crops, sustaining man and beast, grow luxuriantly: but as its hopeful tenants prepare themselves for the rich harvest, down comes Our scourge upon it, by night or in broad day, laying it waste, even though it blossomed but yesterday.»[14]

The dethronement of matter is eloquent of the doubt that surrounds our earthly existence, in which every activity is vain diversion, «but a sport and a pastime.»[15] This is the source of indifference to the model, to the barely suggested relief and the rejection of unfilled space.

In the eyes of Islam man is not the measure of all things. God has placed him above many other creatures not for his merits but from sheer benevolence because man in himself was created «out of a void.»[16] The beauty of the human body is undisputed: «We moulded man into a most noble image,»[17] but this beauty is ephemeral and empty.

As with architecture, so with decoration; the fragile art of the arabesque springs from the same spiritual source, from an ascetic retreat into himself in the course of which man can only bow down before the unattainable divinity, aware of his insignificance: «It is We who ordain life and death. To Us all shall return.»[18]

Notes

[1]   Ibn Sa'id, *Tabaqât al-uman*, ed. L. Cheiko, Beirut 1912, I, 181.

[2]   *The Koran*, Eng. tr. by N.J. Dawood, Penguin Books 1956, V, p. 386.

[3]   *The Koran*, VI, p. 420.

[4]   *The Bible*, Dt., 5. v. 8.

[5]   H. Lammens, «Journal Asiatique», 1915, 350.

[6]   Al-Bukhârî, in A. Papadopoulo, *L'Islam et l'art musulman*, Paris 1976, 53.

[7]   Bishr Farès, *Essai sur l'esprit de la décoration islamique*, Cairo 1952, 25.

[8]   G. Wiet, *Les mosquées du Caire*, Paris 1932, I 182.

[9]   *The Koran*, II, p. 336.

[10]   *The Koran*, XXX, p. 191.

[11]   *The Koran*, XVIII, p. 93.

[12]   *The Koran*, XXVIII, p. 78; LVII, p. 107.

[13]   *The Koran*, XXXV, p. 175.

[14]   *The Koran*, X, p. 65-66.

[15]   *The Koran*, XXIX, p. 197.

[16]   *The Koran*, XIX, p. 36.

[17]   *The Koran*, XCV, p. 23.

[18]   *The Koran*, L, p. 121.

On the preceding page and facing: a detail in close-up and
a general view of a doorway on the east front of the Great
Mosque of Cordoba. Above: the entire east front seen in
perspective (Oronoz). Overleaf: the nave of 'Abd
al-Rahmân I in the Great Mosque (Oronoz).

Cordoba, the Great Mosque: extension built by al-Hakam II al-Mustansir (Oronoz). Facing: interlaced and hexafoil arches of the same epoch.

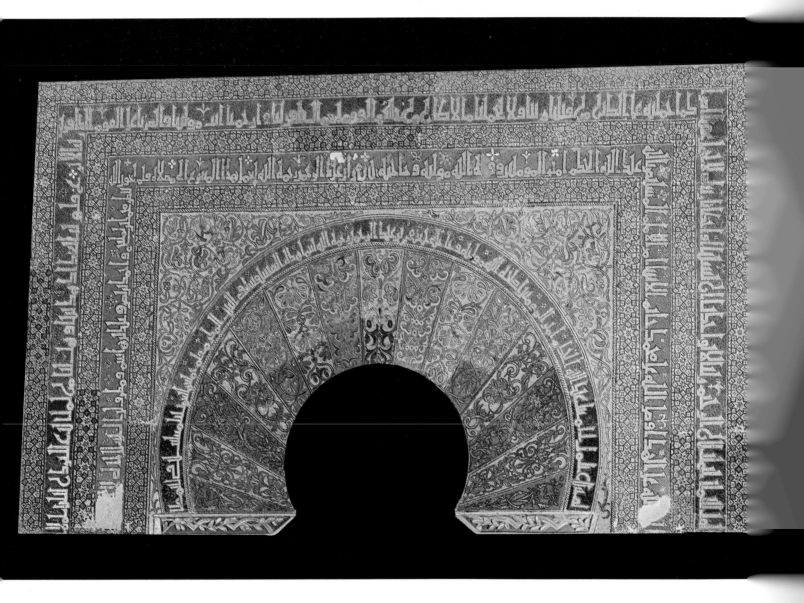

Cordoba, the Great Mosque: arch at the side of the mihrab
(Oronoz). On the left: the nave approaching the qibla.
Facing: vault of transept approaching the arch (Oronoz).
On the following pages: the dome above the mihrab and
the mihrab itself. The entrance arch to the mihrab is
framed by a Kufic inscription, in praise of the Lord, carried
out in gold mosaic against a blue background. (Oronoz)

*On the preceding pages:
Saragozza, Aljaferia: entrance
arch and the interior of the
Oratory. (Oronoz)*

*On the left: Seville. Two views of the east doorway of the
Great Mosque (twelfth century). Above and facing: the
Giralda Tower, Seville (twelfth century). On the following
page, a further detail of the Giralda: a multilobed arch.*

134

The black and white photographs on the preceding pages and here, on the left, illustrate details of both external and internal structures of the Great Mosque of Cordoba. The first photograph shows a marble plaque set into the wall on the right of the Puerta de las Palmas leading into the Patio de los Naranjos. The inscription reads: "In the name of God, the Compassionate and Merciful. All this was carried out with the aid of Allah in the month of dhu higga of the year 346 (February 958)..."

A frontal view of the Aljaferia Prayer-hall at Saragossa. On the following page: a close-up of interlaced arches (Oronoz).

143

Madinat az-Zahra' (Cordoba). A glimpse of the highlands of Giabal al-'Arûs, the Mountain of the Bride, seen from a road in the ancient caliphal town built by an-Nasir in honour of his favorite, in the tenth century.

Madinat az-Zahra': a road in the town, and the remains of an ablution chamber. On the following pages: architectural details enhanced by recent careful restoration.

Madinat az-Zahra': the central hall of the Caliph's Palace (Oronoz). Facing, and overleaf, two details of the interlaced floral decoration that adorned the walls of the building.

CHAPTER FIVE
THE ISLAMIC ART OF AL-ANDALUS

Religious Architecture

a) THE AGE OF THE EMIRS AND OF THE CALIPHS

The political and religious life of the State revolved around the Masgid al-gâmi', the mosque-cathedral still known to Spaniards today as Mezquita Aljamá and, from the artistic point of view, the forerunner of all the mosques in Spain.[1]

When the Muslims moved into the peninsula they followed the practice established by the caliph 'Umar for the Christian church of St. John in Damascus and came to an agreement with the Christians whereby the largest church in the town, that of S. Vincent, should be shared between them.[2] In their own half the Muslims built a mosque and the Christians were allowed to carry on the celebration of their cult in the other. All other churches were destroyed. But as Muslim numbers grew the prayer hall became too small for them and had to be enlarged nave by nave. Things changed under 'Abd al-Rahmân al-Dâkhil, who decided to build a new mosque in emulation the one in Damascus. After summoning a meeting of the leaders of the Christian community in Cordoba and offering them a handsome sum to sell him their half in exchange for permission to rebuild their church elsewhere, he set about the work of demolition in 179/785 and, financed from the coffers of war, the new mosque was completed within a year. The building was certainly still an oratory; enlargement began under his son, Hishâm I, who added a gallery for women, a basin for ritual ablutions and a minaret for the call to prayer.[3]

The building remained unchanged until the reign of 'Abd al-Rahmân II. In 218/833, he had nine naves built, at right angles to the *qibla* wall for a depth of twenty-five metres, incorporating eighty columns.[4] From then onwards every prince was to leave some trace of himself on the mosque. The emir Muhammad made his contribution in the decorative work and sculpture on the lateral façades, as well as in the *maqsura* with three entrances that he had prepared for the sovereign. His name, together with the date and mention of work of

155

consolidation, appears in the form of an epigraphic fascia running round the tympanum above the doorway of San Esteban which gives central access to the oratory of 'Abd al-Rahmân I.[5] Al-Mundhir added the chamber known as the Treasury, so called because the money of the *waqf* (charitable foundations) was stored there, and his brother, 'Abd Allâh, linked the palace to the mosque by means of a covered walk (*sâbât*) bridging the street, thus allowing the ruler access to the *mihrâb* without being seen.[6]

The great builder of civil and military edifices, 'Abd al-Rahmân al-Nâsir, also had to leave his imprint on the Great Mosque. He had Hishâm's minaret razed to the ground and replaced it with a new one which remained unchanged until the sixteenth century. Subsequently he made alterations to the north façade of the prayer hall, as we learn from a commemorative inscription set into the right-hand side of the Puerta de las Palmas, inside the courtyard. The work was carried out by Sa'îd ibn 'Ayyûb under the supervision of the intendant for building, the freedman 'Abd Allâh, the son of Badr.[7]

Al-Hakam II, who has passed into history as a pious and wise caliph, dedicated much of his reign to the embellishment of the sanctuary, thereby bringing it to its culminant splendor.[8] In the interests of enlargement he had the south wall moved nearer to the banks of the Guadalquivir, destroying the covered walk. This made it necessary to build a new *mihrâb* at the end of the edifice to mark the direction of the *qibla*. Work, begun in 350/961, was carried out under the joint supervision of the *hâgib*, Ga'far ibn 'Abd al-Rahmân, the three *ashâb ash-shurta* (prefects of police) of Cordoba, and the secretary, Mutarrif ibn 'Abd al-Rahmân. Their names are still inscribed in gold letters on the mosaic tesserae above the *mihrâb*.[9] The great innovation was the construction of the domes, one at the beginning of the central nave and one at its end, tangential to the *mihrâb* and in proximity to two further domes, in accordance with the typical layout of the mosques of 'Ifrîqiya. The walls of the *qibla* and the *qibla* itself, as well as the *mihrâb* and the doorways flanking it, were all embellished with carved marbles and mosaic work. The contribution of the mosaic workers, commemorated in inscriptions and by the writings of ibn 'Idhâri, is not only of significance for a better understanding of the history of mosque architecture but also provides us with a valuable insight into the international relations of the caliphate.

Just as al-Walîd had requested the Byzantine emperor to send him artists to decorate the mosques of Damascus, Medina and Jerusalem, al-Hakam too, requested Nicephorus Phocas to send him expert craftsmen in this typically Byzantine technique. This is how Ibn 'Idhârî tells the story: «Work began on the mosaic decoration of the edifice. Al-Hakam had written to the king of the Rûm, commanding him to send him a skilled worker, just as al-Walîd ibn 'Abd al-Malik before him had done at the time of the building of the mosque of Damascus. The caliph's envoys returned with a mosaic-worker and, as a gift from the king of the Rûm, three-hundred and twenty quintals of mosaic tesserae. The prince housed the craftsman, treating him handsomely and placing many of his slaves at his disposal as apprentices. Working under the master, these slaves acquired such inventive talent as to surpass him; they carried on working unsupervised after the master craftsman, no longer indispensable, had left the country regaled with gifts and clothing by the prince».[10]

Four slender marble columns, formerly supporting the earlier *mihrâb*, were set up at the

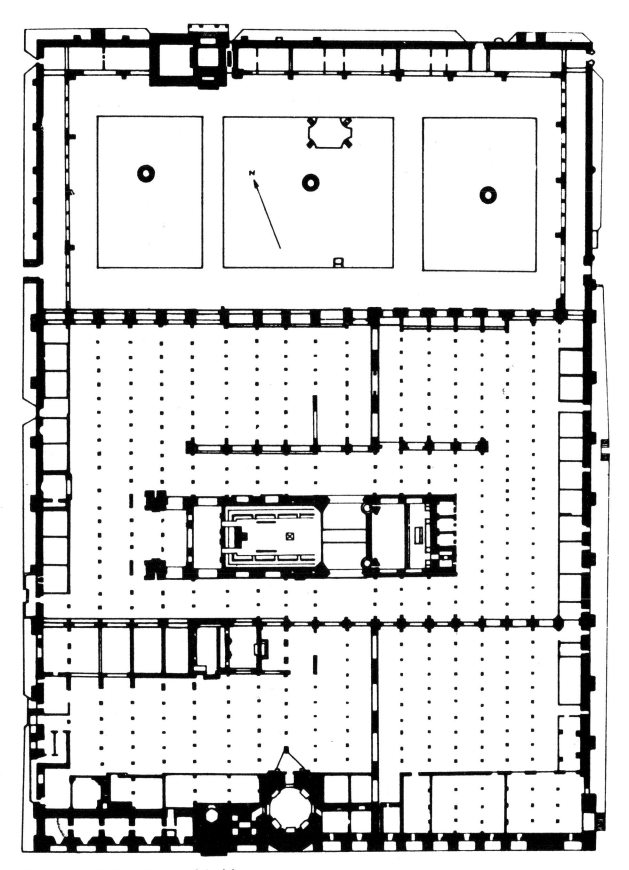

Floor-plan of the Great Mosque of Cordoba.

right of the new one, the ancient *maqsura*, five naves wide, carved throughout and surmounted with crenelation, was restored, and a new *minbâr* was built, with inlays of ivory and precious woods, sandal-wood, ebony and aloe, costing a sum of at least 35,000 dinâr. In the courtyard, the basin for ablutions, formerly fed with water from a well, was demolished and replaced by new reservoirs and new basins. These were fed by the waters of the Sierra which, after decantation in a great basin, were kept in constant activity day and night. To the east and to the west of the *sahn*, four chambers for ritual purification were built, two for men and two for women.

To the west of the mosque he erected a building to serve the needs of social welfare. Here, alms were distributed to the poor and the destitute. The prince made financial provision for the Koran to be taught in the temple precincts to the sick and the indigent. Remarking on this Ibn Shukhays says: «The crowning glory of the great temple is the schools for the orphans of the district. If the suras of the Koran could speak thay would acclaim you as the one who has best understood their message.»[11]

Twenty years later new extensions began because with the arrival of the Berbers from Africa the Muslim population of Cordoba had greatly increased. Work begun in 377/987 led to enlargement of the mosque to the east where eight naves, slightly smaller than the pre-existing ones, were added. Ibn 'Idhârî comments: «Here, al-Mansûr aimed above all at solidity and careful building, not profusion of decoration, even though the part we owe to him is in no way inferior in quality to any of the subsequent additions to the building.»[12] The Mezquita preserved these forms and characteristics until Christian architects laid hands on the building.

The great al-Idrîsî visited this temple, the most important of Muslim Spain, in the twelfth century, and offers us a detailed and moving account of it: «The covered naves number nineteen; the columns in the covered area, both great and small including those reinforcing the *qibla* and sustaining the great dome, a thousand. Illumination is provided by a hundred and thirteen candelabra, the largest of which have a thousand lights, the smallest, twelve. The ceiling of the building is formed of carved woods nailed to the roof beams. All the wood in the mosque comes from the pines of Tortosa. The dimensions of the beams are the following: the thickness on one side is one span, on the other, one span less three fingers, and the beams are thirty-seven spans long.

The space between the beams equals the breadth of the single beam. The ceilings I am speaking of are entirely flat and covered with hexagonal or round decorations known as *fass* (mosaics) or *dawâyr* (circles). Each painting has received individual decorative treatment and the ornamentation, often in very brilliant color, is in excellent taste. Use has been made of cinnabar red, ceruse white, lapis-lazuli blue, red oxide of lead, subdued green and antimony black. The whole is a feast for the eyes, while the purity of line, the varied and harmonious color combinations animate the spirit...

The *qibla* of this mosque is of indescribable beauty and elegance, its solidity of a perfection surpassing anything of which human intelligence can conceive. The facing throughout is of decorative and colorful mosaics sent to the 'Umayyad 'Abd al-Rahmân, known as an-Nâsir li dîn Allâh, by the emperor of Constantinople. On this side, by which I mean that of the

158

mihrâb, there are seven arches supported by columns; the height of each arch is that of a man's arms outstretched; they are all enamelled and as highly wrought as an earring; the delicacy of this ornamentation is remarkable and surpasses anything the Greeks and Muslims have produced in this extraordinary field. Above, there are two inscriptions framed by gold mosaic cartouches, set against an azure ground. The part below is similarly decorated. The surface itself of the *mihrâb* is covered with ornament and a variety of paintings. At the sides there are four columns, two of them green and two dappled, all of inestimable value. At the back of the *mihrâb* there is a niche cut deep into a single block of marble; it is carved and enriched with admirable ornamentation in gold, azure and other colors. The frontal area is screened by a wooden baluster decorated with precious paintings. To the right of the *mihrâb* there is a pulpit unlike anything else in the world. It is made of ebony, boxwood and sandalwood.

The annals of the 'Umayyad caliphs tell us that the carving and painting of this wood took seven years; six workmen were employed on the job, not including their assistants, and each received daily a half of a *mithqâl muhammadî*.

On the left there is a building to house accessories, gold and silver vases and the candelabra used for lighting on the twenty-seventh night of ramadan. In the treasury there can be seen an exemplar of the Koran that is so heavy that two men would have difficulty in lifting it; four pages come from the Koran that 'Uthmâ, son of 'Affân (may God show him favor), wrote with his own hand; one can see numerous drops of blood on it. This exemplar is used every Friday. Two custodians of the mosque, preceded by a third bearing a torch, are encharged with the transport of the Book, which is enclosed in a casket enriched with paintings and delicately wrought ornaments. There is a special lectern for it in the prayer hall. When the imam has read the half of a section of the Koran, it is taken back to the treasury. There are sixty persons employed in the mosque, all under the supervision of an intendant».[13]

A few days after the victorious entry of the Christian troops of Ferdinand III, the mosque was consecrated to the Catholic cult and dedicated to the Virgin Mary with the name of Santa Maria Maggiore. No serious alterations were made to the monument until 1523 when, on the initiative of the bishop, Alonso Manrique, the cathedral chapter decided to erect an entire church in the center of the sanctuary to outshine the work of the caliphs in beauty and sumptuousness.

When the emperor Charles V saw the work the Catholic clergy had obtained his authorization to carry out, he expressed bitter displeasure: «If I had known your intentions, you should not have done this, because what you have done can be seen anywhere, but what you once possessed was something unique to the world».[14]

In the ninth century important mosques, albeit less imposing than that of the capital, were also built in the provinces. 'Abd al-Rahmân II had mosques built at Baena and Jaén, though these have not survived. But, buried beneath baroque structures, there are traces of the ancient mosque of Seville that the Normans tried to burn down in 844. When Ya'qûb al-Mansûr restored it in the twelfth century it was already in grave disrepair and Ferdinand III later transformed it into a Christian church, San Salvador. The ruins of the mosque of the Alcazaba at Badajoz are of the same period. In 1230 this building, after the Reconquest under Alfonso

XI, became Santa Maria del Castiglio.[15]

There must have been numerous places of worship on the Muslim acropolis of Serrania di Ronda before Christian conquest in the fifteenth century by Ferdinand the Catholic. The great Mosque became the church of Santa Maria de la Encarnación; others, Sancti Spiritus, Santiago Apostolo and S. John the Evangelist. Little remains of them. A small, slender tower in the narrow streets of Marchese di Salvatierra, all that survives of the church of San Sebastiano, was once perhaps, a minaret.[16]

The mosque of Bib Mardûm at Toledo, extensively remodelled over the course of time, dates from the end of the century. It was formed of three naves, each divided into three spans to form nine square tambours each crowned with a dome. The central dome was higher than the others. Stone was adopted only for the pilasters on the north front. The rest is brickwork including the arches, round, horse-shoe and trilobated — a distinct pointer to reliance on an oriental prototype. On the interior, the capitals of the four columns bear architraves that delineate a cruciform plan. A kufic inscription on the façade commemorates its building: «In the name of God the Compassionate and Merciful. Ahmad ibn Hadîdî had this mosque built at his own expense, trusting in the reward of Allâh. It was completed, with the aid of the Lord, under the direction of the architect, Musâ ibn 'Alî, and of Sâ'ada, in the month of muharrâm of the year three hundred and ninety (13 December 999 / 11 January 1000).»[17] The mosque later became a Christian church with the name of Cristo de la Luz.

b) FROM THE REYES DE TAIFAS TO NASRID RULE

Spain withdrew into itself during the epoch of the reyes de Taifas (the Taifas kingdoms). The caliphate had fallen and Cordoba was no longer the catalyst it had been, yet the country revealed an admirable unity, even in its art forms. It proved itself capable of coming to terms with the widening gulf that separated it from the Orient. The characteristics of monumental art and the aesthetics of decoration underwent no change. The same techniques continued to be used in building mosques and palaces; the exterior forms retained the simplicity of straight lines and elementary volumes.

The religious foundations of the *mulûk at-tawâ* were not numerous. All that remains to us is the tiny oratory of the Aljaferia at Saragossa,[18] built by Abû Ga'far Ahmad al-Muqtadir, of the family that ruled the town for a period of time, the Banû Hûd. The palace itself was a later addition to the existing rectangular, tenth-century Homenaje tower. The interior is most elaborate; interlaced multi-lobed arches in stucco like those of Cordoba but already providing a foretaste of the pointed form of the horseshoe arch adopted by the Almoravids; acanthus leaves and colorful fascias add to the ornamentation. In the small oratory, now much restored, the arches are interlaced in the lower order and multi-lobed in the upper. The letters of the inscriptions are elongated and split up, the better to form an interwoven geometric pattern which terminates in palm motifs. These inscriptions sing the praises of God: «Everything that exists in the heavens and on earth, belongs to the Lord.»[19]

The religious zeal of the Almoravids made them great builders of mosques. Few of those

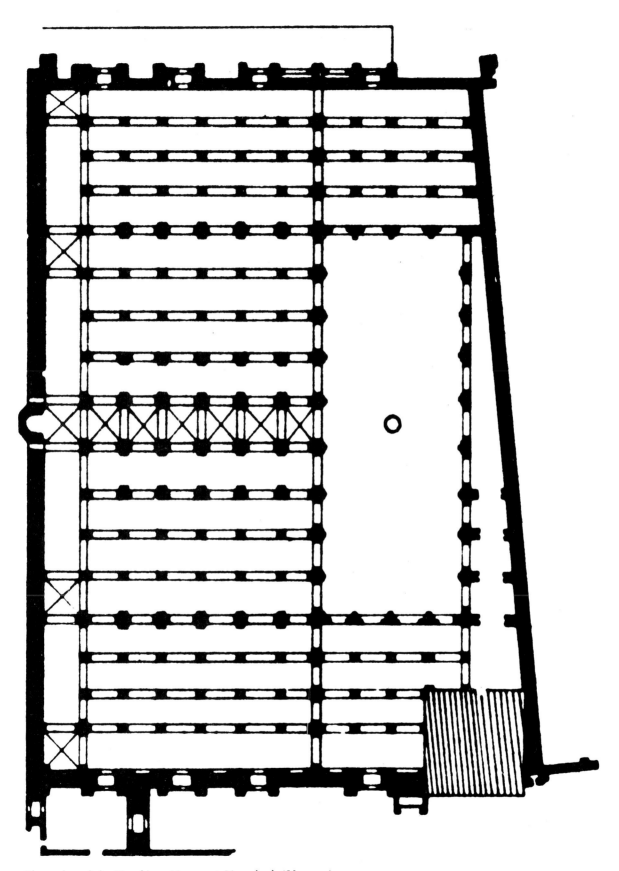

Floor-plan of the Kutubiyya Mosque at Marrakesh (Morocco).

in Morocco can be attributed to them with certainty whereas they are more numerous in Algeria: the simple, handsome structures of the Great Mosque of Algiers, as well as those of Nedroma and Tlemsen.[20] No mosque surviving in Spain can be attributed to the Almoravid period. It is almost as if the effects of a deep social and economic crisis had promptly curtailed artistic creation. But this does not by any means signify that the Saharan warriors had suffocated the art of al-Andalus. Ibn Tashfîn's activities were primarily military and political. He himself was a builder of fortresses but he invited the inhabitants of his empire to build mosques. The most interesting offspring of the Muslim art of Morocco must have been the Great Mosque of Granada built by the Berber emirs of the Banû Zîzî family and, unfortunately, no longer in existence. It would seem to have been built on the T plan which was later to triumph in Almohad religious architecture.[21]

In this initial phase, it was mainly from Ifrîqiya that Muslim art spread to Andalusia and gained widespread acceptance. Then, under the rule of 'Alî ibn Yûsuf, the Muslim art of Spain penetrated the Maghrib, having rediscovered, in times of peace, the joys of life and the desire to create. The Almoravids thus became patrons of an art that in those times, with its constant pursuit of equilibrium and rhythm, was still capable of yielding up masterpieces in a tradition that would soon be compelled to seek refuge on African soil to be able to survive. One of the major artistic glories of these soldier monks lies in their readiness to understand and to avoid without imposing limits and restrictions.

The Almohads, enemies of luxury, contemptuous almost, of any artistic expression, kept faith with the intransigent puritanism of ibn Tûmart. There was no ornamentation on the little mosque of Tinmal,[22] a village in the Moroccan High Atlas where ibn Tûmart drew up the new social structure. The tomb of the Mahdî observed the utmost austerity. One of the chief features of the decoration of the mosque at Taza[23] must have been its great sobriety.

Where the Dâr al-Hagar, the Almoravid palace at Marrakesh, once stood, 'Abd al-Mu'min had a great mosque built, the Kutubiyya,[24] from which the Almohads banished the luxuriance of Andalusian decoration. The artists, once again brought by the caliph from Muslim Spain, created a new type of decoration in which allowance is made for empty spaces to rest the eye. There is a refined elegance about it that can attain to an exquisite classic purity.

This artistic reform was not applied to all the Muslim monuments of Spain; not everywhere was the concept of austerity acceptable. Andalusian art remained true to itself while refining its means; it learned how to turn the slightest reflection of light to good effect, and in the harmony of its proportions achieved an impeccable purity of line.

The greatest example of Almohad architecture in Spain is the Great Mosque of Seville which Abû Ya'qûb Yûsuf began building on in 1172 and brought to a conclusion in 1182.[25] It was to be demolished after the Reconquest to make way for the present cathedral, its minaret becoming the bell-tower of the church from a statue on the summit of this tower it acquired the name by which it is popularly known, the Giralda. With the aid of ancient descriptions a reconstruction may be attempted: as with the Kutubiyya, there were seventeen naves at right angles to the *qibla*. The rectangular *sahn*, or court, was framed by three simple galleries. A gate was let into the wall of the façade, after the manner of the mosque of Cordoba. The same architect who had built the mosque, Ahmad ibn Bâsû, began work on the minaret in 1184, the year in which Abû Ya'qûb died.

There remain other traces of Almohad art applied to religious buildings in Spain: the mosque of the casbah at Badajoz,[26] which became the church of Santa Maria del Castillo; the surviving mihrâb[27] of an oratory at Almonaster la Real in the Huelva province; and at Bolullos de la Mitacion in the province of Seville, the Ermita de Cuatrohabitan conserves a pretty, square minaret with mullioned windows and both multi-lobed and horseshoe arches.[28]

Nothing remains of the royal mosque of the Alhambra, built by Muhammad III in c. 1305 on the site now occupied by the church of Santa Maria. Writers praise its beauty and the inestimable value of its decoration.[29]

It was in the Nasrid capital that an oriental institution, the *madrasa*, first flowered. It appeared in Khorasân in c. 1000, and gained ascendancy in Baghdad where Nizâm al-Mulk, the great minister of the Seljuq Turks, founded the Nizâmiya *madrasa*. Then it spread to Damascus in Ayyudid Egypt. The madrasa is a school of religious science and in particular of Muslim law in which the *sunna* of the great orthodox doctors is taught. Its foundation always stemmed from the bounty of the sovereigns. From these seminaries they could recruit officials who would be both well-trained and loyal to the authorities; and it was precisely this political exploitation, turned to the advantage of the prince, that provoked the dissent of the more intransigent. The function of the building dictated the same architectural criteria in both East and West: living quarters for the students, rooms for communal religious life and halls for teaching. Central to these, a court. The *madrasa* had its own prayer hall with its *mihrâb* and, on occasion, a minaret and a *minbar*. An echo of the form of the *ribât* was to make itself felt in the Maghriban version of the *madrasa*.

One was to appear in Muslim Spain, founded by Yûsuf I at Granada in 750/1349. This was almost wholly demolished in the eighteenth century, except for the prayerhall which shows distinct traces of the influence of Merinid art.[30]

In the context of building for religious ends and as a result of oriental influence, the *qubba*, a square-plan tomb, began to appear in the thirteenth through fourteenth centuries. The mausoleum of the Rawda in the Alhambra,[31] is one such building. Here the tombs of the royal family or of those who lived at court created an authentic cemetery in which the sovereign was surrounded by those of his retinue that had accompanied him during his reign on earth.

A perfect example of a domestic oratory,[32] a small rectangular hall with a *mihrâb* facing southeast, has been conserved in the Alhambra Partal between the Lady Tower and the «Los Picos» Tower. It was probably built during the reign of Yûsuf I. The exterior revetments take the form of severely geometrical and vegetal decorations while the interior is divided into two unequal areas by a semicircular transverse arch. The *mihrâb*, rectangular in form, is crowned with an octagonal dome. The arch bears an inscription that reads: «Take care to pray and to observe the hour of prayer.» Above it is the Nasrid motto: «There is no victor but God.» Verses of the Koran on the interior fascia of the niche read: «In the name of God the Compassionate and Merciful. May God bestow his blessings on our lord Muhammad, his family and his companions, and grant them peace. Recite the prayer from sunset to nightfall and recite it at dawn for the angels keep watch over the dawn prayer; and a further part of the night keep vigil in voluntary prayer that the Lord may raise you to a place of glory, and speak thus: 'O Lord! Allow me to enter as a just man and to leave as one and lend me your power to assist me!' And further say: 'The truth has come and error has departed: for indeed, error is an evanescent thing'.»[33]

Urban Development

a) TOWN PLANNING IN MUSLIM SPAIN

Town life always played a considerable role in the history of Islam, the religion of both the sedentary citizen and the nomad. Religious and political life was centered on the mosque which by reason of this became the hub of the Muslim town and gave Islamic civilization its prevalently urban character.

In many respects the Muslim town differs from that of other civilizations. Street layout is irregular: while there does exist a certain number of transversal or radial thoroughfares linking the gates with the urban agglomerate and the outlying districts, these are enmeshed in numerous minor byways, narrow and tortuous streets leading into even smaller ones that form a ramified complex that often resembles a maze with no outlet. This peculiarity was imported from Syria, where the Arabs built their first urban centers of any importance, by Yemenite merchants who settled in al-Andalus.

Above all, the internal structure differs. The Greek town certainly lost its political independence by incorporation into the Hellenistic community and later into the Roman imperial structure but it did preserve the autonomy of its traditional institutions, the curia and the magistrature.

The centralizing Byzantine structure was instrumental in eliminating these often nominal rather than effective forms of independence and the municipal organization of antiquity rapidly declined in consequence. Islamic civilization thus inherited none of the municipal, juridical and political structures of the ancient town. There existed outward associations, such as baths, markets, walls and entry gates and it is true that the craftsmen of Arab dominated Roman and Visigothic towns continued to work as usual with their hereditary techniques. In part, manufacturing and trade continued, but we have little documentation of the conditions under which these activities were carried on prior to the conquest.

Even though the Arab Middle Ages saw the flowering of a splendid urban civilization, comparable with no other, the most important feature of the Islamic town is its absence of municipal institutions. Compared with the Latin West where civic life in early medieval times was submissive, here there existed an intense and multiform urban life devoid of formal, juridical or civil institutions in that power was firmly held by the emir or the caliph who was hostile to the development of any local autonomy whatsoever.

In the West, where the Roman tradition had been engulfed by autarchic feudal structures, it is not until the eleventh century that a revival of economy can be seen. But this is accompanied by the confident foothold gained by the corporative municipal institutions that put up a fight with their feudal overlords to obtain the recognition of privileges. These are often ratified on papers that bear witness to the growing independence attained in respect of monarchic power. Nothing of this kind took place in Islamic civilization, not even after the fall of the caliphate when each single town came under the sway of one of the reyes de Taifas. Corporations did exist in Islamic civilization but the corporative phenomenon experienced as the urge to play an active part in the administration of public institutions was extraneous to Muslim society.

As often happens with forms of thought and of art, so too, the evolution of the Muslim town was uniform; it presented the same administrative characteristics in every part of dâr al-Islâm. The nature of the differences was purely historical and stemmed from the origin of the urban community. The Islamic town might grow out of an earlier conquered town that would be rebuilt and enlarged, or else adapted to suit the needs of the victors by the building of the mosque cathedral and the Government Palace; at times, a completely new town reserved to the structures of power was built not far from the old one. Its physical profile would answer to certain needs: building, water supplies, pubblic health and hygiene, the state of the roads, the siting of shops, markets and of factories, public baths and the burial of the dead. All these responsibilities devolved on the *muhtasib*, but the evolution of the town was left to the free initiative of the private citizen.

The nucleus of the town lay in the medina, the fortified area in which the sovereign resided. In caliphal Cordoba the medina was split into two sectors, a western and an eastern sector, known as *gânib* (pl. *gawânib*). Within this walled nucleus the principal structures of civil life were to be found: the Great Mosque or Cathedral, the *al-qasâriyya*, a closed market for the more valuable merchandise, the warehouses (*fanâdiq*, sing. *funduq*) for goods of foreign provenance, the baths and the more important markets. This was the focal point of the social, religious and economic life of the town. In the mosque cathedral, not only were the ceremonies of the Koranic rite celebrated, but others too, by means of which every act of life acquired religious overtones: the colors were blessed before the troops left on military expeditions, official documents or items of interest to the population were given public reading. On Fridays it was the meeting place of every Muslim for communal prayer. Generally, it stood at the heart of the town, as was the case at Valencia, Seville, Tudela and Toledo. At Cordoba it was built near to the walls because that was the site of the former Visigothic church.

At Cordoba, Seville and Valencia, religious and political life were brought into close conjunction by the siting of the Alcazar in the proximity of the mosque cathedral. When, for topographic reasons, the sovereign's palace was not in the vicinity of the mosque, it was enclosed in a citadel, *al-qasba*, and formed an independent small district on an easily defensible eminence. This was the case at Saragossa, Huesca, Malaga, Almeria and Granada.

The central district where the mosque cathedral stood was also the heart of the world of trade and of business, both a meeting place and a landmark.

In both West and East the Arabic word *al-qaysâriyya*, which has given rise to the Castilian alcaiceria, stood for a commercial institution and the building in which it was housed.

It was built for public use, at times in the form of a court flanked by porches or covered galleries housing shops. The particular characteristic of this building, the property of the sovereign, was that it had locked gates which were opened under the vigilance of guards at set hours. This was where valuable goods were sold. There are examples at Cordoba, Toledo, Seville, Malaga and Granada. The term soon became obsolete in the East, to be replaced by others, such as *khân, wakâla* or *funduq*. This latter term later came into use in al-Andalus.

The few radial arteries, linking the main gates of the town, led into the town center and catered for the passage of heavy traffic. The main road at Cordoba, on a north-south axis, left from the Bâb Luyûn (Puerto del Osario) and, after passing between the Alcazar and the Great Mosque, arrived at the Bâb al-Qantara (Puerta del Puente).

The majority of the inhabitants lived in the suburbs (*arbâd*, sing. *rabad*) and these in their turn were split up into a certain number of *hârât* (sing. *hâra*) or districts, varying in size and at times consisting of a single street. The suburbs and more populous districts formed, within the town boundaries, a small *medina*, built up round a mosque, with a *sûq*, a bath and bakehouse of its own. A district of a certain importance would be cut by a main road. The secondary roads were sometimes so narrow that only one person at a time could pass along them, consequently goods travelled by mule-back. Streets and alleys were often covered by vaults or passages linking the upper floors of houses on opposite sides of the street. Sometimes the streets had gates which were locked at night to ensure the safety of the inhabitants of the area. Twelfth-century Cordoba employed town officials, known as *darrâb*, whose duty it was to lock up the gates of the streets or districts at night. Every gate was guarded by a nightwatchman with his dog and lantern.

The houses, tall and multistoryed, were put up without any concern for town planning.

Every Andalusian town had a broad open space serving a variety of purposes beyond the encircling town walls. Since the early days of Islam people had gathered together for communal prayer before sunrise on open ground known as *musallâ*; the occasions for these gatherings were the two great Koranic feast-days, one on the first day of shawwâl, which coincided with the end of the month of ramadan and the breaking of the fast, the other, on the tenth day of dhû-l-higga, or the Feast of the Sacrifices. The towns of Western Islam also had a *musallâ*, or sometimes two, and here, though not in the East, another name was current, that of *sharî'a*.

Cordoba had two *musallâ*, one on the right bank of the Guadalquivir, with access from the Puerta del Puente, and the other on the left bank of the river, to the south of the town. The *musallâ* was also to be found at Tortosa, Murcia, Valencia and at Malaga. The Gate of Justice at Granada is no other than the Sharî'a Gate, as we learn from the foundation epigraph of 749/1348. There were winding tree-lined avenues beside the *musallâ*, popular locations for meeting and taking walks. There were too, the cemeteries, which stretched out in all directions. On occasion, in the country districts, one might find leper houses (*rabad al-marda*) built beside it.

Town planning also reflects the search for a deeper meaning to life — an intimate, very private life that is expressed in the silence of the streets, in the empty squares animated only by the splashing of fountains, in the hermetically closed houses, shielded from every indiscreet gaze, in obedience to the Koranic message that discourages the Believer from indulgence in pomp and in vainglorious ostentation.

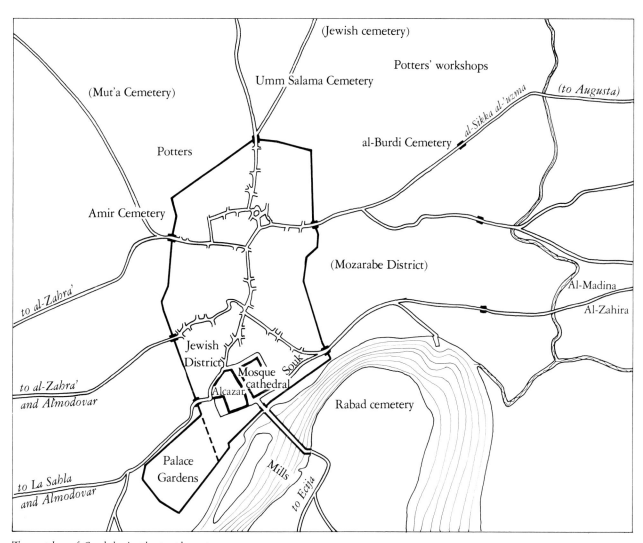

(Jewish cemetery)

Potters' workshops

(Mut'a Cemetery)

Umm Salama Cemetery

al-Sikka al-'uzma (to Augusta)

Potters

al-Burdi Cemetery

Amir Cemetery

to al-Zahra'

(Mozarabe District)

Al-Madina

Al-Zahira

to al-Zahra'
and Almodovar

Jewish
District

Mosque
cathedral

Souk

Alcazar

Rabad cemetery

to La Sahla
and Almodovar

Palace
Gardens

Mills

to Ecija

Town plan of Cordoba in the tenth century.

b) PROVINCIAL TOWNS AND THOSE OF THE MARCHES

One of the characteristics of al-Andalus which never escapes the attention of Arab geographers in that it represents an element of diversity in respect of the Maghrib, is the large number of urban centers. Important towns and villages were distinguished in hierarchic fashion by according the name of *umm* (metropolis) to the chief settlement and that of *bint* (daughter) to those of secondary importance.

Numerous urban nuclei existing at the time of the conquest retained their Iberian or Latin names but slightly modified by transcription into Arabic. It is the case of Cordoba, Seville, Malaga, Toledo, Valencia, Saragossa, and of others too. Many were founded by the victors, obedient to the prescriptions that the elders had established as criteria for the creation of a town that aimed to prosper: running water, fertile soil, trees and meadows, solid building and a leader capable of making himself respected, of taking on the responsibility of the development of the community and the defence of the highways.

Ibn Khaldûn deals at length with the process of birth, life and death of towns. He declares that one of the most important conditions to be observed is the choice of a site with a river and plentiful supplies of pure spring water; a factor of capital importance in as much as water is a «gift of God.» The neighbouring land should be such as to free the inhabitants who cultivate it of any concern for the replenishment of food supplies and the woodland on it should provide an adequate and accessible source of timber for building. But the main concern should be for military defense. To this end, the town should be built on an eminence, on a peninsula or on the banks of a river and its houses congregate within an encircling wall that, in the case of aggression, might provide the peasants of the outlying districts with protection.

The foundation and building of the town was entrusted to the sovereign. The Abbasid caliph al-Mutawakkil, having concluded the building of al-Ga'farriyya, the present-day Mutawakkiliyya, to the north of Samarra, exclaimed: «At last I feel a king, now that I have built a town to be lived in.»

In Muslim Spain every big village might aspire to the appellation of *madîna* by providing itself with encircling walls, a mosque cathedral and districts and suburbs within and beyond its boundaries. Villages of the plain, mountain villages, citadels, seaports, all took on the same undifferentiated appearance because all obeyed the criteria that inspired Muslim town planning. This was so as much in the East as in the West, for social and economic life followed the same rhythm and produced the same results whether it was the Cordoba of the Caliphs, Almohad Seville or Nasrid Granada.

From Umayyad times, the most important town of western Andalusia was Seville, on the banks of the Guadalquivir river which still today retains its Arabic name. Lodestar and exemplar in the political and cultural life of the peninsula during the reign of the Abbasids, after the fall of the caliphate it became the favorite town of the Almohads, who settled there in preference to Cordoba.

Its territory embraced over eight thousand villages, all of which were endowed with numerous bathhouses and dwelling houses worthy of consideration. The traveller along the

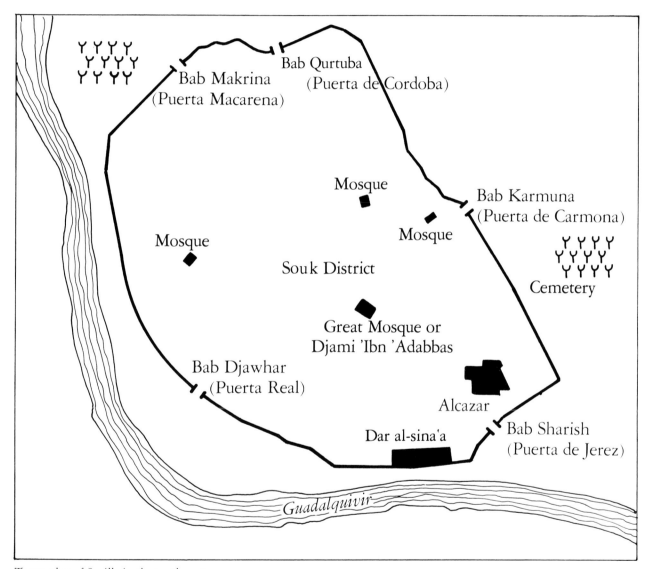

Town plan of Seville in the tenth century.

Cordoba road encountered two main towns. Ecija stood on the right bank of the river Genil, with defense walls dating from pre-Muslim times inset with numerous gates of access, busy markets, a mosque cathedral with five naves and many well kept gardens. Girdled by Roman walls, on the side of what was considered to be an impregnable hill stood Carmona, which possessed a mosque with seven naves. To the south of Seville, in the direction of Gibraltar, stood Calsena and Madînat ibn al-Salîm, the present-day Medina-Sidonia. In the province that takes its name from the lake of Janda there stand the fortress of Tarifa, and Algeciras, the «Green Isle» of the Muslims. It is sited overlooking a bay and was one of the most important mercantile and military ports.

«This latter town has a large population; its walls are built in stone and bonded with lime; it has three harbors and an arsenal situated further inland. A stream known as the River of Honey runs through Algeciras, providing the inhabitants with good, fresh water supplies. There are gardens and orchards on its banks. This is a shipbuilding town; people embark and disembark here... It was the first town in Andalusia to be conquered by the Muslims, in the early days, that is to say, in the year 90 of the hegira.»[34]

To the west, after crossing the Guadiana, the Algarve road led into the Ocsonoba district and to its chief town Silves, lying amongst orchards «Silves is a pretty town, built in the plain and encircled with stout walls. The neighboring land is laid out as gardens and orchards. The water that laps the shores of the town to the south and turns the mills is pure enough to drink. There is a harbor on the river and shipyards, too. The Ocean sea is three miles away to the west. The great quantities of timber produced by the surrounding mountains is exported to the most distant places. The town is handsome and fine buildings and well-furnished markets are to be seen. Its inhabitants, like those of the surrounding villages, are Yemenite Arabs and others who speak a very pure Arabic dialect. They know how to compose verses, eloquence of speech and spiritual refinement is common to all of them, whether they be of the people or of the educated classes.»[35]

From here roads branch off to Santarem, built on a steep hill, Coimbra, set in a fertile zone on the banks of the Mondego, which from there flows due west to the sea, and Lisbon. This latter town, on the Tagus, girdled by strong walls and protected by a fortress, was well known to the Arab geographers because from its port sailors navigated the waters of the Atlantic, animated by the desire to learn what they contained.

In the vicinity of the thermal baths, in the times of al-Idrîsî, there was a road that bore the name of the Adventurers Road.

Following the coast road from Algeciras, one reached Malaga, a magnificent town set in well-cultivated surroundings and with flourishing markets. «The town has two suburbs, one of which is called Fontanella, the other, known as that of the Straw Merchants. The inhabitants of Malaga drink the pure and plentiful waters of their wells, which lie just below the surface of the earth. There is also a torrent whose waters flow in winter and spring but for the rest of the year its bed lies dry.»[36] In the caliphal era there used to be a stout Alcazaba on the hills of Gibralfaro whereas the Great Mosque lay in the direction of the sea, where the Cathedral stands today.

Beyond the last ramifications of the Sierra Nevada lay the great port of Almeria, built by

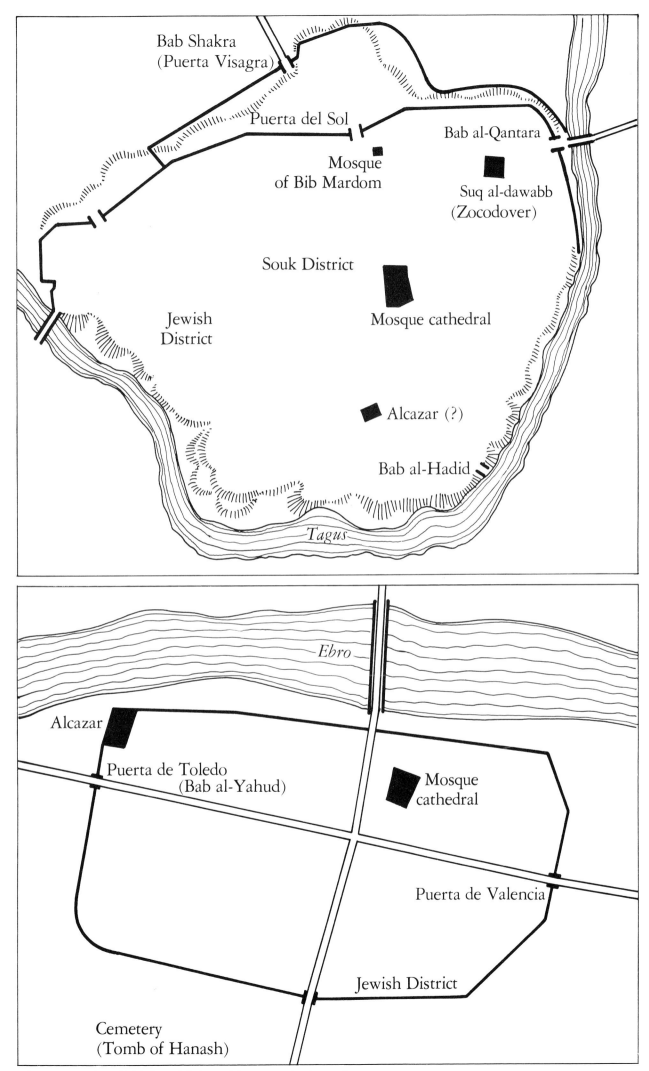

Bab Shakra
(Puerta Visagra)

Puerta del Sol

Bab al-Qantara

Mosque
of Bib Mardom

Suq al-dawabb
(Zocodover)

Souk District

Jewish
District

Mosque cathedral

Alcazar (?)

Bab al-Hadid

Tagus

Ebro

Alcazar

Puerta de Toledo
(Bab al-Yahud)

Mosque
cathedral

Puerta de Valencia

Jewish District

Cemetery
(Tomb of Hanash)

Above, town plan of Toledo and, below, of Saragossa, in the tenth century.

al-Nâsir in the tenth century, and later to become the seafaring port of Pechina.

«Almeria was the main Muslim town at the time of the Almoravids, when it was a very industrious place with, among other activities, eight hundred looms at work weaving silk and producing cloths known by the names of *holla*, *dîbâg*, *siglaton*, *isfahânî* and *giurgiâni* as well as curtains with floral motifs, embroidered silks, and textiles with such names as *'attâbî*, *mi'giar*, etc. Today Almeria is noted for its production of leather goods, of iron-ware and objects of an entirely different nature... The town harbor sheltered ships from Alexandria and from the whole of Syria. Nowhere in Spain might one have found a richer, more industrious population, or one more skilled at business, more inclined to luxury, to spending, and to love of money... As I write this work, Almeria has fallen into the hands of the Christians. Nothing remains of what made it such a pleasurable place, its inhabitants have become slaves, the houses and public buildings have been demolished and there no longer remains anything.»[37]

On the other side of the Sierra Nevada, in the Genil valley, stands the town of Elvira and, a few kilometers away, near the confluence of the Genil and the Darro, Granada, a town that developed under Zirid and, above all, under Nasrid rule. Two roads provided Elvira with its contacts with two important centres: Guadix, a road junction, and Baza, a fortified town and the seat of flourishing industries. To the east stood Jaen, in the midst of fertile land where the breeding of the silkworm was highly developed. In the province of Tudmir one encountered the chief town, Murcia, on the banks of the White River. «This town has a flourishing suburb with a large population and, like the town itself, this too is protected by stout walls and fortifications and is crossed by a waterway. As for the town itself, it is built on the banks of a river and one reaches it by crossing a bridge of boats. There are mills built on boats, like those of Saragossa, transportable from one place to another. Moreover there are numerous gardens, orchards, stretches of land suitable for cultivation as well as vineyards where they also grow figs.»[38] Still keeping to the coast, and moving towards the estuary of the Ebro, one came to Alicante, where there was «a mosque cathedral, as well as a smaller one. Esparto grass which grows here is exported throughout the Mediterranean. The area produces great quantities of fruits and vegetables, especially figs and grapes. There is a castle, built to defend the town, well fortified and standing on a mountain that can be crossed only with difficulty. Although it is not an important place, trading vessels and boats are built at Alicante.»[39] Further to the north stood Denia, then a pretty township by the sea, protected by a fortified castle; Tortosa, where there were shipyards, and Valencia, a flourishing commercial center with one of the largest populations in the Levant.

Along the course of the Guadiana stood the town of Merida, still showing traces of its past grandeur and, on the same river, Badajoz. One of the richest and most prosperous towns in the kingdom was Toledo, sited on an inlet of the river Tagus, where many monuments of the Roman epoch were still to be seen. «At the time of the ancient Christians Toledo was the capital of their empire and a center of communications. When the Muslims became the rulers of Andalusia they found immense riches here. Among these there were a hundred and seventy gold crowns adorned with pearls and precious stones, a thousand royal swords encrusted with jewels, quantities of pearls and rubies, a vast number of gold and silver vases, the table of Solomon, son of David, said to be formed of a single emerald and now preserved in Rome.»[40]

All that remains of the Muslim epoch are two gates, that of the Bridge and the Vieja de Visagra, formerly known as Bab Shakra.

The most important town of the Upper Marches was Saragossa, «It is one of the most remarkable towns in Spain, large and well-populated with broad streets and very handsome houses; the whole surrounded by orchards and gardens. The town walls are built in stone and are very solid. It stands on the banks of a great river, the Ebro, the source of which lies partly in the land of the Christians, partly in the Calatayud mountains and partly in the Calahorra neighborhood. The confluence of all these water courses takes place above Tudela and from thence the river flows towards Saragossa and beyond it in the direction of the Gibra fortress. Here, its waters are joined by those of the River of the Olives and it continues its course towards Tortosa where, to the west, it flows out into the sea. Saragossa is also known as the «White Town» because the majority of its houses are colorwashed with chalk or lime. It must be said that snakes are never to be found here.»[41]

There were many newly founded towns. Certain of them on hills, the better to defend the region in which they were sited, such as Uclés, in the Santaver district, Tudela, built to protect the fertile plain of the central stretch of the Ebro, Lerida, on the left bank of the Segre and Gibraltar, a natural fortress of Islamism, not far from Africa.

Others were founded in the Meseta, like Madrid, built by the emir Muhammad I to the right of the Manzares; Ubeda, in the valley of the Guadalquivir; Medinaceli (Madînat Sâlim), on the site of ancient Ocilis, a military base for summer expeditions against the Christians; and Aznalfarache (Hisn al-farag), so called for the vast panorama to be admired from its walls.

In keeping with Muslim tradition the names of the architects responsible for building all these solid and well-organized towns have not, for the most part, been preserved.

c) HOUSES AND PALACES

The Palace of the Muslim overlords of Spain was built by 'Abd al-Rahmân I who had previously lived on the outskirts of the town in the residence of al-Rusafa.[42] The perimeter of the ancient palace once embraced the lands on which the seminary and the episcopal palace stand today; it was built in 784 on the site of the ancient residence of the Visigoth governors, and their successors, down to an-Nâsir, embellished and enlarged it. In this way the Alcazar became the center of political life in Muslim Spain. Documents provide us with conflicting information on the layout of the building. Ibn 'Idhârî tells us that in the times of al-Masûr there were two gates leading into the palace: Bâb al-Hadîd and Bâb as-Sudda.[43] Ibn Bashquwâl on the other hand counts five; the Iron Gate, the Garden Gate (*bâb al-ginân*), the River Gate (*bâb al-wâdî*), the Bâb Qûrîya, to the north, and the Bâb Gâmi', by which the caliphs entered the mosque.[44]

However, the most important exemplar of caliphal civil architecture is the Madînat az-Zahra'. It was built in 325/936, on the orders of an-Nâsir, on the Giabal al-'arûs, the «Mountain of the Bride», where the buttresses of the Sierra de Cordoba overlook the right bank of the Gudalquivir. Ibn 'Idhârî provides us with valuable information: «Six thousand squared blocks of stone were utilized every day, excluding those used for the foundations. The marble was brought from Carthage in Ifrîqiya and from Tunis, by such trustworthy men as 'Abd Allâh ibn Yûnus, Hasan Qurtubi and 'Alî ibn Ga'far Iskandarâni. An-Nâsir paid them three dinar for each block of marble and eight dinar for each column. The building called for 4313 columns, 1013 of which came from Ifrîqiya and 140 were sent by the king of the Rûm; the remainder was of Spanish provenance... It is said that four hundred rooms in the az-Zahra' were planned to house the sultan, his court and his family, that there were 3750 eunuch slaves and 6300 women both old and young, including servants.»[45] Its origins are legendary. One of the sovereign's concubines is said to have died leaving a great fortune to be used to ransom Muslim prisoners on Christian soil in the north of the peninsula. But the caliph's envoys scoured the province without finding a single one. Consequently, with the money at his disposal, an-Nâsir built a town, named after his Favorite. A statue of a woman, once standing on the main gate, was later removed on the orders of al-Mansûr. The town was laid out on three levels. The uppermost level, formed of the most important buildings; preceded by a court, was reserved to the caliph and his suite; the central area was laid out as vast gardens; the lowest level contained the guardrooms, houses for officials and the barracks, all receiving light from the courts which were for the most part without porches, and the Great Mosque.

During the revolts that led to the fall of the caliphate the Madînat was used by the Berbers as their headquarters and was ultimately looted and burned down. Al-Idrîsî, who visited it in 1010, describes it as follows: «The town still exists, with its walls and the ruins of its palaces. A small number of men and families still live there. It was once a great town, built on various levels, one above the other, in such a way that the ground level of the highest point of the town was parallel to the roofs of the median level which lay parallel to the roofs of the lowest level. All of them were surrounded by walls. At the upper level there were palaces of such great beauty as defies description. There were gardens and orchards at the centre, and dwellings and the great mosque below these. Everything lies in ruin today and is on the point of disappearing.»[46] In the Alcazar of Seville,[47] not far from the Patio de las Banderas, there is the Patio de Yeso, a court surviving from the times of the Reyes de Taifas.

Excavations have brought to light the remains of a palace, in the qasba of Malaga, which can be attributed to the Zirid emir Bâdîs (1053-1063); together with this there are the remains of private residences dating from the eleventh century.[48]

These are small dwellings, built one up against the other, and they stand on the highest area of the fortress. But in this same town, close by these private dwellings, there were more important, spacious buildings.[49] One contains a reception hall, giving on to a court with a tripartite entrance of elliptical arches, each flanked by two columns.

Standing on a spur of rock in the plain, four kilometers away from the town in a northeasterly direction, there is the palace known as Castillejo, built by Ibn Mardanish (1147-1171), which long resisted the African conquerors.[50] There are architectural elements in the symmetrical rectangular plan which were later to become typical features of the Alhambra. Two square pavilions at the centres of the short sides of the court foreshadow the Court of the Lions and illustrate a theme that will be repeated, at a much later date, in the Qarawîyyn

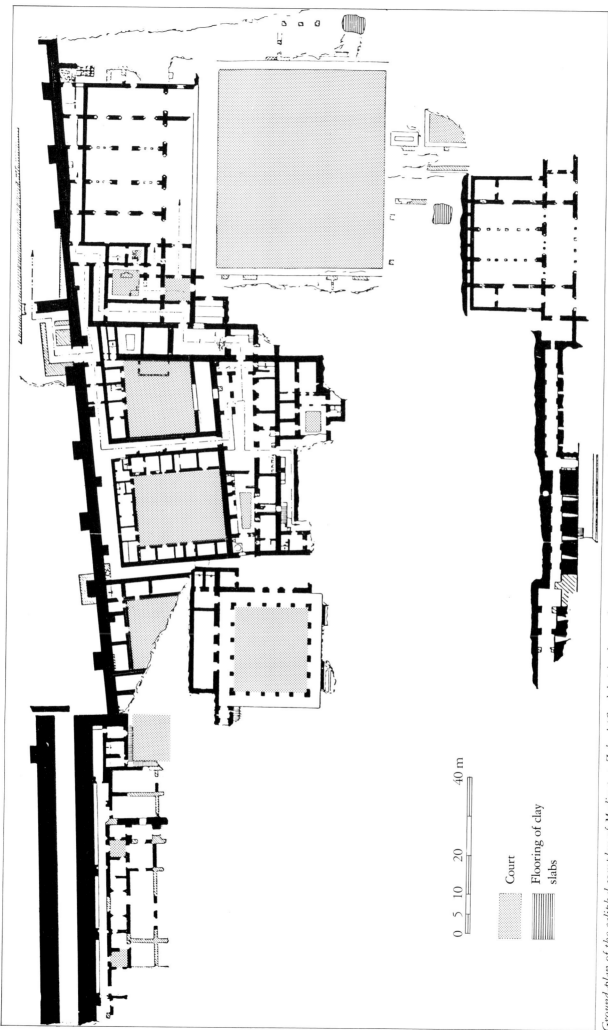

Ground-plan of the caliphal complex of Madinat az-Zahra' (Cordoba) in the tenth century.

Court

Flooring of clay
slabs

0 5 10   20   40 m

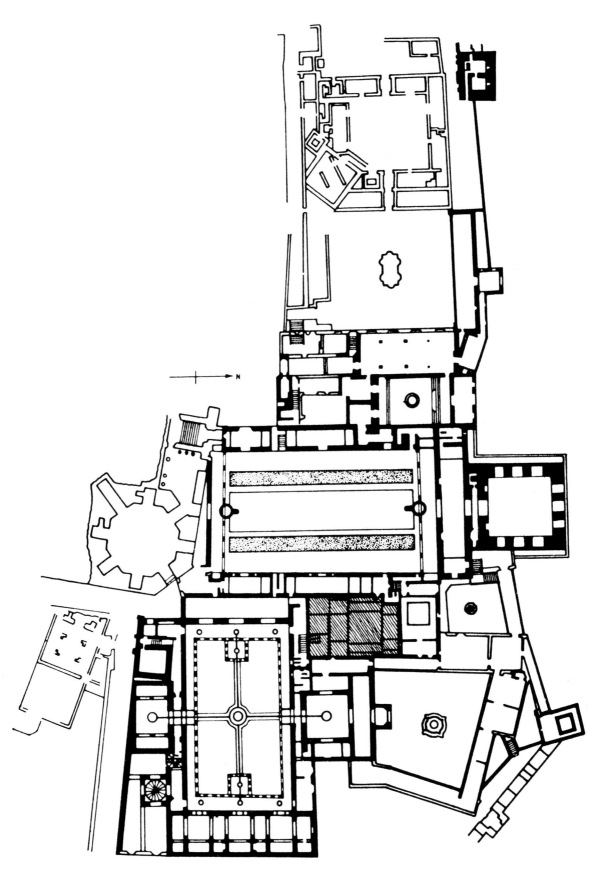

Ground-plan of the Nasrid royal palace, the Alhambra (Granada).

On the preceding page: Granada, the Alhambra. The excavations seen from the Homenaje Tower (Oronoz). On this page: left, a general view of the Alhambra from the northeast; above, the Los Picos Tower (reign of Muhammad II), thirteenth century, and the Wine Gate, let into the second enclosure walls during the reign of Muhammad V.

The Alhambra. Above: two views of the interior of the mihrab tower. Facing: the oratory of the Daraxa meshvar (Oronoz). On the following pages: the Myrtles Court seen from opposite ends (reign of Yusuf I), fourteenth century; the Comares Tower can be seen in the background of the first picture. (Oronoz)

On the preceding pages, the Alhambra: the Hall of the Two Sisters, fourteenth century, and a detail of the dome from below; beyond the entrance the fountain in the Court of the Lions can be seen. On this page: the Court of the Lions seen from the palace of Charles V. Below: the dome of the east pavilion. Facing: arcaded walk flanking the court. (Oronoz)

Two more evocative views of the Court of the Lions (reign of Muhammad V), fourteenth century. The lions, of evident eastern derivation, support a basin carved with a poem by Ibn Zamrak. On the following pages, the Alhambra; left: Mirador de Lindaraja, fourteenth century; right: the Chamber of the Kings (or of Justice). The ceilings of the three alcoves are decorated with paintings attributed to Christian artists from Seville. (Oronoz)

189

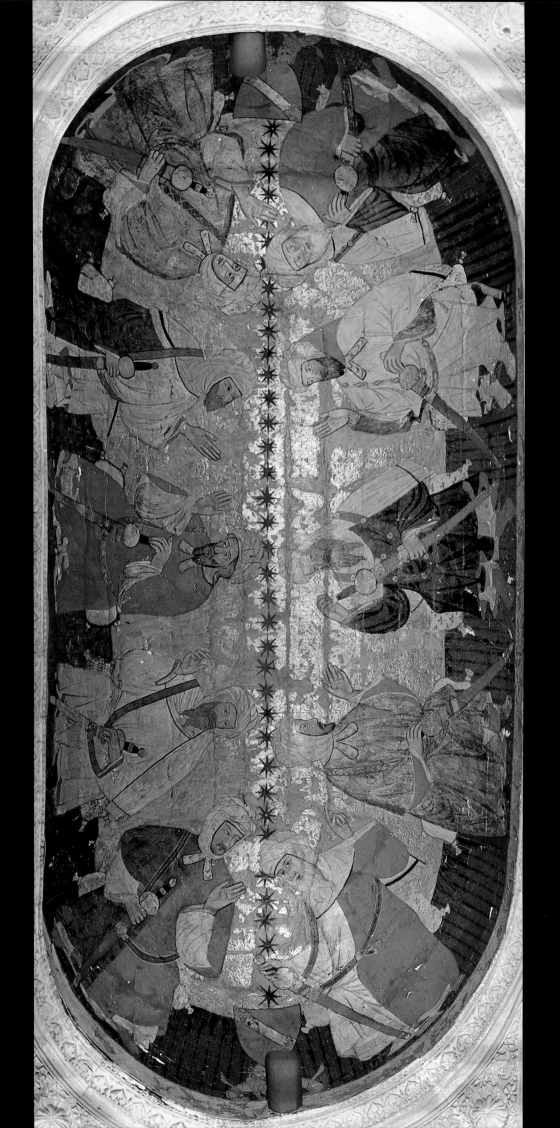

On the preceding pages: The Alhambra; left: ceiling of the central alcove in the Chamber of the Kings portraying the members of the Nasrid dynasty; right: detail of same. Facing, and above: ceiling and detail of same from the left-hand alcove in the Chamber of the Kings. Overleaf, left: another ceiling in the Chamber of the Kings, depicting scenes of knights and ladies. (Oronoz). Right: the dome of the Tower of the Infanta in the Alhambra (reign of Muhammad V), fourteenth century.

The Alhambra. Above: entrance to the Comares Hall. Facing: facade of the entrance to the Comares Palace. (Oronoz)

Details of wooden ceilings. Facing: the Comares Tower; above left: dome of the Comares Hall (Oronoz); right: another example of wooden decoration. Overleaf: painted figures on walls in the Comares Tower.

The Alhambra. Facing: the Ambassadors' Hall, a niche; above: the façade of the Cuarto Dorado. (Oronoz)

The Alhambra. The Royal Baths built during the reign of Yusuf I, fourteenth century. Above left: the "tepidarium"; on the right: the rest room; above right: ceiling of the same, from below. Facing: the great bath and two details of decorative work, above, in stucco, and below, in wood.
(Oronoz)

The Alhambra: the Partal Gardens. Facing: detail of stucco decoration on the Esplanada Gateway. (Oronoz)

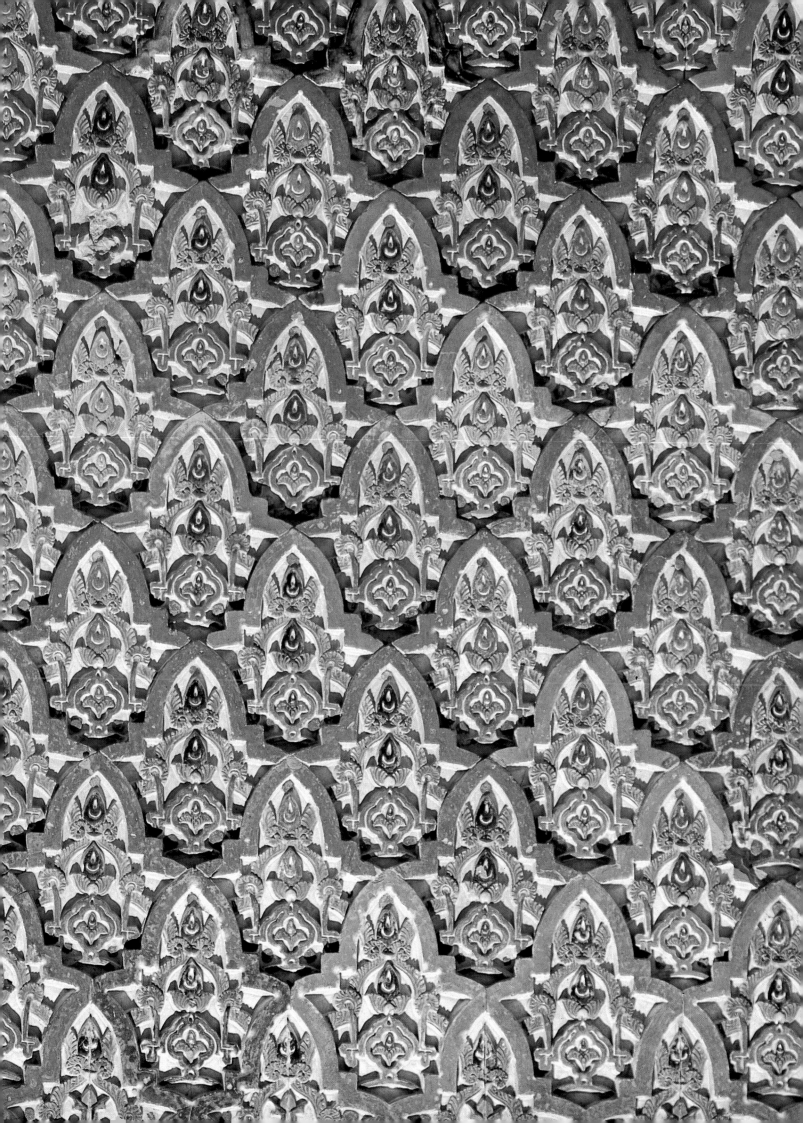

Granada. The Generalife: a general view of the complex, restored during the reign of Abu l-Walid Isma'il (1314-1325). Top right: the Court of the Sultana's Cypress; above right: the gardens. On the following pages: the Partal Garden seen from both ends. (Oronoz)

Seville. The Alcazar, fourteenth century. On the left: the facade;
above: the Los Yesos Court. (Oronoz)

217

The Alcazar. Facing and top right: the Court of the Maidens; above right: flight of arches seen from the Doll's Court.

The Alcazar. Above: the dome of the Ambassadors' Hall. Facing page, right: the arch opening on to the hall; left: arches in the Doll's Court (Oronoz). On the following pages, two details of azulejos, polychrome lustre tile wall revetments to be seen in the halls and courtyards. The last photograph in color shows the Golden Tower, in Seville, first half of the thirteenth century.

221

The Alhambra: remains of dwellings, looking down from the Alcazaba.

The Alhambra. Top: a mingling of muqarnos and azulejos that endow the walls almost with the delicacy of transparent lacework. Above: the basin in the Abencerrajes Hall. Facing: a glimpse of the Mirador de Lindaraja. (Olivella)

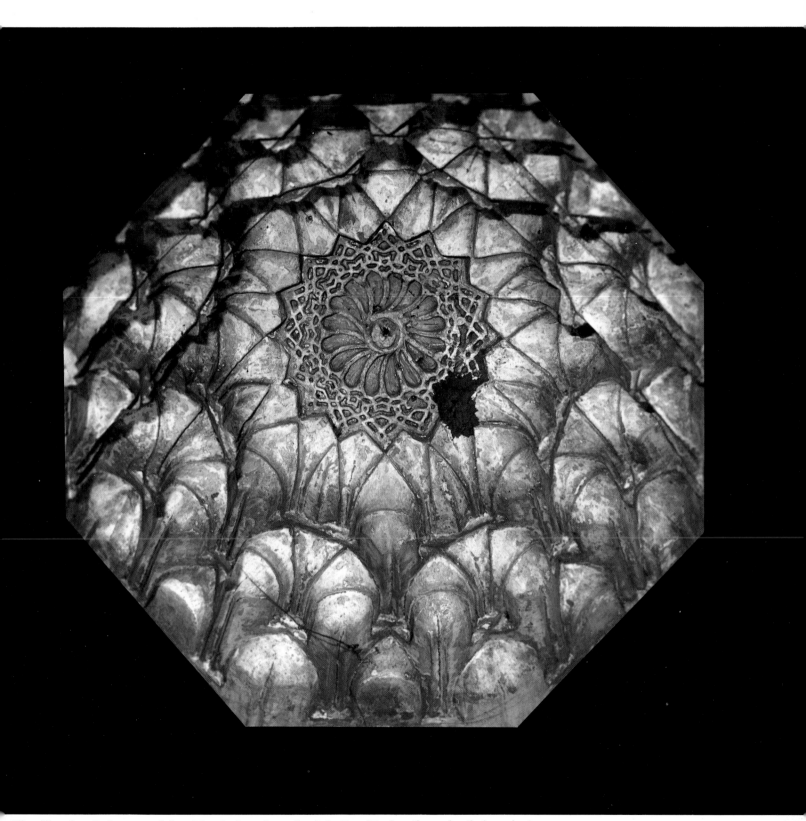

The Alhambra. Facing: one of the niches let into the walls of the Royal Baths. Above: detail of a stalactite ornamented dome in the same baths.

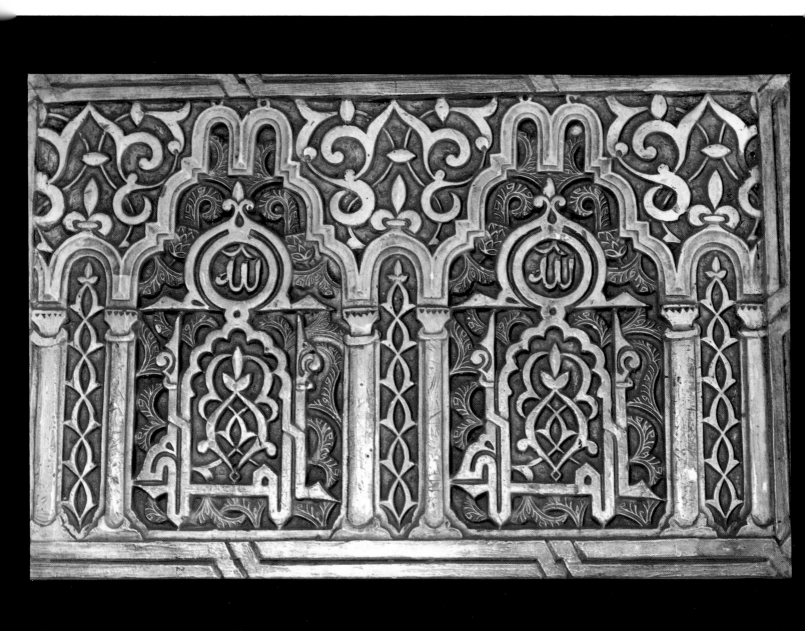

The Alhambra: stucco-work panel with the monogram of Allah.

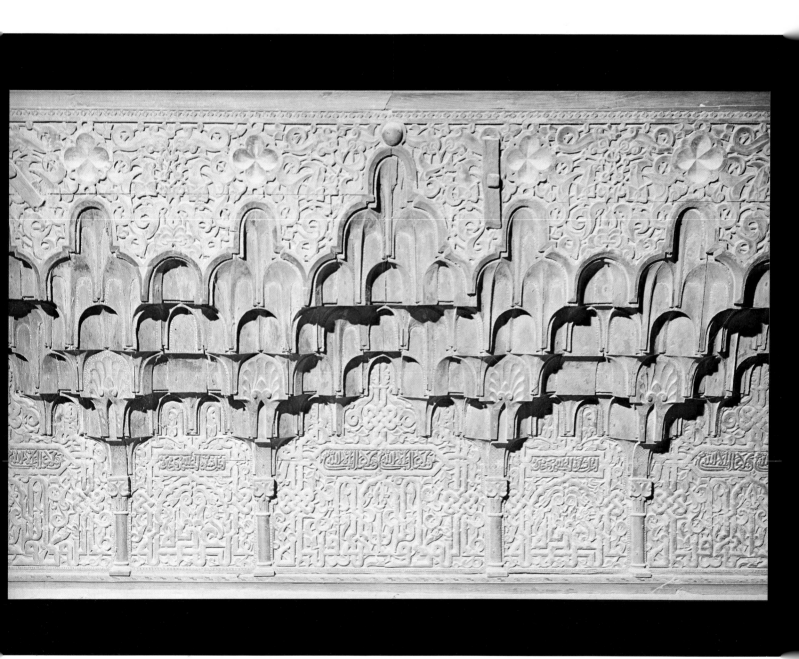

*The Alhambra. Above: muqarnas decorations along the walls of the Ambassadors' Hall (Oronoz). Overleaf, left:
the ceiling of the Comares Tower; right: a detail from the Ambassadors' Hall.*

: a panel with floral decoration.

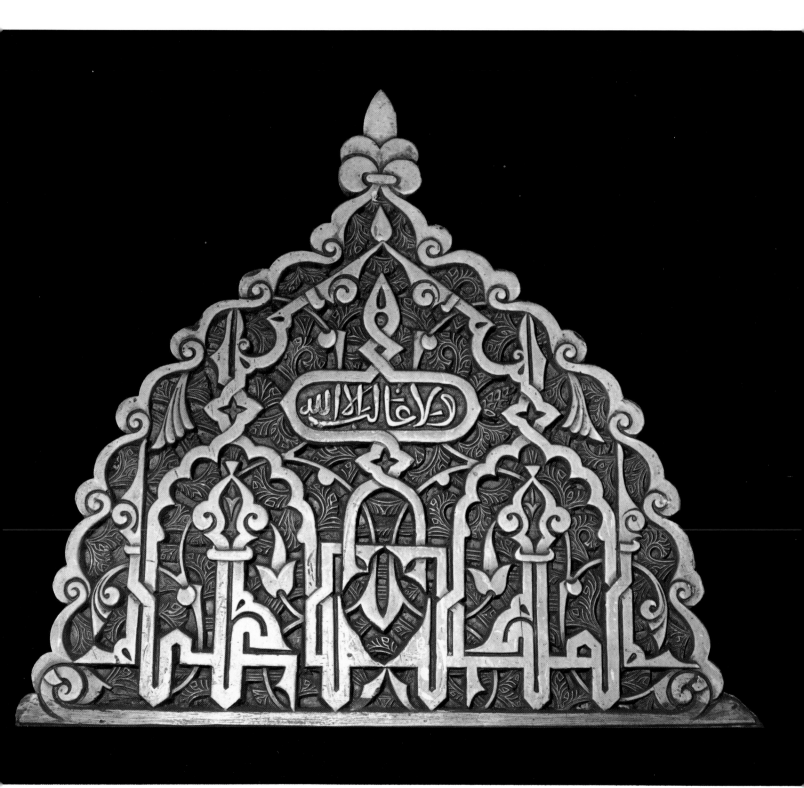

In fragile stucco the omnipresent motto of the Nasrids: "There is no victor but God." Overleaf, left: a detail of geometric decoration; right: a photographic reconstruction of the Fountain of the Lions. The basin is bordered with a poem by Ibn Zamrak: "Do you not see how the water courses along the sides and, unintercepted, conceals itself in the channels? / Like the lover's eyelids brimming with tears, yet concealed from fear of exposure".

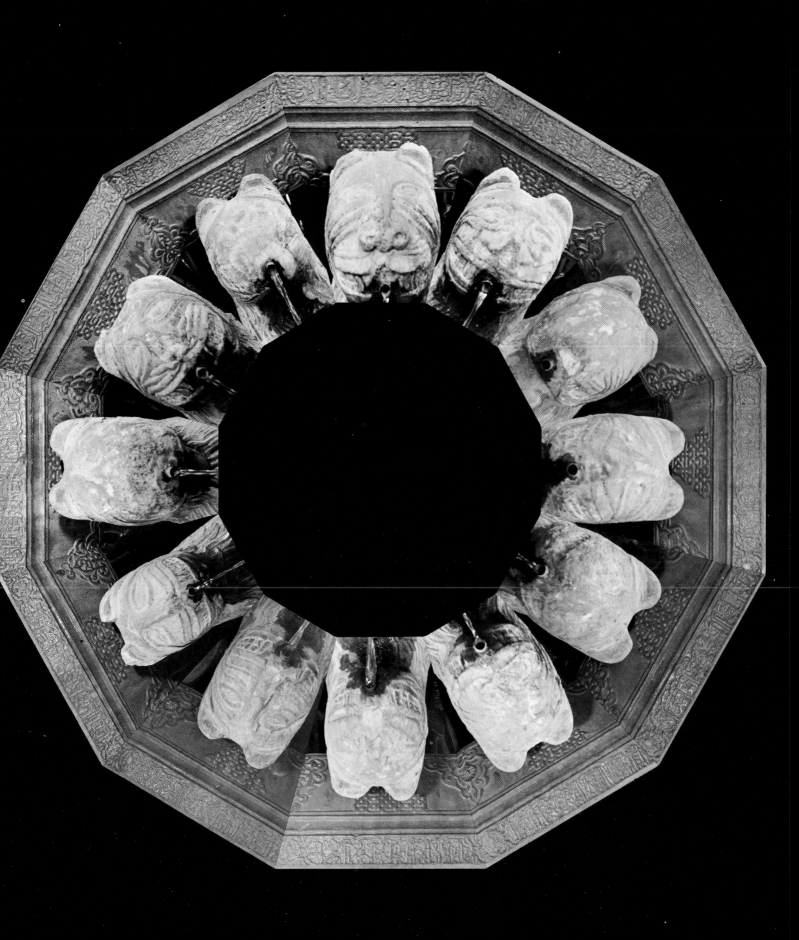

Toledo. Facing: the Puerta del sol, a masterpiece of Mudejar architecture, fourteenth century. Above: the Bab Shakra, later called the Puerta Vieja de Visagra, ninth century. Overleaf: the Bib Mardum Mosque, tenth century. Transformed into a Christian church; it was given the name of Cristo de la Luz.

mosque at Fez. Alleys cut the space into the form of a cross, a formula deriving from Persian gardens and surviving in the Morrocan *riâdh*.

With so many residences and palaces destroyed after the Reconquest, the monument that seems best to epitomize the fantasy and elegance of the civil architecture of Spain as a whole is the al-Qal'at al-Hamra, the citadel that rears up from the red clay hill of Sabîka at Granada; a spur of land that juts out between the Darro valley and the Vega, irrigated by the waters of the Genil.[51]

The Zirids, the Berber rulers of the town, had already built a *qasba* on the western extremity of the highland in the eleventh century. This first military nucleus was the beginning of what was to become the fortress and residence of the Nasrid sultans, the Alhambra.

When Muhammad I took possession of Granada in 1238 and made it his capital, he built fortifications and laid the foundations to the palace that he had in mind to build. Muhammad II continued the work of his father by building the greater part of the enclosure walls. The building of the Lady Tower and the Los Picos Tower on the north front is attributed to the second Nasrid ruler. By the beginning of the fourteenth century the Alhambra had already taken on the appearance of a royal residence and was gradually acquiring the characteristics of a true urban center. It is almost certain that the thirteenth-century palaces were demolished to make way for the new buildings of Yûsûf I (1335-1354) and Muhammad V (1354-1391) that are so much admired today.

Without changing the form of the enclosure walls, Yûsûf built the Military Gate on the north flank and the Justice Gate, known today as De Siete Suelos, on the south flank. Four bastions were built where the land rises perpendicularly from the river Darro: the Captive's Tower, Candil, Machuca, and Comares. This latter contains the Hall of the Ambassadors, the most splendid chamber in the royal residence. A magnificent portico, together with a small oratory nearby are the surviving structures of the Partal palace that once adjoined the Lady Tower. Between the Comares Tower and the Throne Room lies the transversal Barca Gallery, communicating with the Alberca Patio, the Court of the Myrtle Trees, with its central pool. To the east of the Alberca Courtyard the baths are to be found. Leaving the area where the cisterns (algibes) were housed, one encounters three successive courts. Only ruins remain of the first of these, but a mosque and minaret once stood in the south-east corner. The second courtyard, known as the Machuca Court, after the name of Charles V's architect, is not far from the handsome, columned Mexuar Chamber. The third, with its porticoed entrance, is the great hall known as the Cuarto Dorado. Yûsûf's son, Muhammad V, added a new palace whose apartments frame the Court of the Lions.

Like the Alberca Court, the Court of the Lions was built on a rectangular plan, but on a smaller scale. It is framed by the marble columns of four porches providing access to the apartments beyond. To the west, the rectangular Mocàrabes Gallery with its vaulted stalactite ceiling; to the east, the Kings' Chamber or Hall of Justice, divided into three parts, each of which is framed by other, smaller rooms; to the south, the Abencerrajes Gallery with a small central fountain; to the north, the Hall of the Two Sisters, covered by a stalactite ceiling, which communicates with another chamber ending in an alcove in the form of a belvedere,

241

the Mirador de Daraxa (*Dâr 'A'isha*). The Court of the Lions, reverting to the older oriental model of the residence built round a central courtyard, is crossed by two paved walks; at the center where these cross, stands the basin supported by twelve marble lions from which the court derives its name. The central *riâdh* motif which has already been met with in the Marrakesh excavations, dating from the first half of the twelfth century, would seem to be of Iranian derivation.

To the northeast of the citadel stands the Generalife (*Ganna al-'arîf*). This is one of the country houses that the Nasrids had built on the highlands dominating the Alhambra to provide a refuge against the hot summer weather.[52] It was reached from the Puerta de Hierro (the Iron Gate). An inscription praising Ismâ'îl, incorporated in a decoration in one of its pavilions, tells us that the residence was built in the first part of the fourteenth century. The essential feature of the building is the long Canal Court, the Patio de la Acequia, which is cut by a narrow slit of water animated by a fountain and other inventive water displays.[53] Each of the shorter sides of the rectangle is bordered by a pavilion. Beyond the Generalife, to the north, stood the Bride's House (Dâr al'Arusa)[54] with a large court surrounded by dwellings with smaller central courts. Another example of a Muslim garden can be seen at Velez de Benaudalla, on the Motril road from Granada.

Another very important civil foundation at Granada was the *mâristân* or «refuge for the sick.» It was founded by Muhammad V,[55] following the illustrious example of numerous others which had been built in previous centuries at Baghdad, Cairo, Aleppo, Marrakesh, and Fez. The building, demolished in the nineteenth century after having been used for industrial purposes, was articulated around a large rectangular court with a central basin into which the water flowed from two lions, an example of the oriental style that had already borne fruit at the Alhambra, here further enlivened by flowers, plants, and carpets hanging from the walls.

The Alcazar of Seville[56] on the other hand, belongs to what had become Mudejar art. Arab chroniclers make use of the word *mudaggân* to indicate the Muslim who remained on Christian soil. Mudejar art is therefore the expression of those Muslims who continued to live in Christian Spain after the Reconquest, carrying on their ancient techniques and traditions in the employment of the Christian princes, who were not indifferent to the seductions of Muslim culture.

With the exception of a few surviving traces of Almohad overlordship and a number of rooms in pure Gothic style, the Alcazar is the work of Pedro I the Cruel who, after conquering the town, established his residency there in 1363. An inscription in Kufic script framing a fascia on the façade, reads: «There is no victor but God.» The familiar motto of the Nasrids confirms the presence in Seville of Granadine artists sent by Muhammad V to his friend and ally Pedro. Names of Muslim artists are recorded in later centuries too. In 1373, under Henry II, 'Alî worked here; in 1438, under John, Ahmad supervised operations. The complex was partially rebuilt by Charles V's architects in the Italian style, and completely restored in the eighteenth century by Philip IV. However, it was mainly the modifications introduced by the duke of Montpensier that changed the original character of the place. These took place in the nineteenth century when he married a Spanish princess and came to live in Andalusia.

The feature of the central court is found here once again in the Court of the Maidens.

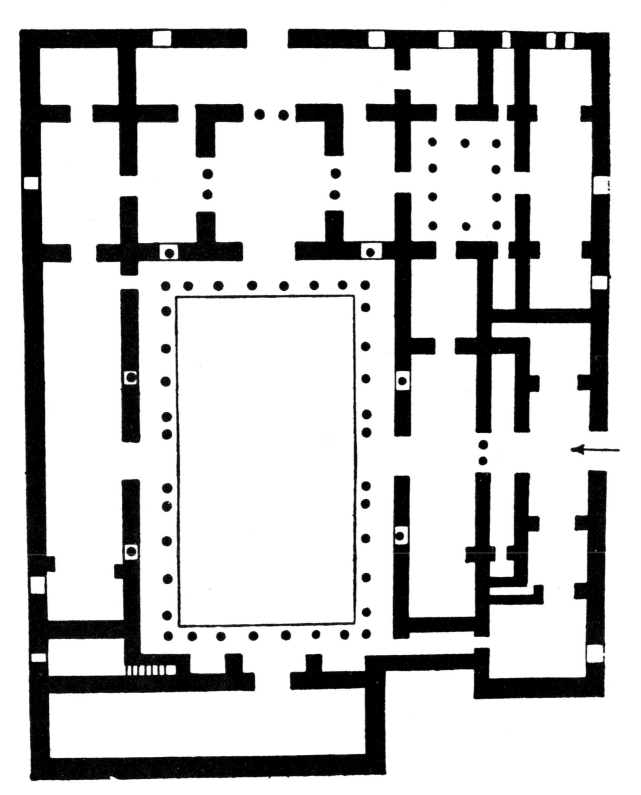

Ground-plan of the Alcazar of Seville.

Several rooms open off it: Charles V's saloon, the Bedroom of the Moorish King, the Prince's Hall and the Hall of the Ambassadors. The entrance to this last hall bears an inscription that reads: «Our lord the Sultan, the great, the supreme, Don Pedro, king of Castile and Leon (May God perpetuate his happiness) ordered his architect, al-Galabi, to make doors of carved wood for this magnificent gateway of happiness. He ordered this to honor the Ambassadors... Their construction and resulting splendor has been a source of joy. Toledan artists created the sculpture. This was carried out in the year of grace 1404.»[57]

But it was Granada which always evoked deep emotion, marvelling admiration, and stunned amazement. In a Castilian poem written on the threshold of the fifteenth century the Nasrid prince, Ibn al-Ahmar, proudly describes the town to the daughters of John II:

> Abenámar, Abenámar, moro de la moreriá!
> ¿Qué castillos son aquéllos? Altos son y reluciàn!
> — El Alhambra era señor y la otra la Mezquita;
> los otros son alijares, labrados a maravilla.
> El moro que los labraba, cien doblas ganaba al dia.
> La otra era Granada, Granada la enoblecida,
> de los muchos caballeros y de la gran ballesterìa.—
> Allì habla el rey don Juan, bien oiréis lo que decìa:
> — Granada, si tú quisieras, contigo me casarìa;
> darte he yo en arras y dote, a Córdoba y Sevilla.
> — Casata soy, el rey don Juan, casada soy que no viuda;
> el moro que a mi me tiene, muy grande bien me querìa.[58]

d) CASTLES AND FORTRESSES

The prolonged hostility between the Muslims of Spain and the Christians of the north contributed to an uncommon development of military architecture in the form of enclosure walls, towers, strongholds, castles and fortresses. These often served a secondary purpose as shelters for travelers and expeditionary forces on the frontiers or the busier highways.

When sites offered fairly level ground, castles in the ninth through tenth centuries generally conformed to a square plan. An excellent example of this is the El-Vacar on the Estremadura road from Cordoba. A much larger fortress is the handsome building known as the Conventual di Merida, which has numerous towers on each façade. Along the Toledo road from Cordoba one encounters the castles of Baños de la Encina and Las Navas di Tolosa, in the province of Jaen.

However, the most important caliphal fortress surviving today is that of Gormaz,[59] in the Upper Marches; it is sited along the course of the river Duero in a magnificent, naturally strategic position. The castle was taken by the Arabs in 925 and later destroyed by the Christians. In the reign of al-Hakam II, in 965, the Muslims rebuilt it, as we learn from a tablet to be seen today walled into the Romanesque San Miguel at Gormaz. After it had changed hands several times, Alfonso VI gave it to the Cid in 1087.

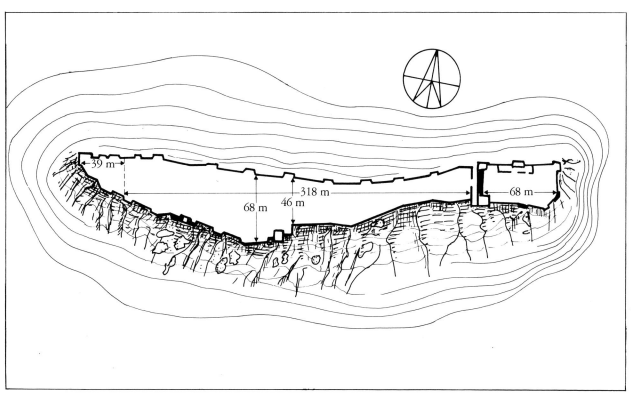

Ground-plan of the Castle of Gormaz (Soria).

It was used by the Christians as a strategic defense work until the fifteenth century but then, like all medieval fortifications, was abandoned and fell into ruin.

Roman tradition, modified by Byzantine and Syrian influences, was observed in the Gormaz plan: a quadrilateral with towers at the corners and others set out at regular intervals along the walls. Two entrance arches remain, one at the center of the south wall and another on the north side. The interior courtyard has a covered rectangular well and a basin for water, designed on a square plan.

Standing on an impregnable site in the upper valley of the Guadalhorce, the castle of Bobastro,[60] the refuge of Ibn Hafsûn, still retains the ruins of its enclosure walls and of the citadel that dominated the tiny agglomerate.

The fall of the caliphate led to a widespread feeling of insecurity that encouraged the proliferation of defense works. The solid walls with which every town ringed itself for fear of raids were constantly added to. A double fortification enclosed the castle of Monteagudo in the vicinity of Murcia. The town center was often linked to the citadel by two long walls, as at Jativa and Denia. More elaborate defense measures can be seen on the Visagra Gate at Toledo, which has a system of closure consisting of two gates with a portcullis between them.

Fortifications built during the Almoravid period were systematically destroyed by the Almohads. Today, surviving examples are only to be found in Morocco. The fortifications of Gibraltar date from the times of 'Abd al-Mu'mîn. Ibn Ya'qûb gave the order to build the two *qasba* at Seville and to fortify Caceres and Badajoz, two frontier towns in the Estremadura.[61] The surviving walls at Cordoba and Seville are Almohad work.[62] An addition to the Alcazar of this latter town was made, on the orders of Abû l-Ula, in 617/1220. This was the Golden Tower,[63] which stands on the left bank of the Guadalquivir. At the time it was built, a similar tower already stood on the opposite bank and a chain used to be stretched between the two to close the entrance to the town harbour.

On a fine strategic site a few kilometers to the southeast of Seville stands the fortress of Alcala de Guadaira, which may have been built by al-Mansûr. Despite remodelling by Ferdinando III, who conquered it in 1246, it still preserves the original Muslim walls.

As examples of Nasrid military architecture, mention may be made of the Calahorra of Gibraltar,[64] built by the Merinid Abû 'Inân in c. 1344, standing in the northeast corner of the old Arab town; the citadel of Antequera, on the road between Seville and Granada and the successive additions to the *qasba* of Malaga.[65] Many isolated towers were built in the Granadine Vega to protect the roads into the town from all-too-frequent Christian attacks.

c) BATHS

Care of the body and attention to cleanliness are a religious duty in Islam, so much so that ceremonial washing is prescribed by rite before the appointed hour of prayer. Consequently the bath has always been of great importance in the Muslim household. The ordinary household made do with hand basins containing cold and lukewarm water while the wealthier families had proper bathrooms which were, however, very costly. It thus became customary in

Muslim countries to build public baths or *hammâm*. Even the smallest village would have its own *hammâm* alongside the mosque. In towns they were more numerous; thirteenth century Baghdad contained over five thousand and there were 1170 in Cairo. What survives today of Muslim baths in Spain can give no idea of how numerous they were. At the end of the tenth century there were about 600 in Cordoba alone.

The architectural model seems to have been established in the eighth century by the baths of Qusayr 'Amra and as-Sarakh. These consisted of a great audience hall with three naves, a smaller *tepidarium* and a *calidarium* roofed with a dome. The baths were built of brick, stone or marble according to the region and area of the town in which they were to be found. Glass panes in the domes provided a source of light and the layout followed an established pattern. After crossing a hall, one undressed in the first chamber, which contained cupboards for storing clothes, and then moved on through the *frigidarium* and the *tepidarium* to reach the *calidarium*. This was divided into two areas: one containing alcoves fitted with stone tables on which one was soaped and rubbed down, the other, and the warmer of the two, housed a brick boiler and was supplied with wooden buckets to pour out the hot water. There were barbers plying their trade in all the rooms. The Alhambra baths were adorned with decorative work in tiles, wood, and carved plaster and had all the air of a residence with a central court and small columns. An epigraphic frieze running round the walls of the Las Camas chamber sings the praises of Yûsuf I. Older bathhouses, simpler in style, are the Banuelo at Granada and the baths of Juderia, Baza, Valencia and Palma de Mallorca.

The bath house generally belonged to the *waqf* and was in the charge of people appointed to the job, who enforced the austere regulations. The Faithful were not to stay on the premises too long and were to avoid eating meals or reciting the Koran there. The men usually went to the baths early in the morning or in the evening. The afternoon was reserved for women, who attended these public institutions most assiduously. Christians might use the baths every day except Friday or an appointed feast day but in the late Middle Ages they spontaneously gave up the practice in the belief that use of the *hammâm* was a sign of weak character.

The Art of Decoration

a) EPIGRAPHY

The sole ornament of the Koran is the grace of its letters. This fact endowed calligraphy with supreme importance, for by association with the sacred scriptures it became the preeminent artistic expression of the Muslim spirit. Calligraphy takes on a monumental dimension, as it does in no other civilization, in the form of the epigraphic fascia, in architecture, mosaic, and painting.

Epigraphy belongs to the non-figurative arts of Islam. It appeared early in the Muslim era in religious inscriptions, graffiti, cut into the rocks of the Arabian desert. At the end of the seventh century it acquired a more dignified architectural setting in the friezes of the Dome of the Rock in Jerusalem and, a few years later, in the mosque of Medina. Henceforward the purpose of epigraphy would be the glorification of the Muslim faith. The friezes not simply affirming the concept of divine power but standing as significant evidence of the fruit of experience and choice, an authentic religious sentiment and not an abstract faith.

The characters, set in the bands framing the *mihrâb*, the doors and windows, in the friezes on the ceilings and the façades, are not restricted to quotations from the Koran. One finds echoes of theological debate, proverbs of wisdom and mystical union, poetic quotations and allusions to the political vicissitudes of the medieval centuries. Nonetheless, the verses of the Book and the passages of the *hadîth* are constantly present, witnessing the depth of religious sentiment, serving as a reminder that the purpose of all art is religious, that everything created by man is to the ultimate glory of God and, withal, of the certainty that whatever man's invention, the product is but vain and ephemeral.

A second category of inscriptions commemorates mankind and its undertakings. Here there appear not only figures whose lives feature in the political and social history of the community, but also obscure pilgrims, travelers and merchants unrecorded by the chronicles, humble inhabitants of towns and villages whose lives are summed up in the brief eulogies adorning modest tombs. Other texts celebrate the construction of a building, though these rarely indicate the names of the artists and the craftsmen who worked on it; unswerving is the belief that what counts is not the individual himself but the product of his labors, offered up as proof of his faith. Man, both creature and servant (*'abd*) of God, does not exalt himself since he knows full well that ontologically speaking he is a mere nothing, totally dependent on his Creator. The commemorative tablet of the Puerta de las Palmas in the Great Mosque of Cordoba reads: «In the name of God the Compassionate and Merciful. The servant of God, 'Abd Allâh al-Rahmân, Lord of the Faithful, an-Nâsir li din Allâh may God grant him long life, gave orders to build this façade and to strengthen its foundations.»[66] In Kufic script, worked in gold mosaic on an azure ground, the long inscription around the mihrâb contains the following: «Believers, fulfill your duties to Allâh and bear true witness. Do not allow your hatred for other men to turn you away from justice. Deal justly; justice is nearer to true piety. Have fear of Allâh; He is cognizant of all your actions.»[67]

Sometimes inscriptions give news of social convictions, of economic and intellectual life, of fame attained by men of science and of letters, or offer praise for the conduct of the caliph; elsewhere, on coins, weights and measures, they indicate the norms of administration, or appear on panels, caskets, ivories, stuccoes, bricks, ceramic wares and metals, to commemorate a gift, an event, or a kind thought.

The inherent nature of Arabic script lends itself to these purposes, both in the occasion it offers to vary the relationships between vertical and horizontal spacing, and in the inexhaustible aesthetic potential, detached from meaning, that it possesses. For this reason it was exploited for purely decorative use by the Byzantines, by Italian painters, and by French artists in the Middle Ages to decorate church doorways such as that at Puy.

When the Muslims invaded the Iberian peninsula the use of Kufic as the preeminent script for sacred texts was already widely established.

The Kûfî script of al-Andalus was modelled on the typical script, termed archaic, of the town of Kûfa. The sobriety of its rectilinear and angular forms interspersed with the occasional small rosette was admirably suited to stone carving and brickwork, or for mosaic compositions. Consequently, this form alone was used in the field of architecture for centuries and, though slight regional variations are to be met with, it remained substantially the same in all Islamic centers. In Muslim Spain, during the last years of Muhammad I, the uprights of the letters became shorter and took on the rounder, lighter and more stylized forms, with floral decorations, known as floriated Kufic, an epigraphic form which was to become very popular throughout Arab countries.

The floral motifs were to be condemned by the strictly orthodox caliph al-Mustansir who attempted to reinstate the earlier simplicity of the classical tradition and to discourage the growing taste for ornamentation. This intervention resulted in Simple Kufic, a form less ornate than the floriated style but lacking the austerity of the earlier form in which the letter sufficed in itself. Simple Kufic survived until the fall of the caliphate.

Political unity, once upheld by central power at Cordoba, broke down under the reyes de Taifas. Thenceforward each province developed autonomous tendencies, as much in epigraphy as elsewhere. The most important innovations came from Seville, which continued to follow the rules of Simple Kufic but lengthened the letters; from Toledo, which revived Floriated Kufic with a particular predilection for an abundance of vegetal motifs, and from Saragossa. Here, artists decorating the Aljaferia, the palace of Abû Gia'far, adopted a strongly stylized letter form, articulated with extreme elegance against a floral ground, to evoke the Fatimid art of Africa.

The Almoravids brought about no marked changes in ornamental writing but the Almohads introduced the use of Naskhî, a cursive script that derives from the movement of the hand in the act of writing. Preference was shown to this new script because it was easier to read, although, compared with Kufic, it is less solemn and imposing. The earlier script was therefore restricted to religious texts in monumental inscriptions. The artistic taste and sensibility of the Andalusians led them to cultivate the stylization of floral motifs, which gradually absorbed all the space between the letters. This was how Geometric Kufic came into being. The style is splendidly exemplified in the decorations of the Nasrid palace at Granada which testify to the victory of Naskhî over the official script.

Extracts from the Koran as well as verse and prose writings in praise of the princely founders and their works cover the walls of the Alhambra. A poem in twelve verses celebrating the purity of the water and the sultan Muhammad V is inscribed on the twelve panels of the basin of the Lions fountain:

> Liquid silver flowing among jewels, candid and transparent
> beauty to which nothing may be compared.
> Water and marble fuse before our eyes and we cannot distinguish
> which of the two flows swiftly.
> Do you not see how the water courses along the sides and, unintercepted,
> conceals itself in the channels?
> Like the lover's eyelids brimming with tears, yet concealed
> for fear of exposure.

What can it be, if not a cloud that sprinkles the lions with
its bounty?
Like the caliph's hand, by day outstretched to bestow
gifts on the lions of war
Though you may take aim, respect for the caliph curbs
the hostility of the lions in wait.
O heir of the *ansâr*, in direct descent, the heredity of grandeur
allows you to crush those who stand on high!
The peace of God be eternally with you, in the plenitude of joys,
in the affliction of your enemies.[68]

«Lâ ghâlib illa-l-lâh,» «There is no other victor but God,» the motto repeated a thousand
times over, is to be seen everywhere. Framing the niches at the entrance to the Hall of the
Two Sisters is a text explaining the use of these «*babucheros*»: the visitor will be greeted by a
refreshing drink, prompting him to bless the house just as one blesses the rainbow that
heralds the sun. Within, there is a poem by Ibn Zamrak:

We have never seen a garden with finer flowers,
so rich in fruit and so scented.
Offer twofold, in ready money, the sum that
the *qâdî* of beauty has assigned to it.
Then, at dawn, the zephyr will place in your hands
ten *dirhâm* of light, sufficing for the tithe,
and in the garden, the sun's *dinâr*
will garland the branches.[69]
The same poet, enchanted by the beauty of the *meshwar*, writes:
«Here the birds of hope fly, to gather the fruits of desire
in the garden of magnificence.»[70]

But even in this Garden of Felicities it is not the contemplation of this world below that
beckons to mankind. Believers are reminded of the faith and the prophetic message contained
in the Koran on entering the Patio of the Generalife: «We have sent you forth as a witness
and as a bearer of news and warnings, so that you may have faith in Allah and His apostle
and that you may assist him, honor him, and praise Him morning and evening. Those that
swear fealty to you swear fealty to Allah Himself. The hand of Allah is above their hands. He
that breaks his oath breaks it at his own peril, but he that keeps his pledge to Allah shall be
richly rewarded.»[71]

b) PAINTING

Muslim authors have debated at length on the legitimacy of representing living beings in
painting and sculpture, establishing laws that were not always universally observed. The
evolution of the figurative arts can be divided into two periods. It the first of these there is a
continuation of Greco-Roman and, even more, of Byzantine aesthetics. In the second, painting

attempts to come to terms with the new proscriptions of the *hadîth*.

Illustrative of the first period are the mosaics in which landscape rather than the human figure is the center of interest and these show a prediliction for geometric motifs. The majority of mural paintings of the early centuries of Islam have disappeared, with the exception of the cycle at the eighth-century castle of Qusair Amra in which the frescoes depict hunting and battle scenes, baths and, a very rare thing for Muslim art, naked women. In this cycle, so close in spirit to the Byzantine world, there is no Muslim influence whatsoever.

In the tenth century the image spreads throughout the Islamic world, as much in the East as in the West, both in Spain and in Egypt. Animal and human figures are celebrated in Fatimid art which plays a leading role throughout the following century. By the twelfth century however, fauna and the human figure, though still used in the East, have almost disappeared in the West and will become even rarer in the centuries to come.

An explanation for this attitude towards the figurative arts is certainly to be sought in the strict and radical monotheism of Islam, which views the representation of living beings with disfavor. But here perhaps we are confronted with one of the components of Arab genius, a genius that has never produced, for example, the sweeping fresco of the epic poem but, instead, has richly flowered in essentially lyrical poetry. The tales of treasure and spells, of magicians and genii of *The Thousand and One Nights* confirm this thesis because this anthology is not a typical creation of the Arab spirit to which the narrative genre was unknown until the literary revolution of our own times.

A strictly spiritualist people like the Muslims can have no interest for the composition of scenes. The objective reality of nature is never represented, however vast the space allowed to vegetal forms in decoration. But the acanthus and the vine, the palm and the garden herb, the geranium and the tulip, the rose and the daisy, have here become emanations of the spirit, forms of the arabesque, an invention of the hand. The artist does not imitate, eschewing deformation he transfigures, and represents an idea. His scenes respect the picture plane, architecture is without perspective, space acquires a life of its own in the arabesque and in the spiral, and colour, however important it may be, is also extraneous to reality. Divergence from the classical tradition could not be greater. After the fall of the caliphate and the ephemeral aegis of the reyes de Taifas, power in Muslim Spain passed into the hands of Saharan nomads, of Berbers from the Atlas regions, representatives of an austere Islam, rigidly observant of the Tradition. They were great builders, patrons of the arts, paladins of orthodoxy who could not be expected to tolerate paintings representing living beings. They built mosques, founded schools, colleges and hospitals, but allowed no space to the human figure. The historian, Ibn Khaldûn, states that images are prohibited by religion which must be the sole source of artistic inspiration for the Believer.

In the West we find figural representations only under the sultans of Granada, whose life style was an occasional cause for scandal in the Muslim world. The paintings may be seen in the Kings' Chamber in the Alhambra. One scene represents ten men in oriental costume grouped around a fountain; laterally placed to this are illustrations of legendary tales of chivalry, probably the work of a Christian artist from Seville.

Muslim work is to be seen in the figures painted on the walls of the Lady Tower in the

251

Partal, one of the most evocatory settings in the Alhambra. The style is that of miniature painting. The tiny figures, without perspective, animate a variety of scenes, arranged in horizontal bands against a glossy white ground. The scenes illustrate moments of daily life, with men and women gathered together to celebrate some event, princes receiving dignitaries and subjects at court, horsemen hunting wild beasts, knights returning victorious from a campaign against the infidels, riding towards the field with their banners unfurled in the wind and bringing with them camels loaded with booty, a female captive or two and prisoners in chains.

The beauty of the scene is enhanced by the skilful use of colors, white, carmine, ochre, red, green, intense black, azure, cobalt blue and gold. The floral motifs and the epigraphic fascias in cursive script carefully pick up the main chromatic tones.

c) CERAMICS

The potters's art, in which Muslim taste for decoration found a ready outlet, was transformed under Islamic domination even in those regions where this art had been in existence since ancient times, such as Mesopotamia and Egypt. The first examples bore simple decorations consisting of friezes of stylized palms in dark green or opaque white. These soon became translucent, the forms grew in complexity, the decorations became more elaborate; then the enamelling process, known as *mînâ'î*, appeared.

The art of ceramics passed from Baghdad to Kairouan and soon penetrated the western area of the Mediterranean, to reach Muslim Spain in the early years of the invasion.

What we know of caliphal ceramic ware is chiefly due to the excavations at Madînat az-Zahra' and at Elvira which have yielded up many examples inspired by oriental art. The most prized productions were covered with a layer of lead sulphide that gave them a surface similar to that of enamel and with the addition of iron, copper and manganese oxides a variety of colors was obtained. Al-Idrîsî, writing in the twelfth century, declares that the production of the Calatayud factories was exported everywhere. The elements of decoration comprised small arches, epigraphic fascias often repeating the word *al-malik* in elegant letters, and occasionally, figures of men or animals. There was no frequent use of geometrical motifs.

After the Almohad domination Malaga became the center for ceramic art, its craftsmen worked extensively for the Granadine sovereigns. From the twelfth century onwards ceramic ware became extremely important in Spain as a means of architectural ornamentation. The craftsmen were particularly skilled in cutting the monochrome blocks that were used to compose geometric, epigraphic and floral motifs. By means of the technique, known to the Spaniards as «*cuerda seca*», they obtained interlaced geometrical patterns that from the distance give the impression of inlay work. One of the most important illustrations of the architectural use of ceramic tiling is the eastern arch of the Puerta del Vino in the Alhambra, where white, green, black, azure and yellow are separated by black lines which define the contours.

The use of mosaic tiling to decorate the dados was popular at Granada; the earliest examples can be seen in the Lady Tower in the Partal. The technique was perfected in the Comares Hall during the reign of Yûsuf I, in the Captive's Tower and, much later, in the Hall of the Two Sisters and the Mirador de Daraxa.

There are admirable examples of this art of azulejos at the Alhambra, in the House of Pilate in Granada, and in the Alcazar at Seville where it brings color and life to the walls. Colored tiles were also frequently used in place of marble for paving floors. There are fine examples to be seen around the fountain in the Las Camas Chamber, in the Alhambra royal baths and in the tower known as Peinador de la Reina, where a white ground sets off a decoration in green, azure, cobalt, violet and gold, inset with octagonal medallions in which figures of men and animals appear.

d) STUCCOS AND RELIEFS

Stucco was commonly used in the caliphal epoch but it really came into its own after the twelfth century when, with the adoption of techniques imported from the East, it came to play an essential part in monumental art by enriching not only the interiors but also the exteriors of buildings.

In Nasrid Granada and particularly in the Alhambra it almost entirely dominated the wall surface, replacing stonework in the halls and on the façades facing the courtyards. As a decorative medium it provided a simple and economical method of reveting structures and the orich polychromic effects that resulted were of great beauty. In the main rooms stucco work covered the walls from dado to wooden ceiling; in rooms of secondary importance and in the courts it was confined to panels and friezes. It was used, additionally, to hide the wooden supporting structures of the building.

The most original and artistic creations are those of the palace of Yûsuf I and of Muhammad V. The floral motifs are more realistic, the workmanship shows greater command of technique, as may be seen in the friezes running along the entrance gate to the Comares Court and on the entrance to the Barca Gallery.

The arabesque is applied to this medium too, chiefly using geometrical and vegetal motifs. Polygons are utilized, especially the octagon, the sides of which form a new and similar polygon and thus by repetition all the available space is readily covered. The leaf motif, flat, undulating or rounded, is widely used although never in isolation; it is always accompanied by a branch that completes it and which, in its turn, forms volutes and inlays that set up a counterbalancing rhythmic movement. To such an aesthetic scheme the two main variants of calligraphy adapt with ease. Whoever contemplates the complex lines of the Nasrid royal palace stuccos is conquered, first and foremost, by the logic of form which, by endless repetition, proclaims its victory over mere vacant space.

The Industrial Arts

a) MOSQUE FURNISHINGS

The Cordoban court did not cnfine its patronage to the building of mosques and palaces. It also showed an appreciation of the industrial arts, especially those that led to the manufacture of luxury goods. It was a tradition inherited from the Eastern Islamic world, a world which had a strong influence on al-Andalus during the ninth and tenth centuries, particularly at the time of 'Abd al-Rahmân II who surrounded himself with refinements similar to those of the Abbasids at Baghdad and imported into Spain from Constantinople, Egypt, Syria and Iraq, objects that might gratify the lordly taste of his Western court.

In this way local craftsmen were furnished with models for their own production. However, by and large, evidence of mutual influence has still to be established. This is due both to the scarcity and poor condition of surviving objects and to the lack of exemplars that can be reliably attributed to definite periods. There is nothing, for example, that can be attributed with any certainty to the ninth century. Nonetheless, the development of these arts owed much to the splendor of Eastern production, filtered through Byzantine, Sassanian and Coptic mediation.

What was made, especially furnishings intended for religious use, has largely disappeared. There remain, however, numerous *minbâr*, to be found in all the principal mosques and used for prayer readings and orations. Highly praised by Muslim writers, the *minbâr* of the Cordoban mosque, according to al-Idrîsî, required seven years work for its carving and painted decoration. Inlaid with ivory and precious woods, red and yellow sandalwood, ebony, boxwood and aloe, the *minbâr* was kept on the right of the *mihrâb* and brought into use every Friday. Even in the fourteenth century, the *minbâr* of Cordoba together with that of the Kutubiyya of Marrakesh were still acclaimed for the perfection of their workmanship and degree of artistry. Much later, in the Almoravid epoch a *minbâr* splendidly inlaid with ivory was made at Cordoba for the Kutubiyya.

An even earlier product of cabinetmaking was the *masqûra*, made during the reign of Muhammad to isolate the sovereign from the faithful during prayer. The *masqûra* stood before the *qibla* wall in proximity to the *mihrâb*.

There were fewer wooden objects in the mosque than in the Christian churches; there was no call for seats, choirstalls and organs. Wood was employed for decorative friezes, ceilings, lecterns to hold the Koran and the cupboard doors behind which cult objects were preserved.

Another handsome *minbâr*, created in 1182 for the Great Mosque of Seville, had inlaywork of mosaic and ivory embellished with gold and silver in addition to solid gold figures that shone like moons from the shadows.

b) JEWELERY

The great majority of Muslims certainly observed the strict precepts of the Prophet inequivocably condemning the use of gold ornaments but Arab chroniclers tell us of the enormous quantities of precious stones that were to be found in the treasure chests of the caliphs and of the court princesses.

At Cordoba too, this art, subject though it was to sumptuary laws, met with great success; numerous examples of it survive in the safekeeping of the cathedral treasuries where they were preserved against the dispersion that, instead, was to be the fate of oriental production. One of the most valuable pieces comes from the treasury of Garruche (Almeria). This is a silver bracelet, made in two parts and joined by a hinge. On the inner surface it bears the inscription «Perfect Blessing.» We possess necklaces of the finest silver on gold, decorated with clasps representing lions, peacocks, deer and hares. It was principally in the reign of the Nasrids that the jewelers' art flourished. The ladies of the nobility and of the important families adorned themselves with rich necklaces, bracelets, earrings, ankle rings, diadems and gold and silver girdles.

The jewelers were often employed in decorating caskets. One of these, from Gerona, is plated with gilded silver embellished with a leaf motif outlined in pearls.

c) METALS

Decoration excepted, very few plastic works of Muslim art have survived. The bronzes of al-Andalus, mostly produced during the tenth century, bear traces of the Byzantine and Coptic cultures that mediate the original oriental tradition which itself drew inspiration from Sassanian forms.

There was frequent use of bronze for fountain spouts, as we learn from al-Maqqarî, who remarks that there were stone, marble, silver or copper animals spouting water in many of the palaces at Cordoba. Many works have emerged from the ruins of Elvira and from those of the caliphal town of az-Zahra', which had been deserted in favor of Granada after the Berbers set fire to it at the beginning of the eleventh century. Ancient Illiberis has yielded a hexagonal fountain with twelve columns once supporting small domes, towers and birds at the corners.

In the al-Na'ura palace, built by al-Nâsir, there was a monumental fountain fed by the waters of the Sierra which gushed into the basin from the mouth of a great lion, sheathed in pure gold, its eyes formed of precious stones,

It was not unusual to find dogs, peacocks, gazelles and doves spouting hot and cold water in the baths.

There survive circular or polygonal bronze mortars inscribed with Kufic script, containers and candlesticks. These often took the form of stylized animals with elaborately incised surface decoration and were also widely used in Syria and Egypt. Bronze, copper or brass might be used for braziers, which were polygonal in form and decorated with geometrical, vegetal and animal motifs. Bronze plates often formed the revetment of Mosque doors, while iron or copper was used for the door knockers of private houses.

Silver was also used to decorate wooden caskets like the one al-Hakam had made for his son Hishâm, preserved in the Gerona Cathedral treasury, or for tiny scent containers. Lamps made chiefly for mosque lighting varied in shape, size and type of metal used. The three great lamps that illuminated the interior of the *masqûra* of the Great Mosque at Cordoba were made of silver. Metalwork also prospered under the Almoravids, as we may see from the bronze door panels from the Qarawiyyin mosque at Fez, with its polygonal relief decorations. A high degree of artistry is shown in the bronze revetments of the wooden doors of the Puerta del Perdon in the Great Mosque of Seville. Here, polygonal decorations alternate with floral motifs and the ubiquitous Kufic inscription, «Power belongs to God.»

Ibn Sa'îd tells us that brass and iron objects produced in al-Andalus were still exported to Africa in the thirteenth century. Little has been preserved of this art form from the Nasrid epoch however, exception made for the mechanisms regulating the opening of city gates and fortresses, together with keys and nails. Small objects in brass, such as cylindrical boxes decorated with cursive script, are more frequently to be seen. On the other hand, we do have a bronze lamp which was made during the reign of Muhammad III for the royal mosque at the Alhambra.

Metals were widely used in the manufacture of weapons and armor. The great center for this work was Damascus but Muslim Spain soon challenged the primacy of the orient for perfection of workmanship.

Following ancient traditions, steel was tempered at Bilbilis and Toledo; it was 'Abd al-Rahmân II who reestablished the Toledan workshops, and others followed in Almeria, Murcia, and at Granada. Al-Maqqarî tells us that Seville's steel was of the first quality. The surviving weapons of Muslim Spain are all of Granadine provenance and without exception date from no earlier than the fifteenth century. The most famous of these is the sword of Boabdil, who was captured at the battle of Lucena in 1482. It has a gold hilt, enamelled in azure, red and white; a Kufic inscription running along each side exhorts: «Serve your purpose by saving life.»

d) EMBROIDERIES AND CARPETS

Tapestry weaving, a derivation of the simpler art or embroidery, brings a pictorial approach to the art of the textile which allows the imagery to develop in absolute creative freedom.

The sole surviving example of an embroidered fabric of the caliphal age is a cloth of colored silks once used as a covering for the ark of the relics of St. Isidore of Leon. The unsophisticated treatment of the decorative elements offsets figures of deer and eagles with circular, polygonal and floral motifs. The cloth is certainly of Andalusian origin.

The outstanding work of caliphal wallhanging comes, instead, from a Pyrenean church. It is composed of medallions in typical Cordoban style, inset with human and animal figures of oriental derivation. These are embroidered in colored silks of white, azure, crimson and dark green. Later in date is the embroidered silk border of what is known as the St. Valerius mitre in the cathedral of Rhodes. This is a perfect example of the Andalusian style with a peacock motif and a Kufic inscription praising God.

On the preceding page: Ivory casket (caliphal art) in the Archeological Museum, Madrid (Oronoz). On this page: an Arab bottle with a figure of a musician. Archeological Museum, Cordoba (Oronoz). Facing: Amphora, fourteenth-century Nasrid art. The Alhambra, Granada; Museum of Hispano-Muslim Art.

Overleaf, left: detail of Handbasin in beaten brass (second half of the thirteenth century), Galleria Nazionale della Sicilia in Palermo (Archives of Credito Italiano / Libri Scheiwiller). Overleaf, right: detail of Hispano-Arab ivory casket, of particular interest for the portrayal of musical instruments; Museum of Navarra, Pamplona. (Oronoz)

Facing: Two bowls in beaten brass; Galleria Nazionale della Sicilia in Palermo (Archives of Credito Italiano / Libri Scheiwiller). On this page, above left and below left: Bronze ewer and candlestick of the caliphal period; the Archeological Museum of Granada. Below right: Copper ferrule (XI century); Alhambra Museum of Hispano-Muslim Art.

On the following pages: Examples of sheet-ivory caskets with gilded bronze locks; from Italian museums. Lower left: Ivory pyx. Civica Raccolta d'Arte Applicata; Castello Sforzesco, Milan. (Archives of Credito Italiano / Libri Scheiwiller).

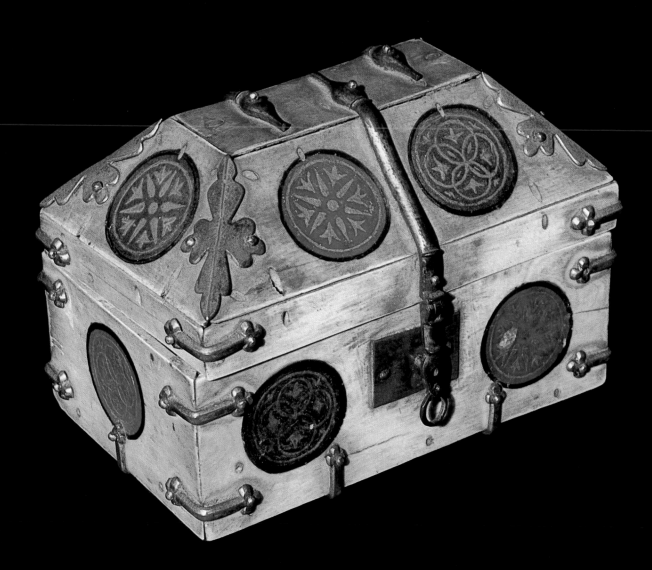

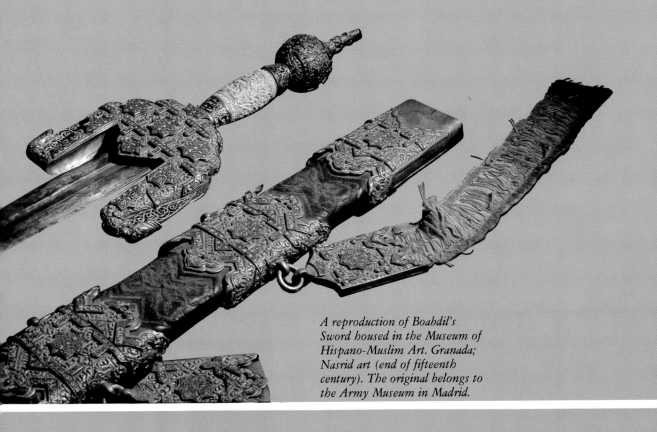

A reproduction of Boabdil's Sword housed in the Museum of Hispano-Muslim Art. Granada; Nasrid art (end of fifteenth century). The original belongs to the Army Museum in Madrid.

Wooden casket, inlaid with ivory. Archeological Museum, Granada.

Footwear. Convent of Santa Croce di Sassonia (Viterbo). (Archives of Credito Italiano / Libri Scheiwiller.

Engraved ewer. Archeological Museum, Granada.

مما اعتنى بجمعه العبد الفقير الى الله تعالى
علي بن محمد بن عبد العزيز بن ابي الفتح
الدريهم الموصلي عامله الله بلطفه
وكان الفراغ من تزويقه
البديعة الغريبة ونقوشه

الْخَيْلُ

الْفُرَسُ طَاعَهُ الرهوى الْمَشْىُ وَلْجَدِّ فِي الْاحضار تَحْت فَارِسه وَيُعْجِبُهُ رُكُوبُهُ اياهُ وَيَعْرِفُ الْمُصَيْبه مُحِبُّ للنَّزْو عِنْهُ مُحِتِ الْاوْلاد عَبُوزٌ ۞ وَمِن خَاصِيَّتِه أنَّهُ اذَا اوْطِى عَلى اثُرو طى الذِّيْب ارْعَد وَخَرجَ مِن جِسْدِه بُخَار وَالبرْذُون يُحِبُّ سَابه وَالرمَكَه دَات شَبَق شَدِيد وَكَثرَةِ اكْل

المتمره

*Bronze stag. Museum of
Cordoba (Oronoz).*

*On the following page:
Female figure in wood.
Provincial Archeological
Museum, Granada.*

Carpets played an important part in Muslim furnishing. They were used not only as floorcoverings but also as wallhangings to create a pleasant and cheerful environment in even the simplest home. The floor of the sacred enclosure was covered from wall to wall with carpets. The purpose of the Muslim prayer rug is, as is known, to purify the place in which the *salât* is being observed.

Al-Idrîsî writes of the great technical ability and artistic skill attained in this field at Murcia and Chinchilla. Al-Shaqundî, writing in the first half of the thirteenth century, tells us that carpets from Murcia and Albanilla were exported to the East. In the same epoch Baza and Granada were also famed for their production. But despite this, only one badly preserved example of the al-Andalus carpet has come down to us. This survivor is woven in wool and decorated with medallions and stars in white, azure, green and yellow against a red ground. The weaving technique is what is known as Persian, very different from the Andalusian technique used for all Mudejar carpets.

e) GLASS AND CRYSTAL WARES

The art of glassmaking must certainly have been a flourishing one in Muslim Spain because al-Maqqarî tells us that there were factories at Murcia and Almeria and, moreover, that the musician Ziryâb taught the Cordobans the use of glass vases and other vessels. But only rare examples have come down to us and these were mostly found in the ruins of Madînat az-Zahra'.

Al-Himyarî speaks of the existence of a seam of rock crystal about forty miles to the north of Badajoz. One of the most important pieces surviving today is the spherical ampulla in transparent crystal, known as the Chalice of St. Toribius, preserved in the cathedral of Astorga. Ampullas or bottles of this type are to be seen in ivory decorations. Examples of carved crystal work have chiefly been preserved in monastic shrines; the usual decoration is of floral motifs but there are occasionally Kufic inscriptions.

No example of Andalusian colored glass has survived although we know that the Muslim world was familiar with this kind of work of the examples from the Qubba of Marrakesh, the Bû Inania *madrasa* at Fez and the ruins of the Umayyad castle of Qasr al-Hair al-Gharbi in the Palmyra desert.

f) IVORY AND ORNAMENTS

There was an ancient tradition of ivory carving in Islamic countries but nothing has survived from the more remote times. The technique was handed on, virtually unchanged, from the Alesandrian workshops to those of Fatimid Egypt.

In Muslim Spain, where the material was imported mainly from African countries, the carving techniques clearly reflect the influences of Baghdad and Byzantium. Numerous examples have come down to us. There are many cylindrical boxes and rectangular caskets that provide evidence of the great skill and imagination with which the decorative themes were handled. They were mainly intended for women, who used them as jewel caskets and scent containers. As inscriptions confirm, they occasionally contained musk, camphor and aloe.

The earliest surviving example is a small container which was made for the daughter of al-Nasîr in the first half of the tenth century; the interior has three compartments which once contained balls of perfume.

Casket decoration was usually more elaborate than the architectural decoration of the period but the vocabulary of ornamentation of the earliest pieces drew on this latter source for its forms. One finds inscriptions, geometrical designs, floral motifs—chiefly palms and leaves forming arabesques—but never human or animal figures. The Kufic characters often terminate in floral motifs. A casket in the Victoria and Albert Museum in London is inscribed in splendid letters: «In the name of God, this box was ordered by Sayydat Allâh, bride of 'Abd al-Rahmân, Commander of the Faithful, may God show him mercy.»

Animals, and occasionally human beings, play a part in the decorative schemes of later times. We find court scenes, knights, enthroned sovereigns, men on foot hunting with falcons, others gathering dates from a palm, women traveling on elephants, musicians and their instruments in garden scenes with women and servants carrying chalices and bottles, eagles with spread wings, seated griffins, dogs chasing hares, camels, deer, antelopes, gazelles and peacocks. These are free interpretations of the familiar decorative themes of Mesopotamian art.

Perhaps none of the ivory objects surpasses in beauty the rectangular casket that once belonged to the queen, Blanche of Navarre, and subsequently passed into the safekeeping of the Pamplona cathedral treasury. The ivory revetment covering the entire surface is decorated with multilobed medallions framing scenes of men hunting with the falcon, struggling with wild beasts or seated oriental fashion among animals, in the midst of luuriant vegetation. It carries the following inscription: «May the blessing of God, happiness, good fortune, the promise of deeds well done and deferment of the fatal hour be granted to the chamberlain Sayf al-Dawla 'Abd al-Malik al-Mansûr. This casket was made to his order, under the supervision of his chief eunuch, Numair ibn Muhammad Alaumer, his slave, in the year 395 (1005).»

After the fall of the caliphate, ivory caskets and boxes cease to bear the indications of dating and provenance that are essential to precise attribution. It is believed that in this period there were two main factories, one in Spain and the other in Sicily where, despite Christian domination, Islamic influences were still strong. Subsequently, in the centuries to come, production was commercialized; quality often being neglected and precedence granted to quantity. This was an evolution that places the objects outside the domain of art.

Ivory carving continued even in fourteenth and fifteenth century Granada when the hilts of swords and daggers were decorated with geometric forms and cursive scripts. Ivory alternates with gold, silver and enamel to create precious works of the goldsmith's art, an example of which is the hilt of the magnificent weapon known as Boabdil's Sword.

There was no decline in the production of caskets, whose decorative treatment picks up motifs that had been characteristic of the caliphal age.

c) DOMESTIC OBJECTS

Caliphal ceramic work, whether rustic or glazed, drew on Oriental and, occasionally, on earlier Roman tradition to satisfy the needs of daily life in the domestic sphere.

The majority of the finds come from the excavations at Madîna Elvira and at Madînat az-Zaha', in addition to the ruins of Mesas de Asta and the fortress of Alcalà la Vieja. In recent years important finds, illustrative of ninth and tenth century production, have come to light in Almeria.

In the rustic or glazed version we find storage jars, wine bottles, bowls, plates, candleholders and lamps with several spouts. The eye meets with echoes of Oriental models both in the forms and in their decoration. At times, this may be confined to the repetition of a simple white or dark gray motif; at others, greater complexity is sought for in the elaborate play of arcs, rhomboids, dots, vegetal and animal motifs. Letters are frequently found because in the Orient the letter provided the Islamic world with its first expression of epigraphic art. Kufic letters forming the words *al-Mulk* (Power) and *al-Yumn* (Happiness) frequently appear on the plates from al-Andalus. They are usually centrally placed and surrounded by floral motifs. Byzantine influences notwithstanding, many themes, above all in vegetal decoration and in representations of the human figure, recall the arts of Syria and of Iraq. Palm leaves, peacocks, doves and Kufic fascias were also used in the decoration of vases and storage jars. The Alhambra yielded many examples, particularly of large vases, often with light decorations against a dark ground or with black or green motifs offsetting the pale ground of the baked terracotta. Objects in glazed pottery, dark green on the inside, were also widely used in daily life.

Gilded pottery, on the other hand, was a luxury product. It gave the impression of owning objects in precious metal, especially when the novelty of combining gilded decoration on a white enamelled ground with others of an azure-cobalt blue tint was introduced. The main center for the production of these objects, in the Nasrid period, was Malaga. In the fourteenth century the town exported its wares not only to Egypt and Italy but also to Great Britain. Receptacles and plates are numerous at the Alhambra and in the Alcazaba of Malaga. The most handsome pieces of this type of production are undoubtedly the large vases; a magnificent example of these is to be seen in the Alhambra museum. It is probably a fourteenth century work, covered with decorations and splendid arabesques interspersed with ornamental inscriptions. At the center, above two antelopes, the maximum circumference is marked by a broad epigraphic fascia. The cursive script spells out: «Prosperity and health belong to God alone,» - «Happiness and prosperity.»

h) WOODS

Few examples of wood carving for domestic or, in broader terms, for secular use, have come down to us. Doors, cupboards and other furnishings, as well as latticed windows (*mashrabiyya*) in private houses were carved and decorated, often built up of small panels.

There was already an illustrious tradition in the field of wood carving when the Almoravids came to power, but under their rule, as was to be the case later under the Almohads, it was mainly the production linked to religious needs that developed, Islamic society having always attached but small importance to the requirements of secular life.

A marquetry casket originally from the Collegiate church of St. Isidore of Leon would seem to date from 1200. Wooden caskets of this kind were sometimes painted and decorated with geometrical and floral motifs, often bore Kufic inscriptions and were additionally inlaid with ivory and tortoiseshell.

Cabinet making of the Nasrid period is worthily represented by two items. The first of these, a door leaf from the Casa de los Infantes, with geometric decorations very similar to fourteenth century work from Seville, witnesses to the perfection attained in the Oriental technique of inlay in al-Andalus. The second, the scepter of the Granadine sultans, later to become the staff of Cardinal Cisneros, is carved in cursive script with the familiar Nasrid motto: «There is no victor but God.»

A number of luxurious octagonal boxes have survived from the same period. These are delicately inlaid with gold, ebony, lemon and cedar woods.

i) TEXTILES

The Muslim art of weaving stems from Sassanian, Coptic and Byzantine sources. It slowly developed autonomous processes to meet the requirements of national markets differing from those of the places of origin.

In conformity with Koranic proscription it immediately rejected the figural motifs that the Copts had derived from Byzantium and showed a preference for geometrical ones, often interspersed with fascias composed of words of praise for the intended recipient, or of Koranic verses.

After the invasion, the Arabs introduced these weaving techniques already familiar in the Orient to Muslim Spain where, of all the provinces, Almeria proved most receptive to this art. We learn from Al-Maqqarî that in this town of al-Andalus, textiles of extraordinary beauty known as *dibâg* were produced. Cloth of silver, in many colors and known as *tirâz*, was made especially for the prince and was inscribed with his name; another type of cloth, known as *hulûl*, was intended for the general market. Sumptuous clothing was initially brought into favour by 'Abd al-Rahmân II at his luxurious court. Robes were made from Cordoban tirâz in imitation of that of Baghdad.

The silk worm had been introduced in Spain in the tenth century and the widespread popularity of silk encouraged the development of weaving; so much so that Spanish silks were exported not only to the Orient but also to such Christian countries as France and Flanders.

The Andalusian weavers, who reproduced Egyptian and Mesopotamian models, used their skills to create ceremonial wear, brocade and silk tunics, veils with delicate golden fringes, tissues interwoven with gold and silver embroideries, stylized figures of animals and vegetal motifs, white letters to decorate borders of azure, white, mauve, yellow and pale green silk.

One of the earliest examples of their work is decorated with medallions inset with seated figures, a king or a queen perhaps, flanked by lions and birds; Kufic letters on the fascias read: «In the name of God, the Compassionate and Merciful. May the blessing of God and happiness be bestowed on the caliph, the imâm 'Abd Allâh Hishâm II, the favorite of God.»

Ibn al-Khatîb tells us that in the fourteenth century the factories of Andarax, Dalias and Jubiles produced gold embroidered fabrics of such excellent quality that the Nasrid sultan Muhammad V sent examples of their work adorned with poetry composed for the occasion by Ibn Zamrak, to the Merinid al-Mustansir.

The strictly observant did not approve of the unbridled luxury of the Granadine court where ladies wore gowns, girdles and veils covered with gold and silver fronds. Granadine textiles may be recognized by a certain uniformity of decoration but, over and above this, by the unrivaled splendour of color. The hues of gold, azure and red, the favourite colors of the sultans, black green and white, the identical colours used in their azulejos and painted stuccoes—all are woven together to create motifs and inscriptions that evoke the impalpable shimmer of the Alhambra walls.

Notes

1   Al-Maqqarî, *Nahf at-tîb gusn al-Andalus ar-ratîb wa dhikr wazîrihâ Lisân ad-Dîn Ibn al-Khatîb*, abridged ed. R. Dozy - G. Dugat - L. Krehl - W. Wright, Leiden 1855-'61, 2 vol., I, 297-462. (complete ed. Bûlâq 1279 H./1862); partial Eng. tr. by P. De Gayangos, *The Mohammedan Dynasties in Spain*, London 1840-'43, 1, 200-249; Cfr. E. Lévi - Provençal, *L'Espagne musulmane au $x^{ème}$ siècle. Institutions et vie sociale*, Paris 1932, 195-236; Ibn 'Idhârî, *al-Bayân al-mughrib fî akhbâr al-Maghrib*, ed. R. Dozy, Leiden 1848-'51, II, 60, 70, 86, 159, 244, 247, 250, 253, 254, 257, 307, 309; Fr. tr. by E. Fagnan, *Histoire de l'Afrique et de l'Espagne*, Algiers 1901; Al-Idrîsî, *Description de l'Afrique et de l'Espagne*, ed. and Fr. tr. by R. Dozy - J. De Goeje, Leiden 1866; Al-Idrîsî, *Wast al-masgid al-gâmi' bi Qurtuba*, Algiers 1949. Ibn al-Qutîya, *Iftitâh: ta'rîkh iftitâh al-Andalus*, ed. and partial tr. by E. Fagnan, *Extraits inédits relatifs au Maghreb. Géographie et Histoire*, Algiers 1924, 209-218; K.A.C. Creswell, *Early Muslim Architecture*, Oxford 1932-'40, II, 138-161; H. Terrasse, *L'art hispano-mauresque des origines au XIIIe siècle*, Paris 1932, 58-151; L. Torres-Balbas, *La Mezquita de Cordoba y las ruinas de Madînat al-Zahra*, Madrid 1952.

2   M. Ocaña Jimenez, *La Basilica de San Vicente y la Gran Mezquita de Cordoba*, «Al-Andalus», 1942, 347-366.

3   Ibn 'Idhârî, *al-Bayân...*, II, 245.

4   Ibn 'Idhârî, *al-Bayân...*, II, 8245.

5   E. Lévi-Provençal, *Inscriptions Arabes d'Espagne*, Leiden-Paris 1931, 1-2, plate I.

6   Al-Idrîsî, *Description de la Grande Mosquée de Cordoue*, ed. and Fr. tr. Dessus-Lamare, 10-11.

7   E. Lévi-Provençal, *Inscriptions...*, 8-9.

8   G. Marçais, *L'architecture musulmane d'occident*, Paris 1954, 139-145.

9   E. Lévi-Provençal, *Inscriptions...*, 10-11.

10 Ibn 'Idhârî, *al-Bayân...*, II, 53.

11 Ibn 'Idhârî, *al-Bayân...*, II, 256.

12 Ibn 'Idhârî, *al-Bayân...*, II, 307-308.

13 Al-Idrîsî, *Description de l'Afrique...*, 208-212.

14 L. Torres-Balbas, *La Mezquita de Cordoba...*, 100-106.

15 L. Torres-Balbas, *La Mezquita de la Alcazaba de Badajoz*, «Al-Andalus», 1943, 466-470.

16 L. Torres-Balbas, *La acropoli musulmana de Ronda*, «Al-Andalus», 1944, 449-481.

17 E. Lévi-Provençal, *Inscriptions...*, 62; M. Ocaña Jimenez, *Inscription de la mezquita de Bîb al-Mardûm*, «Al-Andalus», 1949, 181-183.

18 L. Torres-Balbas, *Cronica Arqueologica*, «Al-Andalus», 1945, 409.

19 H. Terrasse, *L'art hispano-mauresque...*, 176.

20 G. Marçais, *L'architecture...*, 191-199.

21 L. Torres-Balbas, *La Mezquita Mayor de Granada*, «Al-Andalus», 1945, 420-432.

22 H. Basset - H. Terrasse, *Timnel, Sanctuaires et forteresses almohades*, «Hespéris», 1924, 9-91.

23   H. Terrasse, *La grande Mosquée de Taza*, Paris 1943.

24   G. Marçais, *L'architecture...*, 202-206.

25   L. Torres-Balbas, *Cronica Arqueologica*, «Al-Andalus», 1946, 425-439.

26   L. Torres-Balbas, *Cronica Arqueologica*, «Al-Andalus», 1941, 193; 1943, 466.

27   L. Rodriquez Cano, *Cronica Arqueologica*, «Al-Andalus», 1934, 364.

28   L. Torres-Balbas, *Cronica Arqueologica*, «Al-Andalus», 1941, 204.

29   L. Torres-Balbas, *Cronica Arqueologica*, «Al-Andalus», 1949, 196.

30   Almagro Cardenas, «Boletin de la Real Academia de la Historia», 27, 490.

31   L. Torres-Balbas, *Paseos por la Alhambra: la Rauda*, «Archivio Español de Arte y Arcqueologia», 6, 1926.

32   L. Torres-Balbas, *Oratorio y casa de Astasia Bracamonte ed el Partal de la Alhambra*, «Al-Andalus», 1945, 440-449.

33   *The Koran*, XVII, p. 234; Eng. tr. by N.J. Dawood, Penguin Books 1956.

34   Al-Idrîsî, *Description de l'Afrique et de l'Espagne*, ed. R. Dozy - J. De Goeje, Leiden 1866, 176.

35   Al-Idrîsî, *Description...*, 180.

36   Al-Idrîsî, *Description...*, 200.

37   Al-Idrîsî, *Description...*, 197-198.

38   Al-Idrîsî, *Description...*, 194.

39   Al-Idrîsî, *Description...*, 193.

40   Al-Idrîsî, *Description...*, 186.

41   Al-Idrîsî, *Description...*, 190.

42   Ibn Khallikân, *Wafayât al-a'yân*, Cairo 1310; Eng. tr. de Slane, Paris-London 1843-1871, III 134; Ibn 'Idhârî, *al-Bayân al-mughrib fî akhbâr al-Maghrib*, ed. R. Dozy, Leiden 1848-'51, II, 62; E. Lévi-Provençal, *L'Espagne musulmane au Xème siècle. Institutions et vie sociale*, Paris 1932, 221-224.

43   Ibn 'Idhârî, *al-Bayân...*, 280; Al-Maqqârî, *Analectes...*, I, 303.

44   E. Lévi-Provençal, *L'Espagne musulmane...*, 223.

45   Ibn 'Idhârî, al-Bayân..., II, 245-247.

46   Al-Idrîsî, *Description...*, 212.

47   L. Torres-Balbas, *Arte almohade, arte nazarî, arte mudejar*, Madrid 1949, v. IV of the *Ars Hispaniae* series, 30-31.

48   L. Torres-Balbas, *Cronica Arqueologica*, «Al-Andalus», 1945, 398-409.

49   M. Gomez-Moreno, *Arte árabe hasta los Almohades, arte mozárabe*, Madrid 1951, v. III of the *Ars Hispaniae* series, 248.

50   L. Torres-Balbas, *Cronica Arqueologica*, «Al-Andalus», 1934, 366-370.

51   E. Lévi-Provençal, *Granade musulmane*, in *Annales Universitaires d'Algérie*, Algiers 1937; E. Lambert, *L'Alhambra de Grenade*, «Revue de l'art ancien et moderne», 1933, 145-164.

52   L. Torres-Balbas, *Cronica Arqueologica*, «Al-Andalus», 1939, 434-445.

53   G. Marçais, *Les jardins de l'Islam*, in *Mélanges d'histoire et d'archéologie de l'occident musulman*, Algiers 1957, I, 233-244.

54   L. Torres-Balbas, *Cronica Arqueologica*, «Al-Andalus», 1948, 185-203.

55   L. Torres-Balbas, *Cronica Arqueologica*, «Al-Andalus», 1944, 481-498.

56   Velasquez Bosco, *El Alcazar y la arquitectura sevillana*, «Arquitectura», 1933, 284ss.

57   R. Amador de los Rios, *Inscripciones árabes de Sevilla*, Madrid 1875.

58   J. Vernet, *La cultura hispanoarabe en orient y occidente*, Barcelona 1978, 198-299; I. Seco de Lucena, *Investigaciones sobre el romancero. Estudio de tres romances fronterizos*, Granada 1958.

59   Gaya Nuno, *Gormaz, Castillo califal*, «Al-Andalus», 1943, 431-450.

60   E. Lévi-Provençal, *Histoire de l'Espagne musulmane*, Paris-Leiden 1950, I, 210ss.

61   L. Torres-Balbas, *Caceres y su cerca almohade*, «Al-Andalus», 1948, 446ss; L. Torres-Balbas, *La Alcazaba almohade de Badajoz*, «Al-Andalus», 1941, 168ss.

62   L. Torres-Balbas, *Cronica Arqueologica*, «Al-Andalus», 1941, 199-200.

63   L. Torres-Balbas, *Las Torres del Oro y de la Plata*, «Al-Andalus», 1934, 372.

64   L. Torres-Balbas, *Cronica Arqueologica*, «Al-Andalus», 1942, 193-201.

65   L. Torres-Balbas, *Arte almohade, arte nazari...*, 165-167.

66   R. Amador de los Rios, *Inscripciones árabes de Cordoba*, Madrid 1879, 188-191.

67   *The Koran*, V, p. 378; Eng. tr. by N.J. Dawood, Penguin Books 1956.

68   A.N. Nykl, *Inscripciones árabes de la Alhambra*, «Al-Andalus», 1936, 193-194; Lafuente y Alcantara, *Estudio sobre las inscripciones árabes de Granada*, Madrid 1979, 120-173.

69   Lafuente y Alcantara, *Estudio sobre...*, 126-131.

70   Ibn Zamrak, in E. Garcia Gomez, *Cinco Poetas Musulmanes*, Madrid 1944, 214.

71   *The Koran*, XLVIII, p. 270.

CHAPTER SIX

MUSLIM SICILY
AND ITS HERITAGE

The Descriptions of Muslim Travellers

We have little first-hand information about social organization, economic structure and daily life in Muslim Sicily. Only after visits to the island in successive epochs of three geographers, Ibn Hawqal (d.c. 981), al-Idrîsî (d. 1165) and Ibn Gubayr (d. 1217), do we find the arguments examined in any detail. Their works provide us with precise accounts of, respectively, Kalbite Palermo, the Palermo that produced the Arab-Norman synthesis and Palermo during the decadence of Arabism, in the last years of the Hauteville dynasty.

The Iraqi traveler Ibn Hawqal, who visited Sicily in 973, has left us a generous description of this town: «Palermo consists of five districts; there is not much distance (between them) but since each has very characteristic features the boundaries can be seen clearly. (The first of these) is the great town, Palermo properly speaking, girdled by stone walls and defendable, inhabited by merchants. Here there is the *gâmî* mosque, formerly the church of the Rûm, in which (there may be seen) a great sanctuary. A certain logician tells me that within this sanctuary, transformed into a mosque by the Muslims, there lie the remains of Aristotle, the ancient Greek philosopher, in a suspended wooden (coffin). The Christians held the tomb of this (philosopher) in great honor and used to invoke his aid to make rain fall, laying great store by certain traditions (inherited) from the Greeks concerning the great merits and virtues (of his intellect). (The logician) related that the coffin had been suspended in mid-air so that the people might pray for rain, or for the well-being (of the community) and (for deliverance from all) those calamities that drive (man) to turn to God and to propitiate Him, as happens in times of famine, plague or civil strife. (In all truth) I saw a great wooden (coffin) hanging there, and perhaps it did contain the corpse.

The (other town) is called al-Khâlisah (the Chosen). This too is encircled by a stone wall, but no rival to the one (we have described). The sultan and his followers live in al-Khâlisah. There are no markets or storehouses, but there are two bath houses, a *gâmî* mosque, small but well attended, the sultan's prison, the shipyard and the *dîwân*. The town has four gates, to the south, north and west, but the east wall is gateless.

The district called Harat as-Saqâlibah (the Slavonian District) is bigger than the two towns previously mentioned and it has a larger population. It contains the harbor and several fountains fed by the waters that flow between this district and the old town; the waterway is the only boundary mark there is.

The district known as Harat al-Masgid (the Mosque District), that of Ibn Siqlâb I mean, is also spacious but lacks fresh running water so the inhabitants drink from wells. To the south of the district (runs) a great river called wâdî' Abbâs with numerous mills set up along its course, but (its waters) are used neither to irrigate the crops nor to water the gardens.

Harat al-Gadidah (the New District) is also a big place. It stands close by the Mosque District, and nothing divides them, not even a wall like that of the Slavonian District. Most of the markets are to be found between the mosque of Ibn Siqlâb and this New District: for example, the oilvendors' market, which houses all the shops and stalls selling this commodity. The moneychangers and the spiceries are also established outside the town walls, as are the tailors, the gunsmiths, the coppersmiths, the corn merchants and all the other trades. But inside the town walls the butchers have over a hundred and fifty shops for the sale of meat whilst here (in the two districts just mentioned) there are very few of them. The great number of shops shows the importance of this trade and how many people are involved in it. This may similarly be argued from the vast scale of their mosque, in which, on a day when it was full of people, I counted more than seven thousand persons present since there were more than thirty six rows lined up for prayer, with about two hundred people to a row.

There are more than three hundred mosques in the town of Khâlisah and in the outlying districts beyond the walls; the majority are well provided for and have roofs, walls and gateways. Well-informed people locally, all making a rough estimate, agree on the number (of the mosques)... There are many *ribât* along the sea shores, crowded with ruffians, dishonest and seditious people, both young and old, rogues of every tongue who decry honest women, yet from prostrating themselves to win alms have raised bumps on their foreheads. The majority are pimps of filth or addicted to infamous vice. Worthless men that they are, vagabonds and scoundrels, these are the habitués of the *ribât*...

The town, oblong (in shape), is crossed by a market known as *as-simât* (the row) that runs from west to east, paved in stone from one end to the other, a fine emporium for all kinds of wares.

The countryside around Palermo is plentifully supplied with waters, flowing in an east-westerly direction, each waterway with a current strong enough to turn two millwheels; consequently there are numerous watermills built along the banks. From the source inland, all the way down to the sea, the streams are flanked by broad areas of swampland where bamboo (grows), ponds have been built and gourds (are cultivated).

There is also a low-lying area here entirely covered with *birbîr* (papyrus), that is to say *bardî*, which is (the very plant) they use to make *tûmâr* (rolls of papyrus for writing on). I do not know whether the Egyptian papyrus has any other companion on the face of this earth besides this Sicilian one. Most of which is twisted to form rigging for ships and a little is set aside to make writing material for the sultan, just as much as serves his purposes...

Channels are the most usual means of garden irrigation because, just as in Syria and other countries, many gardens as well as fields are not naturally supplied with moisture. Nonetheless, there are wells in most districts and in the town itself but the water is heavy and polluted. They have taken to drinking it for lack of fresh running water, from lack of foresight and an over-addiction to eating onions. And truly this nutriment, which they are very fond of and eat raw, harms the senses. There is no man of whatever station in life who does not eat some every day, who does not have some served at table both morning and evening in his home. This is what has diminished their imaginative faculties, dulled their wits, disordered their senses, distorted their intelligence, doused their spirits, clouded their visages and so distempered their constitutions that they hardly ever see things as they are.»[1]

There then follow reflections on the economic conditions of the island: «The living conditions of the inhabitant of the town and of the provinces is evaluated according to capital, taxes and real estate, as well as social standing and intrinsic merit, etc. But the wealth of the island of Sicily that in our times, which for her above all are the most prosperous and plentiful from every point of view, including taxation, which comprises a fifth part of the crops, revenue on wine, poll taxes, maritime dues, the annual tribute paid by the Calabrians, hunting rights and every other source of income, her wealth amounts in all to... Whereas in ancient times her crops and her fertility, her production of food and drink were just as generally plentiful as in such places as I have mentioned at the beginning of my book, when I was there all this prosperity was replaced by famine.

The habits of the country lords are much like those of the islanders in general, men of barbaric and indecorous tongue, entirely unresponsive; as far as the (rural) inhabitants are concerned, travel not having induced any sort of refinement in them, they live like animals, in a condition of obtusity and neglect of every obligation, as is evident from their bearing, their unbalanced opinions and their violent aversion to any foreigner and stranger who chances among them, being as they are, entirely unsociable.»[2]

Such, according to Ibn Hawqal, was the situation in Kalbite Sicily in the second half of the tenth century. The island had been Islamized for little more than a century, it was bound to seem to him poor in possessions and mental vivacity compared with the great Muslim metropolises of Iraq, Egypt and 'Umayyad Spain, but we need not believe that conditions were as bad as he makes them out to be. We know that other geographers considered the island to be one of the most fertile lands of the Islamic world, comparable with the Campiña of Cordoba for the fertility of its soil and the rich harvest it yielded. Although the Arabs as a people have little inclination for the agricultural life, they did introduce the orange tree, the mulberry tree, the sugar cane, the date palm and the cotton plant while, in virtue of the rights of conquest, expropriating the rich landowners and redistributing their lands. Among their industrial activities, the *tirâz*, the textile industry, was particularly important, producing fabrics of very fine quality and, moreover, supplying the court with its special needs. Close by Balhâra, in the vicinity of present-day Monreale, there was an iron mine rich enough to make the island self-sufficient.

With the island by now a point of convergence for Christianity and Islam, Roger II entrusted al-Idrisî with the task of composing a vast geographical conspectus of it. His description is very different from that of Ibn Hawqal. Here is how the great geographer describes the Sicily of 1154: «Let us say then that for fruitfulness and beauty, the island is the jewel of the century; she is unsurpassed (in the world) for profusion (of natural resources and density of) buildings and (distinguished) antiquities. Travelers come here from every corner of the world and the merchants of the towns and the metropolises, all of whom extol her to a man, (testify) to her riches, praise the splendors of her beauty, speak of her fortunate circumstances, of the many and varied merits she is endowed with and of the merchandise from every other country (in the world) that Sicily attracts to herself... Palermo contains buildings of such beauty that travelers are drawn here by the fame of the architectural marvels (the town offers), the exquisite workmanship, (the ornament of so much) rare, (artistic) invention. The town is divided into two parts: the *qasr* (Cassaro castle) and township. The Cassaro is the ancient fortress, renowned in every town and every region. It is composed of three districts, the central one of which is richly provided with towering palaces and lofty, noble dwellings, with mosques, storehouses, bath houses and the shops of great merchants.»[3]

The kindness and courtesy of the islanders made an impression on Ibn Gubayr, an Arab from Spain who set out from Valencia on the holy pilgrimage in 1183. On his return in December 1185, he traveled along the north coast of Sicily from Messina to Trapani. During his stay, which lasted until February 1185, he had occasion to meet the Muslim notables who confided in him the nature of their circumstances and the fears that overshadowed their hopes for a serene future. He was a keen observer of the moral atmosphere and the material conditions of the land and freely expressed his opinions not only of the government of William II but also of the lives of the peasants, the town dwellers and the merchants who crossed his path, without ever forgetting however that he was a Muslim and, moreover, that his position was that of the *hagg* the pilgrim returning from Mecca.

«The finest town in Sicily, where the king resides, is known to the Muslims as al-Madînah, and to the Christians as Palermo. It has a large Muslim population with its own mosques and markets as well as numerous districts reserved to it.

The other Muslims on the island are scattered about the farms and the villages or in such towns as Syracuse. The biggest town and the most densely populated is, however, the capital, the residence of their king, William, and after this comes Messina. If God be willing, we shall stay in Palermo and from there, with God's consent (glory be to His name!), we hope to set sail for whichever of the countries of the West that He may choose for us.

King Williams is famed for his impartiality because he keeps Muslim retainers and confides in his eunuch pages. Although it is true that they must conceal their faith, they are all, or almost all, believers in Islam. The king lays great store by the Muslims and entrusts them with even the most delicate matters, so much so that even the person who tastes his food is a Muslim. Moreover he keeps a battalion of black Muslim troops under the command of a Muslim. He selects his viziers and chamberlains as well as his courtiers and the state employees from among his pages.

The king has magnificent palaces and delightful gardens, above all in the capital of his kingdom. He owns a palace, as white as a dove, on the sea shore at Messina. Many pages and maidens live here in attendance on him. No Christian king is more clement than he in ruling the state; none enjoys such delights or greater material wealth. William throws himself into the pleasures of court life as Muslim rulers do and he follows their style too in his legal system, in manner of governing, in establishing the social hierarchy, in the regal magnificence of his way of life and the luxury he surrounds himself with. His kingdom is vast. Such is his predilection for physicians and astrologers that on learning that one such is traveling in his territories he will give orders for him to be detained. The man will be offered such a princely sum to accept employment as to make him forget his native land. May God in his goodness protect all Muslims from such a temptation. The king is about thirty years of age. May God grant the Muslims that his life be prolonged in perfect health.

One of the most extraordinary things related of this king is that he reads and writes Arabic. One of his retainers who is well acquainted with him told me in confidence that he has adopted the *alâmah* 'Praise be to God! Worthy is He of praise.' His father's *alâmah* was 'Praise be to God in thanksgiving for His favors.' Moreover, all the palace women and concubines are Muslims. Yahyâ, the page just mentioned, who works in the *tirâz* trimming the king's clothes with gold told me another extraordinary thing: the Frankish Christian women who live in the palace have all been converted to the Muslim faith by the other young women of whom I spoke. He added that all this had taken place unbeknown to the king and that the ladies were very active in charitable works...

The king's pages, who come to hold the key positions in his government, are all Muslims, and so are the administration employees. All of them, without exception, observe both voluntary and commendatary fasting and give alms to gain merit in the eyes of God; they ransom prisoners, educate Muslim children and arrange marriages for them, making provision for them in every possible way. This is one of God's mysteries (Glory be unto Him!) and one of his many works in favour of the island's Muslims. May God always come to their aid!...»

After a digression on the amiability of the inhabitants, who waylay him in the streets to pay their respects, and his satisfaction on hearing the *adhân* in the mosque of the Qasr Sa'd castle, the present-day Cannita, not far from Palermo, he returns to the subject of the capital. «Both in appearance and in reality it offers all that the heart may desire, the flowers and the nectar of life. Ancient and elegant, magnificent and pleasing, wholly seductive to the eyes, the town lies among hills and plains that are one great garden... The Muslims of Palermo are still devout. They are attentive to the maintenance of the majority of their mosques, heed the muezzin's call to prayer, own the districts in which they and their families live and avoid contact with the Christian. On feastdays they recite the *khutba* with the invocation for the Abbasid caliphs but since the *khutba* is, strictly speaking, forbidden, they do not observe Fridays. At Palermo they have a *qâdî*, the judge at their legal proceedings, and a congregational mosque where they gather together for prayer during the holy month. The other mosques, too numerous to be counted, are used as schools, in most cases by teachers of the Koran. In general, the Palermitan Muslims show little fondness for their brethren who have become subjects of the unbelievers. May God in His munificence console them with His favors!

One of the things about this town that recalls Cordoba—there is, after all, always some common factor that likens one thing to another—is that here too there is an old town called the Qassar situated at the heart of the new town, just as there is at Cordoba, may God protect

285

her! Here one may observe magnificent palaces and castles with towers soaring up to the heavens wherever the eye turns, buildings of astonishing beauty.

One of the most admirable Christian buildings we have seen here is their church called the Antiochian (the Martorana). We saw it on Christmas Day, the day of their great feast, when it was crowded with men and women. One of the various parts of this building that drew our attention is the facade, truly noteworthy, which we are unable to describe and, indeed, would prefer not to, since it is the finest building in the world.

There are marble panels surpassing anything that has ever been seen before, all inset with gold mosaic work and crowned with tree motifs in green mosaic. Above these are solar discs in gilded glass that project rays of light to dazzle the eyes and bring such joy to the spirit that we prayed to God that they should be preserved.»[4]

Muslim Art under Norman Domination

Very few traces survive in Sicily that can be reliably attributed to the long period of Arab rule, but the nature of much of what remains from the period of Norman domination warrants its inclusion in this study of Muslim art of the West.

After the eleventh century, when the island ceased to belong to Islam, the distinguishing features that formerly marked religious, civil, and military architecture vanished. There is no trace of the mosque, except, perhaps, at San Giovanni degli Eremiti (S. John of the Hermits). The monuments of interest are those built for the Normans on Christian soil. They were often designed and built by Muslims, influenced by the styles of Barbary, and eloquent of the vitality of Islamic presence and of the unsevered links between countries of the East and of the West.

Almost nothing survives of the Favara castle at Palermo, founded, according to Amari, by the emir Gia'far. Arab authors describe it as a building articulated around an arcaded courtyard, the whole surrounded by water. This may be why it was called the castle of the freshwater sea and the name Favara (*fawwâra*) is a tribute to the importance of the waters that flowed down from the mountain nearby.

In the upper town of Palermo a palace called Cassaro, from the Arabic qasr, was built for Roger II. It had two powerful square towers attached to the central construction called the Gioaria. Some of the splendid decorations in marble and mosaic can still be seen on the interior of the building.

Art flourished under the Normans, creating masterpieces of synthesis. One of these, the Cappella Palatina (Palatine Chapel), consecrated in 1140, stands on the first floor of the Royal Palace that, before conversion, was an ancient Muslim fortress, Western influence can be seen in the plan and in the Corinthian columns. The gold mosaics are Byzantine. What astonishes, is the marvellous presence of Arab art in the wooden stalactite ceiling which has an intricate painted decoration in Kufic script extolling the king.

The three great medieval cultures are united in that other masterpiece, Santa Maria dell'Ammiragliato, also known as the Martorana in homage to a minor figure, a certain

Goffredo di Marturanu who founded a convent of Benedictine nuns adjacent to it in 1146. What stands as one of the finest Greek churches on the island was, instead, founded by the *amîr al-bahr*, George of Antioch. Girdling the base of the dome is a carved wooden frieze bearing the words of an ancient Byzantine hymn to the Virgin, written in Arabic, and this may have reminded George of his adolescent days in Syria when he would have heard the hymn in this tongue.

Links with the style and building techniques of North Africa are to be seen chiefly in buildings in the neighborhood of the capital, once forming a ring around it. The Cuba pavilion, built on a rectangular plan by William II, recalls the Dâr al-Bahr palace and the Qal'a minaret. The building consisted of a central hall with two side rooms; it gains its name from the dome, inset with niches, that covers it.

Also on a rectangular plan, but on a larger scale, is the Zisa pavilion, begun by William I but completed by William II. Here, there are two great central halls, one above the other, each surrounded by smaller rooms. The lower of the two halls, the most sumptuous room in the palace, was decorated with colonnettes and, set in an alcove facing the entrance, a welcoming and refreshing fountain. A new element is to be seen here in the central hall on the first floor, the stalactites (*muqarnas*), also decorating the ceilings of the adjoining first-floor rooms and reminiscent of those of the great mosque of Tlemsen, the first example of this type of work in the Maghrib.

The Zisa is a marvellous synthesis of Islam, whose meaning is summed up in the Arab inscription in white stucco relief on the entrance arch: «Here, whenever you wish, you may admire the finest treasure of this kingdom, the most splendid among the lands and seas of this earth. The mountain peaks tinged with the color of narcissi... You will see the great king of this age in his handsome residence, a palace of such joy and splendor as befits him. This is the earthly paradise offered to your gaze, this is the glorious king; this palace, the Azîz.»

Not far from the Cuba stands a graceful little pavilion, known for its modest scale as the Piccola Cuba (the Small Cuba). The exterior resembles the pavilion standing in the courtyard of the Fatimid mosque of Sfax. The hemispherical dome surmounting the square plan of the building is supported by pendentives.

Besides these monuments, the Muslim art of Norman Sicily is represented, not unworthily, by the baths of Cefalù a few kilometers outside Palermo, the Christian sanctuaries of San Giovanni degli Eremiti (S. John of the Hermits), San Cataldo, and the cathedrals of Palermo and Cefalù.

In all the monuments dealt with one observes the use of the four-centred arch that, however, never exceeds its span. There are no examples of the horseshoe arch in Sicily. Typically Maghriban architectural features are columns decorated with rings at the base and bas-relief work on the upper surfaces; the honeycombed *muqarnas*, formed of tiny domes inscribed with eight-pointed stars; the use of the cross vault and the tunnel vault; columns that are binated or grouped to form polystylar systems. The pointed arch and much of the taste for decoration derives instead from Egypt. It may have been Persian work that inspired the cycle of paintings on the Palatine Chapel ceiling where there are representations of both men and animals, musicians, hunters, dancers and chess players, camels, lions and gryphons. Greek influence is to be observed in the mosaic decorations, particularly where the essentially Byzantine technique of the gold background has been used.

The ability to create a cohesion of such different styles from the various provinces of Muslim art is not the least of the merits of Norman Sicily.

There is much more evidence available for the study of the applied or the industrial arts than there is for architectural work. We have ceramic ware, painted caskets, enamelled and gilded glass, precious objects created from carved crystal, productions of Fatimid art for the most part, carved and decorated woods and basins and goblets of every kind of metal. It is however, albeit to a lesser extent, to the more general field of culture that Muslim Sicily was to leave her legacy. As the «Daughter of Andalusia» she was to play her part in the Spanish mediation that would be so crucial to the building of Western civilization in the twelfth and thirteenth centuries.

Culture and Administration under Norman Rule

The distinctive Christian-Islamic culture, destined to achieve so much fame and importance, flowered under the new conquerors. Arab spiritual and cultural preeminence was established, a reflection of the great Muslim civilization of that time and, more specifically, of the Fatimid court. There arose an interest for the sciences, al-ulûm al-qadîma, that is to say for logic, geometry, astronomy, music, medicine and alchemy. There were many scientists and scholars who found the tolerant atmosphere of the Norman court congenial to them and the pacific coexistence of so many heterogeneous elements was made possible by its eclecticism.

Abû l-Fidâ says of Roger: «He quartered the Franks on the island together with the Muslims. These he honored, forbidding the others to do them injury, and they became his friends.»[5]

We have the word of Eadmer, disciple of S. Anselm, Archbishop of Canterbury, that Count Roger refused to allow his Muslim troops to be converted to Christianity. Each and all, Normans and Italians, Longobards, Greeks and Saracens had a role to play in the state. Arab writing stayed in current use, especially for official documents. At the Palermitan court one might hear French and Greek, Arabic and Italian. The mosques were crowded while monasteries of the Greek and Latin rites grew in number. To discourage rebellion the king himself made use of his faithful Muslim troops, immune as they were both to the subversive tendencies of the Norman barons and to papal excommunications. From all over Europe, from all over the world, scientists and scholars flocked to the Palermitan court; the most numerous group was composed of the Arabs whose tongue was universally recognized as the preeminent language of science. This source of light attracted many Latins too, among them Adelard of Bath, pioneer of Arabic studies in England and translator from the Arabic of the *Elements* of Euclid.

The Muslim hallmark was visible in administration too; the manner of dividing up the island was identical with Arab military territorial circumscriptions, the *iqlîm*. A number of twelfth century documents confirm this. The Registry, in Arabic *diwân at-tahqiq*, was

These pages show examples of Islamic influences on Italian architecture. The two preceding photographs are, respectively, a detail of the central gallery of Villa Rufolo (thirteenth through fourteenth century) at Ravello (Salerno) and of the Paradise Cloister (thirteenth century) at Amalfi (Salerno). On this page: the Piccola Cuba, in one of the pavilions of William II in Palermo. On the following pages: the Castle of Lucera (thirteenth century) (Foggia), and the summit of the Bell-tower at Amalfi (Salerno). (Archives of Credito Italiano / Libri Scheiwiller)

translated in Latin as *Dohana de Secretis*; tools of office were termed *defetarii*, from *dafâtir*, plural of *diftar* which may be a transcription of the Greek word for «skin» and «codex of parchment.»

Wherever Arabic was the prevalent tongue the region was governed by Muslim *amils*. Justice was administrated by visiting magistrates assisted by a varying number of *boni homines*, both Christian and Muslim, who often worked in collaboration. There was also an Arab record office that used Greek or Arabic or both with impartiality. The king's decrees were headed by the motto (*'alâmah*) chosen by the ruler and written out by a special secretary who, in the process, guaranteed the authenticity of the document. The motto of Roger II was «Praise be to God, in thanksgiving for his favors.» Besides the Western name on coins there was also an Arab title, after the manner of the caliphs. The title of Roger II was «al Malik al-mu'azzam al-mu'tazz bi-llâh» («the revered king, exalted by the grace of God»), or «an-nâsir an-nasraniyya» («defender of Christianity»).

However, during the last years of William II, who earned such praise from the traveler Ibn Gubayr, signs of change began to appear, so much so that the Valencian pilgrim also refers to him as a tyrant and oppressor of the Muslims.

The aggressive force of the culture that had developed in northwestern Europe and reached Sicily with the Normans was beginning to make itself felt. Numerous Catholics, especially French Catholics were installed at court. At their hands, slowly and in secrecy, persecutions began. Meanwhile, relations with the population continued to be of the friendliest. The mosques and the schools that flourished beside them were well-attended; the solemn Friday prayer with the invocation for the Abbasid caliphs continued. Indeed, when looting took place, it was often the Muslims who held back the Christians and prevented them from committing acts of violence and sacrilege against other Christians.

Yet many families sought to sell their worldly goods in the hope that they might thus reach some Muslim country. The Muslim scholars who conversed with Ibn Gubayr during his travels understood that the times were changing and foresaw that before long Islamism would be extinguished in Sicily.

The Dazzling Swabian Era

Relentless persecution of the Muslims began in 1189, on the death of King William II. Survivors took refuge in the mountains of the west, in Val di Mazara. The new ruler was the Hohenstaufen emperor, Henry IV, son of Frederick Barbarossa and the husband of Constance, daughter of Roger II. He entered Palermo in November 1194, the year in which his son, Frederick, was born at Jesi. The Hauteville spirit was not entirely extinguished. But at barely four years of age Frederick was orphaned and became a ward of the Pope. During his minority the island's Muslims were subjected to persecution everywhere and their defeat came with the great massacre at Palermo in 1200. The last act of violence against them was at the hands of the young Sicilian ruler himself, after he came of age: the last rebels were finally rooted out and their leader, Muhammad ibn 'Abbâd, was executed together with his two sons.

Those who survived were deported to Lucera to form a Muslim colony. A colony that was to show lifelong fidelity to the emperor, coming to the aid of King Manfred at Benevento where it was was precisely with the charge of these Saracen horsemen that the battle began. It is possible that such fidelity lasted until the death of Conradin, in 1268, when Swabian domination of South Italy came to an end.

The spirit of Islam in Sicily was not extinguished by the defeat of the last Muslims. Frederick, who had been familiar with the Arab tongue since his youth, took care to keep it alive even in the organization of the state. A thirteenth-century Muslim historian tells us that he was raised by the Muslims' *qâdî*. Certainly, he frequently retired to the baths and his banquets were enlivened by a troup of dancing girls; he kept a harem and his wives were guarded by eunuchs; at his court, just as at the court of William II, the muezzin made the call to prayer. Suspicion and diffidence grew in ecclesiastic circles, he was accused of sympathy for the Muslim faith, of Oriental licentiousness. Frederick was cynical and non-conformist, probably indifferent to religious matters—Ibn al-Gawzî judged him to be a materialist—and what interested him above all in Eastern civilization was the scientific and intellectual aspect. The best scholars of Europe gathered at his court and it became the lodestar of culture. Among these scholars were William Figuerra, Lanfranco Cigala, Sordello himself and Michael Scot, the link between Frederick's circle and the translation center at Toledo. He remained at the court until he died, translating from Arabic the writings of Aristotle together with the comments of Averroes. Aristotle's five books devoted to *Logica*, together with an introduction by Porfirius, were translated from the Arabic into Hebrew on the initiative of the emperor by a disciple of the Spanish Jew Maimonides, Iacob ben Abbamari ben Simson ben Anatoli, a Jew himself. The emperor also commissioned the translation of an Arab treatise on falconry from his astrologer and this became the basis for Frederick's own work on the same subject and the first work of modern natural history. His greatest personal contribution however, was the foundation of the University of Naples, the first state university in Europe. Here he achieved his dream of bringing together the three great medieval culures in a climate of understanding and collaboration. He endowed it with a generous collection of Arab manuscripts, had numerous works translated and sent copies of these to the universities of Paris and Bologna.

Frederick's contacts with Eastern rulers were always frequent. We know that he sent ambassadors to the sultan of Egypt in 1207 because a mosaic, which was still in situ in the sixteenth century, on the portico of Cefalù cathedral, showed him in the act of taking leave of Giovanni Cicala, Bishop of Cefalù, with the following words: «Go to Babylon and to Damascus; there you will find the sons of Saladin and shall speak to them boldly in my name.»[6]

Frederick was a political animal capable of grasping the significance of his times, almost a Renaissance ruler in the autumn of the Middle Ages. He had already accepted the emblem of the cross in 1215 when the Archbishop of Mainz had placed the crown of Germany on his head in the cathedral of Aachen. But his absolutist vision of the Empire, the novelty of his attitude towards non-Christian peoples brought him into serious conflict with the Holy See, fearful of seeing itself surrounded and vanquished by this Empire and of losing its feudal rights over the Southern kingdom. Nevertheless, Frederick continued to maintain diplomatic relations with al-Kâmil, the sultan of Egypt, who enlisted his aid against his brother, al-Mu'azzam, the governor of Damascus.

After lengthy and insistent papal persuasion, culminating in an excommunication, Frederick set sail from Brindisi in June of 1228 on a crusade and disembarked at Acre in the autumn.

This is how Abû l-Fidâ tells the story: «Meanwhile, the emperor had reached Acre with his army. Al-Kâmil had sent a messenger to him, Fakhr ad-Dîn ibn Shaykh, to beg him to enter Syria and challenge his brother al-Mu'azzam. When the emperor arrived al-Mu'azzam was dead, but the sultan was still committed to their agreement. Among the Franks the term Emperor signifies *mâlik al-'umarâ*. In reality, his name is Frederick. He is the lord of the island of Sicily and of Barr at-tawîl, that is to say, of Apulia and Lombardy. The *qâdî*, Gamâl as-Dîn ibn wâsil says: 'I visited these lands when I was al-Mâlik Baybars'ambassador to the emperor. Among the Frankish rulers he is unrivaled for love of philosophy and logic. He is well-disposed towards Muslims, not an unusual thing in the island of Sicily where the greater part of the population is made up of believers'... al-Kâmil agreed to surrender Jerusalem to the emperor on condition that the ruins of the walls should not be rebuilt, the Franks should be forbidden entry to the Qubbah as-Sakhra and the al-Aqsâ mosque, there should only be *wâlî* Muslims in the villages surrounding Jerusalem and the Franks should take possession only of the townships along the road from Jerusalem to Acre. An agreement was reached on these points and both parties swore on oath to observe it.»[7]

The surrender of Jerusalem had aroused the indignation of the caliph of Baghdad and that of the entire Muslim world. Consequently Frederick apologized to the emir Fakhr ad-Dîn assuring him that had his own honor not been at stake he would never have imposed such a sacrifice on the sultan. He had only taken Jerusalem, he declared, to avoid losing face with the Franks. He then begged the sultan's permission to enter Jerusalem.

«On 17 March 1229 the emperor entered the city that had been under Patriarchal interdiction. The following day, after a visit to the church of the Holy Sepulchre wherein he placed the crown on his head, he paid a visit to the Muslim holy places accompanied by the sultan's envoy, the *qâdî* of Nablus. Entering the as-Sakhra mosque he read the great Saladin's inscription on the dome: 'This city of Jerusalem, Salâh ad-Dîn liberated from the unbelievers.' At noon, the hour of prayer, he invited the muezzin to give the customary call. At nightfall, Frederick, shunning the company of the Christian pilgrims, dined among the Saracens at the table of the *qâdî* of Nablus. He talked of the sun and of the moon to the *shaykh* 'Alam ad-Dîn, the astronomer sent to him by the sultan. Finally, with the first call to prayer, morning came and Frederick returned to the Knights of S. John. The impressions he created among the Muslims were conflicting, but they were, withal, full of admiration and respect for a man who spoke their tongue and discussed the greatest problems of science and metaphysics with them, seeking truth and knowledge.

The emperor then left for Acre. This was a scholarly prince, knowledgeable in geometry, arithmetic and the exact sciences. He sent the sultan, al-Mâlik al-Kâmil, numerous arduous problems to resolve concerning geometry, the theory of numbers and mathematics. The sultan showed them to the *shaykh* 'Alam ad-Dîn al-Hanafi, more widely known under the name of

Ta'sîf, and to other scholars, had their answers written down and returned to the emperor. The emperor returned home by sea from Acre at the end of the second gumâda.»[8]

These friendships made in the East were to continue through the exchange of gifts and letters. We have two letters that Frederick wrote from Barletta after his return from the Holy Land, addressed to the emir Fakhr ad-Dîn, relating the circumstances of his victories over the Roman pontiff. In 1232, the sultan's ambassadors, bearing costly gifts, were welcomed at Melfi. Among these gifts, which were placed in storage at Venosa, was a magnificent canopy with rotating images of the sun and the moon indicating the hours of the day and night. One of the Egyptian notables, named Mahlûf, died at Messina where he was given a sumptuous burial.

In the meantime serious disagreement, this time to be irremediable, arose between Frederick and the pontiffs Gregory IX and his successor Innocent IV. The General Council of Lyons confirmed the sentence whereby the emperor shold be deposed and his subjects released from their oath of fidelity. In 1244 Jerusalem was taken by as-Sâlih Ayyûb, but when the pontiff attempted to deal directly with the sultan, to the detriment of the emperor, as-Sâlih rejected his overtures. Once more the friendship and profound loyalty of the Orientals were not to betray the man who honored them.

Frederick returned the courtesy by informing the sultan of the plans and strategies of the crusade that Louis IX would lead to Egypt in the spring of 1249. In the course of the battle in which the King of France himself was taken prisoner, Frederick's friend, the old emir Fakhr ad-Dîn, died, bearing on his standard both the imperial insignia and that of the sultan.

Friendly relations had continued throughout this period. The sultan gave an honorable reception to a Sicilian ship that reached Alexandria in 1241 with a cargo of gifts from Frederick. The Muslim chancellery has preserved for us the titles used by the sultan in his letters to Frederick: «The Great King, the Illustrious, the Most High, the All Powerful King of Germany, Lombardy and Sicily, Custodian of the Holy City (of Jerusalem), Protector of the imam of Rome, King of the Christians, Defender of the Frankish kingdoms, Leader of the Christian army.»[9]

Certainly Frederick admired oriental absolutism, the unlimited power exercised by the sovereign over his subjects without the hindrances of baronial privileges, the autonomies of the communes and papal interference. Above all, in the East there was no papacy, his great enemy and the adversary of the empire.

Frederick died at Castel Fiorentino on the day of S. Lucia; that same year the Ayyubid dynasty in Egypt came to an end. Muslim troops escorted the body of their master, clad in the sovereign's red, down through Italy to Palermo. This is how an Italian chronicler recalled the event: «On the 28 of that month the body of the Emperor passed by on its way to Taranto, and I was at Bitonto to see this. It was borne on a litter covered with carmine velvet, escorted by his Saracen guards on foot and six battalions of armed horsemen; as they entered his lands they wept for the Emperor.»[10] The body of the emperor, wrapped in a white robe covered with Kufic inscriptions in gold, was buried in the Cathedral.

Ibn al-Furât recalls: «In that year there died the emperor Frederick, Lord of Germany and of Sicily, Protector of the Holy City of Jerusalem, King of the Christians, Custodian of the

Frankish kingdoms and Commander of the Army of the Cross People say that the emperor was secretly a Muslim. But what he was and what his beliefs were God knows best.»[11]

The love for Arab culture never declined under Frederick's successors. With the fall of the Ayyubid dynasty in Egypt and the rise to power of the Mamelukes, the sultan Baybars sent an ambassador to the newly enthroned Manfred at a moment in which he was surrounded by enemies. The best testimony is offered by Abû l-Fidâ: «When Frederick died in 648, the kingdom of Sicily and the other countries of continental Italy passed to his son Qurâ ibn Fardarîk (Conrad IV). On his death he was succeeded by another son of Frederick, Manfrîd ibn Fardarîk. All the princes of this dynasty take the title of emperor when they are enthroned. Among all the Frankish kings the emperor was the best friend of the Muslims and he loved wise men. When I joined the entourage of the wise emperor Manfred he treated me with honor and I stayed with him in a town of continental Italy, in the province of Apulia. In the course of our frequent meetings I found him to be a most uncommon person and a lover of the speculative sciences; he knew ten propositions of the book of Euclid by heart. Near to this town there was another, called Lucera, whose population was made up entirely of Muslims from the island of Sicily, who openly declared their allegiance to Islam. I discovered that many of the most important figures at the emperor Manfred's court were Muslims and this they showed at the moment of 'adhân and at prayer in the field. The town I was staying in is a five days' walk from Rome. The pope, Caliph of the Franks, for all that this was a period of friendly relations between him and the emperor, was plotting with the Raydâfrans (the king of the Franks) on ways to fight the emperor and kill him. The emperor had already been excommunicated by the pope. All this because of the sympathy the emperor showed towards the Muslims. For the very same reason the emperor's brother Conrad, and his father Frederick, had in their turn been excommunicated by the pontiff of Rome for their leanings toward Islam.»[12]

The sun was setting on Swabian power: its last rays shone on the struggle to revive it of Conradin, he too recalled with respect by the Muslim chroniclers: «Messengers bearing a letter from the king Conradin, son of the emperor, reached the sultan Baybars. It told of his victory over the king Charles; of how Almighty God had restored to him the rightful patrimony of his ancestors and how he was once more entered into possession of his lands. The sultan wrote to him in reply telling him to be of good heart and asking him to present his respects to all those who had been allies of his uncle and his grandfather.»[13]

The end of Swabian domination brought with it the inexorable decline of Muslim influence in Italy. There remained only the faithful colony at Lucera that was to be ruthlessly exterminated in 1300 by Charles of Anjou.

Sicily Lost

In the first decades following the arrival of the Normans, some of the greatest talents of the island took flight, poets such as al Ballanûbî, who died in Egypt in 1050, and Ibn Hamdîs who fled to Tunisia in 1079 but was later to be warmly received at the Abbasid court in Seville where he stayed until the dynasty was overcome by the Almoravids, forcing him to seek shelter at the court of the Zirids. His poetry not only reflects the adventurous and carefree life he led, it also contains many verses expressing his nostalgia for his lost mother country.

> I remember Sicily, and what sorrow remembering it
> brings to the heart. A place of youthful follies
> now deserted, once animated by the flower of noble souls.
> Since I have been cast out of a paradise, how can I speak of it?
> Were my tears not bitter, I would believe them to be
> the rivers of that paradise.[14]

The poet continues:

> I swear that my head has never bowed in slumber without
> my being visited, despite the distance that separates us,
> by visions of that Vale in which my kin dwell.
> The land whence the plant of honor springs, where
> knights make war on death.
> Long life to that populous and cultivated land,
> may the traces and ruins of her existence survive!
> The scented air, wafted to us by morning and evening,
> may this survive!
> May the living live on among these, and laid in the
> sepulchre their mortal remains,
> Long life to these too![15]

Similar feelings are expressed by a fellow countryman, he too a guest at the 'Abbasid court, Abû l-'Araba Mus'ab al-Qurashî:

> My homeland, since you have withdrawn from me,
> I shall take the saddles of the generous steeds
> for my home.
> Since I sprang from the soil, every land
> is my homeland, and every human creature / my kin.[16]

Others stayed on at the court of the Norman kings, in the period when the island was still Muslim and playing an important role in Italian history. 'Abd al-Rahmân celebrates the island stolen from Islam as follows:

> Hand round the mellowed golden wine, and drink
> from dawn to dusk,
> Drink to the sound of the lute, and of the songs
> worthy of Ma'bad.
> There is no serenity, but in sweet Sicily's shade,
> subject to a dynasty surpassing the imperial
> dynasties of the Kings.
> Here are regal palaces, harboring joy;
> sublime abode, on which God bestows perfect beauty!
> Here is the refulgent setting for every architectural device,

the proud gardens by which the world flowers anew,
the lions of her fountain, that spill out
the waters of paradise.
Spring has robed her purlieu with the resplendent
vestiments of her beauty.
Has crowned their visages with jewel-encrusted
raiments of many hues,
She scents the west winds' breezes,
at dawn and dusk.[17]

Celebrating the beauty of Favàra, at Palermo, Abd al-Rahmân al-Itrabânishî writes:

Twin-laked Favàra, every desire is encompassed by you:
sweet sight and sublime spectacle.
Your waters shed into nine brooks: O most beautiful
branching streams!
Where your two lakes meet, there love tarries,
and by your channel passion sets up her tents.
O resplendent lake of the two palms and sovereign abode
girdled by lake!
The limpid water of the two springs seems liquid pearls,
and the pool, a sea.
The garden branches seem to stretch out, smilingly
to gaze on the fish in your waters.
The great fish swims in the park's limpid waters,
and the birds sing in its gardens.
The proud oranges of the islet seem balls of fire
on their emerald branches.
The lemon tree takes on the pallor of a lover bereft,
one who has passed the night in grief.
And the two palms, two lovers who,
for fear of enemies, have elected a mighty castle
as their abode.
Palms of the twin lakes of Palermo, may showers of rain
never cease to fall on you!
May fortune be yours, every desire attained,
and may adversity slumber!
Prosper and grant shelter to the lovers; in the immunity
of your shade love reigns unprofaned.[18]

But the fall of the Swabian dynasty was a tragic moment for the Muslim community. On the death of Frederick II, when the last torch of Arabism was extinguished in Sicily, a Palermitan *qâdî* gave orders for a lament to be cut on his tombstone, a lament in Kufic script for a world that had disappeared and for his beloved island: «Where is my land?... Alas!»[19]

303

Notes

1   Ibn Hawqal, in M. Amari, *Biblioteca Arabo-Sicula*, Turin-Rome 1880, I, 10-24. [The words in brickets were supplied by Amari in the interest of a clear reading of the text. (*translator note*).]

2   Ibn Hawqal, *Kitâb al-masâlik wa-l-mamâlik*, ed. J.H. Kramers, Leiden 1938, 130-131. It. tr. by F. Gabrieli, *l'Islam nella storia*, Bari 1966, 63-64.

3   Al-Idrîsî, *L'Italia descritta nel «Libro di re Ruggero»*, ed. and It. tr. by M. Amari and C. Schiaparelli, Rome 1883, 22-23, 25-26 in the translation.

4   Ibn Gubayr, *Rihlat al-kinâni*, ed. M. Amari, «Journal Asiatique», 1845, 509-523.

5   Abû l-Fidâ, *Mukhtasar ta'rîkh al-bashar*, ed. J. Reiske-Chr. Adler, Hafniae 1789-'94, V, 144.

6   R. Pirro, *Sicilia Sacra*, Palermo 1773, 805.

7   Abû l-Fidâ, *Mukhtasar...*, IV, 346, 348, 350.

8   Al-Maqrîzî, «Revue de l'orient Latin», 9 (1902), 526-529; Fr. tr. by E. Blochet.

9   Al-'Aynî, in M. Amari, *Biblioteca...*, Lipsia 1857, 517.

10 Matteo di Giovenazzo, in Huillard-Bréholles, *Historia diplomatica Friderici secundi*, Paris 1852-'61, VI, 812-813.

11 Ibn Al-Furât, *Ta'rîkh ad-Duwâl wa l'mulûk*, ed. H. ash-Shamma', Basra 1970, for the period 600-651 H; extracts and Eng. tr. by C. Lyons, Cambridge 1971, 48.

12 Abû l-Fidâ, *Mukhtasar...*, V, 146, 148.

13 Ibn al-Furât, ed. Cambridge, 167.

14 Ibn Hamdîs, It. tr. by F. Gabrieli, *Gli Arabi in Italia*, Milan 1979, 737.

15 Ibn Hamdîs, It. tr. by F. Gabrieli, *Gli Arabi...*, 737.

16 Al-Qurashi, *Gamharat ash'âr al-'Arab*, Bûlâq 1038 H., It. tr. by F. Gabrieli, *Arabi di Sicilia e arabi di Spagna*, «Al-Andalus», 1950, 39.

17 Cfr. F. Gabrieli, *Arabi di Sicilia...*, 41-42.

18 Cfr. F. Gabrieli, *Arabi di Sicilia...*, 42-43.

19 M. Amari, *Le epigrafi arabiche di Sicilia*, Palermo 1879-'85, II, 143-144.

CONCLUSION
THE CONTRIBUTIONS OF MUSLIM CIVILISATION IN THE WEST TO THE REBIRTH OF CHRISTIAN EUROPE

Throughout the Early Middle Ages, when Muslim banners fluttering in the wind announced the presence of the Arabs and Berbers of Africa just beyond the Pyrenees and on Italian soil, the Byzantine and Latin West, which was to experience its formidable capacity for conquest, undoubtedly viewed Islam as the scourge of God. Yet behind the incursions lay Sicily with a social and political structure that would still be influential in the Norman and Swabian epoch and Spain, a beacon of civilization.

It was primarily the word of the Sacred Book, the message of the Prophet, that is to say, the Word of God, that the horsemen who crossed the Straits of Gibraltar in the seventh century brought with them, for this was the command of the Koran. But they were also the harbingers of science, culture and art; of values that the West could avidly draw on in the interests of revival. In the intellectual history of medieval Europe Muslim Spain played a leading role in the transmission and creation of a new culture. The contribution of the Crusades to the introduction of the science, the philosophy and the wisdom of the ancient world has been over-emphasized, mediation was the work of the Andalusians.

Translation gave the West a familiarity with the classics and also kept it abreast of the development of the most significant and original works of Muslim philosophic and scientific thought in the East, where Baghdad rose to become the most important cultural center in the world in the ninth century.

By the tenth century translations from Arabic into Latin were being made in the monastery of Santa Maria at Ripoll in the Spanish Marches. Such was its prestige in the field of learning that Brother Gerbert of Aurillac (945-1003), later to become Pope Sylvester II, was sent to study at Vich.

It was in this period that the West learned the use of the astrolabe and the quadrant and assimilated the skills needed to build sundials and portable time keepers in the form of the clepsydra. The use of optical instruments to study the stars also became popular.

The translations made by the monks of Ripoll, however imperfect they may have been, gave Europe its first taste of Muslim culture. It spread via Lorraine where the leading figure was Herman Contractus (1013-1054), abbot of the Benedictine monastery of Reichenau, who used the translations in his possession to make a study of the astrolabe.

This was only the beginning. In the twelfth century the translators began to transmit to the West not only works of Eastern science but also the works of Aristotle, Ptolemy, Archimedes, Hippocrates, Galen and Plato, that were still unknown in the original Greek.

Plato of Tivoli worked at Barcelona in collaboration with the Jewish Abraham bar Hiyya, known as Savasorda. He translated Ibn al-Saffâr's text on the astrolabe (*Liber Abulcasim de operibus astrolabiae*) and texts on astronomy and geometry. He dedicated his work to John of Spain, or of Seville, the leading intellectual of the first half of the twelfth century who, perhaps elevated to the rank of vizier by al-Mu'tamid and protected by Raymond, archbishop of Toledo, devoted himself to translating the astrological treatises of al-Farghânî and al-Zarqâlî.

This industrious school was joined a few years later by Domenico Gundisalvi, archdeacon of Segovia, who worked in collaboration with John of Spain on the translation of the works of the great Eastern philosophers: the *Liber di Scienciis* and the *De Animalibus* of al-Fârâbî, the *Maqâsid* of al-Ghazâlî (Algazel), the *Metaphisica, De Anima* and *Logica* of Ibn Sînâ (Avicenna), and the *Fons Vitae* of Ibn Gabirol (Avicebron), all works that exercised great influence on Albertus Magnus and S. Bonaventure.

In 1142 Peter the Venerable arrived in Spain on a pilgrimage to the sanctuary of S. James of Compostella and to visit the monasteries of the Cluniac order. Wishing to gain more knowledge of the Koran, the better to disprove it, he encouraged the making of a Latin translation. The task was entrusted to two foreigners, Herman the Dalmatian and Robert of Chester, who completed the work by the usual means: a Jew, a convert, or a Mozarab first translated the text from Arabic into Castilian and it was then rendered in Latin. Another visitor from England was Adelard of Bath, translator of Euclid and of al-Khuwârizmî.

The second half of the twelfth century was dominated by the great figure of Gerard of Cremona (1114-1187), who devoted his austere life to his love for science. He learned Arabic and translated more than seventy works, among them the *Analytica Posteriora* of Aristotle, the *Almagest* of Ptolemy, the *De Intellecto* of al-Kindî, the *Canon of Medicine* of Ibn Sînâ and the *Corpus* of Galen.

The work, sustained by an untiring devotion to learning, continued throughout the thirteenth century. The archbishop of Toledo, Rodrigo Jimenez de Rada, sponsored a second translation of the Koran, Michael Scot translated the *Sphaera* of al-Bitrûgî (Alpetragio), and Herman of Germany translated into Latin Aristotle's study on the Nicomachean Ethics and works by al-Fârâbî and Ibn Rushd.

In the year which saw the death of Frederick II, Alfonso X the Wise was enthroned in Castile where scholars of the two religions would later be drawn to his court. Here, the collection of maxims of Mubashshir ibn Fâtîk, known under the title of *Los Bocados de Oro*, was translated into Castilian, Provençal, French and English. The Muslim religion was studied, chiefly by Dominicans and Franciscans, with apologetical intention in the works of Ramón Martìn, a disciple of S. Albertus Magnus in Paris, and of Raimondo Lullo, who suggested to the Pope that schools of Eastern studies should be set up for the teaching of Arabic, Aramaic and Hebrew, and saw his proposals accepted when the Council of Vienna recommended the creation of such centers in Rome, Bologna, Paris, Oxford and Salamanca.

Great advances made in the mathematical sciences were due to the German Nemorarius who drew inspiration from the works of Nasawî and Leonardo Pisano, known as Fibonacci, whose influence was to be felt right up to the sixteenth century.

John of Holywood, otherwise known as Sacrobosco, and Grosseteste, were familiar with Latin treatises on astronomy that owed much to the works of al-Battânî. We are, moreover, indebted to the Arabs for the skills needed to build astronomical instruments, by which means our knowledge of the earth and the celestial bodies has been furthered.

Works dealing with physics, medicine, optics and surgery were translated. A passion for chemistry developed and became widespread as a result of the translation of the works of al-Râzî and Geber.

Warfare was revolutionized by the use of gunpowder, in Arabic, *bârûd*, *naft* or *dawâ'* and the ancient Arab predilection for travels led to the application of new systems to the art of navigation and to new discoveries in geography.

The *Kitâb al-kulliyât* of Averroes, devoted to the study of anatomy, physiology, pathology, hygiene and general medicine, was translated into Latin by Bonacosa with the title of *Colliget*. The translation of the work of al-Gâfiqî gave Europe its first great treatise of pharmacology.

Contacts with Muslim culture in Spain were not confined to the sciences, for they also penetrated the world of medieval thought and poetry; but there was a different balance to the relationship because an original spirit was brought to the Eastern ideas. Their transformation and adaptation to another pattern of thought resulted in a new creation and this fact, together with the very complex problems that characterized the rise of a vernacular literature in the Christian West does not always make it easy to identify the contributory factors.

By the end of the nineteenth century Orientalists were pointing to the links between the work of Dante and Indian or Persian texts. The first organic approach to the problem is to be found in the work *La escatologia musulmana en la Divina Comedia* by Miguel Asin Palacios, whose initial instigation stems from the Koranic verses that proclaim: «Glory be to Him who made His servant go by night from the Sacred Mosque to the farther Mosque whose surroundings We have blessed, that We might show him some of Our signs.»[1] The *Kitâb al-mi'râg*, an extremely popular religious text in Arab countries, contains a collection of literary works dedicated to the theme of Muhammad's travels in the Other World. In the first half of the thirteenth century Alfonso X had the collection translated into Castilian and, before being lost to us, this work was translated into Latin and early French with the respective titles of *Liber Scalae Machometi* and *Livre de l'Eschiele Mahomet*.

The question is still open to debate, but with due consideration it cannot be denied that there are numerous points in common between the description of Dante's journey in the Other World and that offered by the *Libro della Scala*, which he was certainly familiar with, even though the influence that Muslim eschatology exercised over him is but one facet of the formation of the great poet who brought his own stylistic and spiritual force to bear in remolding his material. It is pertinent at this point to recall that Dante's master, Brunetto Latini, once an envoy of the Florentine Guelph party at the Castilian court, had used Arab sources for the composition of the *Tesoro*, a kind of encyclopedia of medieval knowledge.

The Dantean theory of light is certainly linked to that developed in Spain by Ibn Masarra and later transmitted to the West by Avicebron and Ibn 'Arabî. A passage in the *Convivio* reveals Dante's familiarity with the thought of Averroes.[2] The *Convivio* also contains many points in common with the *Tesori degli amanti* (the «Lovers' Treasury») by Ibn 'Arabî, and this brings us to the great problem of relations between Arab poetry and the developing lyric poetry of Europe.

Petrarch for one had no sympathy for the forms of Arab lyric poetry and indeed, expressed his aversion to anything that might be considered Arabic: You know the Arabs as physicians. I know them as poets: affected in the extreme, mellifluous, lacking in vigor, the epitomy of lasciviousness. It will be hard to persuade me that anything good can come out of Arabia.[3]

The thesis of Arab origin for Provençal lyric poetry stems from the dual problem of metric form and concepts expressed in images that owe their origins to a particular spiritual background. It was certainly from the other side of the Pyrenees that there came the vision of woman as the object of courtly love, not a lure for the senses but for the lover's spirit, a spirit elevated by contemplation of the loved one.

The theme of chaste adoration of the loved woman, already familiar at the Abbasid court, was introduced in Spain by poets like Ibn Zaydûn (d. 463/1071) and reached its zenith with the great Ibn Hazm, the author of the *Tawq al-hamâma* (*The Ring of the Dove*), a treatise on the phenomenology and types of love that for all the differences of faith and cultural background provides numerous parallels with troubadour love lyrics.

New perspectives to the inquiry were opened at the beginning of this present century by the discovery of the works of Ibn Quzmân. The *dîwân* of this twelfth century poet was not composed in classical Arabic but in the spoken form; it rejected the classical meter of the ancient *qasîda* in favour of the popular form of the *zagal*, syllabic strophes that afforded different combinations of rhyme. Confirmation of the origin may be found in a text by al-Tîfâshî that unhesitatingly attributes its invention to Ibn Bâhha, the philosopher known to Christians by the name of Avempace.

There are marked resemblances to the lyrics and themes of the early Provençal troubadours, William IX of Aquitaine, Cercamon, Marcabru and Rudel. It is natural therefore that Arabists should have viewed this kind of composition as the forerunner of European strophic poetry and not simply Provençal, as the Cantigas, Castilian Villancicos and Italian Laudi demonstrate.

Romance poetry is indebted to Arab lyric poetry for another strophic form, the *muwashshaha*. According to Ibn Bassâm, this form was invented in the tenth century by Muhammad of Cabra, the first to use the vernacular tongue, who incorporated Romance words or phrases into the structure of the strophe. This kind of composition is very different from the *zagal*. It was written in classical Arabic that allows for a structure of five or seven strophes formed of two parts, one with verses in independent rhyme varying in relation to the specific theme (*gusn*) and the other in a rhyme common to the whole poem (*qufi*). The final strophe might be in either the classical tongue or in the vernacular (*kharga*). The themes and forms were also adopted by the English and the German Frauenlieder and by the French Chansons de Femmes.

Just how important the contribution of the Arab lyric poetry of Muslim Spain was to the formation of the European opus is still open to debate. Nevertheless it cannot be denied that there was always frequent intercourse between the land of al-Andalus and Christian countries. Soldiers, pilgrims, artists and travelers were undoubtedly purveyors of civilization; on occasion, so were prisoners, as Ibn al-Qattânî reveals in the following sketch of life in eleventh-century Navarre: «There were several Muslim dancers and singers in the hall, a gift from Sulaymân ibn al-Hakam when he was Commander of the Faithful in Cordoba. The Christian woman made a sign to one of them who took up a lute and sang a number of verses... an exquisite performance. Serving maids and lady companions waited on the Christian, captives... of such beauty as might be compared only to the waxing moon. On hearing the verses one of them broke into tears... I approached her and asked what troubled her. She replied that the verses had been written by her father and that on hearing them again her grief was aroused. I spoke to her thus: «Slave of the Lord, who was your father?» «Sulaymân ibn Mihrân of Saragossa. I have long been a captive and know nothing more of my family.»[4]

Arab narrative began to gain a public in the West, thanks once more to the work of translation encouraged by Alfonso X, above all the *Kalîla wa Dimna*, the *Book of Sinbad* (or Syntipas) and *The Thousand and One Nights*. All of these are works inspired by Eastern models.

Kalîla wa Dimna is a collection of allegories deriving from the *Panchatantra*, a fourth century composition written by a brahmin named Bidpaï. The title is taken from the first episode, which tells the story of two brothers. Translated from the original Pahlevi into Arabic and thence into Castilian, the work greatly influenced the *Roman de Renard*, the *Conde Lucanór* of Juan Manuel and the *Tales* of La Fontaine.

References to the *Book of Sinbad* are to be met with in the Leodilla episode in Boiardo's *Orlando Innamorato*, a tale from Boccaccio's *Decameron*: «I tre uomini di Isabella,» and in the work *El Monserrate* by Cristóbal de Virvés.

The *Thousand and One Nights* directly influenced medieval short story writing. The Boccaccio episode of Frederick and the Falcon is simply a variation on the ancient theme of generosity, illustrated by Hâtin al-Tâ'î (night 270) who sacrifices his camel to offer food to his guest; the Wooden Horse (nights 357-371) is to be met again in the *Clavileño* of Cervantes; the story of Qamar al-Zamân (nights 170-249) was used by Carlo Gozzi when writing his Turandot and later, by Schiller and Puccini.

An interesting case illustrating the transmission of Arab themes to Western literature is that of the archpriest of Hita, illegitimate son of the wealthy Arias Gonzales, Lord of Cisneros, who spent twenty-five years in Granada as a Muslim prisoner. His son, Juan Ruiz, the archpriest, was born at Alcalà la Real, the Alcalà of the Arab Banû Sa'îd, entered the Church and wrote the *Libro del Buen Amor*. The book handles themes already dealt with by Ibn Hazm, such as the description of the symptoms of love, which will be met with again in the pages that present Don Quixote enamoured of Dulcinea of Toboso, and that of praise and contempt for money, drawn from a *maqâma* of al-Harîrî. Chaucer was certainly familiar with the work of the archpriest, which was to play a significant role in the development of medieval narrative.

No less important and discernible are the ascetic and mystic infiltrations, exemplified by the «*Book of the Friend and of the Lover*,» a work by Raimondo Lullo who was directly influenced by Shushtarî, a *sûfî* of Guadix.

Islam was thus of decisive importance in the formation of medieval Christian man who, flexible in his approach to forms of art and life differing from his own, was occasionally open to dialogue, always willing to learn. The transmission of knowledge from East to West met with no barrier on either side.

Then the two worlds drew apart, and each sank into a form of self-contemplation. The East, after so much splendor, locked in the contemplation of the grandeur that once was hers, Europe, carried away by the myth of the supremacy of man, preening herself as the Custodian of Civilization and of the Truth.

In our own times Islam, in wholehearted acceptance of the past, affirms man's right to live, not as the measure of all things or a law unto himself, but as a complex spiritual entity perennially bound to God. The message that reaches us from the East even today, is still as it always has been, a passage from the Koran: «In the creation of the heavens and the earth, and in the alternation of night and day, there are signs for men of sense.»[5]

Notes

[1] *The Koran*, XVII, p. 228, Eng. tr. by N.J. Dawood, Penguin Books 1956.
[2] Dante Alighieri, *Il Convivio*, Florence 1964, III, 14.
[3] Francesco Petrarca, *Rerum Senilium Libri*, XII, 2.
[4] H. Pérès, *La poésie andalouse en arabe classique au XIe siècle*, Paris 1953, 386-387.
[5] *The Koran*, III, p. 413.

Dynasties

Califfi

The «Orthodox» Caliphs

1. Abû Bakr: 12 - 13 H.
                                      632 - 634 a.D.

2. 'Umar ibn al-Khattâb: 13 - 23 H.
                                      634 - 644 a.D.

3. 'Uthmân ibn 'Affân: 23 - 36 H.
                                      644 - 656 a.D.

4. 'Alî ibn Abî Tâlib: 36 - 40 H.
                                      656 - 661 a.D.

The 'Umayyad Caliphs of Damascus

1. Mu'âwiya I ibn Abî Sufyân: 40 - 60 H.
                                     661 - 680 a.D.

2. Yazîd I ibn Mu'âwiya: 60 - 64 H.
                                     680 - 683 a.D.

3. Mu'âwiya II ibn Abî Yazîd: 64 H.
                                     684 a.D.

4. Marwân I ibn al-Hakam: 64 - 65 H.
                                     684 - 684 a.D.

5. 'Abd al-Malik ibn Marwân: 65 - 86 H.
                                     685 - 705 a.D.

6. al-Walîd II ibn 'Abd al-Malik: 86 - 96 H.
                                     705 - 715 a.D.

7. Sulaymân ibn 'Abd al-Malik: 96 - 99 H.
                                     715 - 717 a.D.

8. 'Umar ibn 'Abd al-Azîz: 99 - 101 H.
                                     717 - 720 a.D.

9. Yazîd II ibn 'Abd al-Malik: 101 - 106 H.
                                     720 - 724 a.D.

10. Hishâm ibn 'Abd al-Malik: 106 - 125 H.
                                     724 - 743 a.D.

11. al-Walîd II ibn Yazîd ibn 'Abd al-Malik: 125 - 126 H.
                                     743 - 744 a.D.

12. Yazîd III ibn al-Walîd ibn 'Abd al-Malik: 126 H.
                                     744 a.D.

13. Ibrâhîm ibn al-Walîd ibn 'Abd al-Malik: 126 - 127 H.
                                     744 - 745 a.D.

14. Marwân ibn Muhammad ibn Marwân: 127 - 132 H.
                                     745 - 750 a.D.

The 'Abbasid Caliphs of Baghdad

1. al-Saffâh: 132 - 136 H.
                                     750 - 754 a.D.

2. al-Mansûr: 136 - 158 H.
                                     754 - 775 a.D.

3. al-Mahdî: 158 - 169 H.
                                     775 - 785 a.D.

4. al-Hâdî Mûsâ: 169 - 170 H.
                                     785 - 786 a.D.

5. al-Rashîd Hârûn: 170 - 193 H.
                                     786 - 809 a.D.

6. al-Amîn: 193 - 198 H.
                                     809 - 813 a.D.

7. al-Ma'mûn: 198 - 218 H.
                                     813 - 833 a.D.

8. al-Mu'stasim: 218 - 227 H.
                                     833 - 842 a.D.

9. al-Wâthiq: 227 - 232 H.
                                     842 - 847 a.D.

10. al-Mutawakkil: 232 - 247 H.
                                     847 - 861 a.D.

11. al-Muntasir: 247 - 248 H.
                                     861 - 862 a.D.

12. al-Musta'în: 248 - 251 H.
                                     862 - 866 a.D.

13. al-Mu'tazz: 251 - 255 H.
                                     866 - 869 a.D.

14. al-Muhtadî: 255 - 256 H.
                                     869 - 870 a.D.

15. al-Mu'tamid: 256 - 279 H.
                                     870 - 892 a.D.

16. al-Mu'tadid: 279 - 289 H.
                                     892 - 902 a.D.

17. al-Muktafî:	289 - 295 H. 902 - 908 a.D.	28. al-Mustazhir:	487 - 512 H. 1094 - 1118 a.D.
18. al-Muqtadir:	295 - 320 H. 908 - 932 a.D.	29. al-Mustarshid:	512 - 529 H. 1118 - 1135 a.D.
19. al-Qâhir:	320 - 322 H. 932 - 934 a.D.	30. al-Râshid:	529 - 530 H. 1135 - 1136 a.D.
20. al-Râdî:	322 - 329 H. 934 - 940 a.D.	31. al-Muqtafî:	530 - 555 H. 1136 - 1160 a.D.
21. al-Muttaqî:	329 - 333 H. 940 - 944 a.D.	32. al-Mustangid:	555 - 566 H. 1160 - 1170 a.D.
22. al-Mustakfî:	333 - 334 H. 944 - 946 a.D.	33. al-Mustadî:	566 - 575 H. 1170 - 1180 a.D.
23. al-Mutîl:	334 - 363 H. 946 - 974 a.D.	34. al-Nâsir:	575 - 622 H. 1180 - 1225 a.D.
24. al-Tâ'î:	363 - 381 H. 974 - 991 a.D.	35. al-Zâhir:	622 - 623 H. 1225 - 1226 a.D.
25. al-Qâdir:	381 - 422 H. 991 - 1031 a.D.	36. al-Mustansir:	623 - 640 H. 1226 - 1242 a.D.
26. al-Qâ'im:	422 - 467 H. 1031 - 1075 a.D.	37. al-Musta'sim:	640 - 656 H. 1242 - 1258 a.D.
27. al-Muqtadî:	467 - 487 H. 1075 - 1094 a.D.		

The Fatimids of Egypt

1. 'Ubayd Allâh al-Mahdî:	297 - 322 H. 909 - 934 a.D.	8. al-Mustansir:	427 - 487 H. 1036 - 1094 a.D.
2. al-Qâ'îm:	322 - 334 H. 934 - 946 a.D.	9. al-Musta'lî:	487 - 495 H. 1094 - 1101 a.D.
3. al-Mansûr:	334 - 341 H. 946 - 953 a.D.	10. al-Âmir:	495 - 525 H. 1101 - 1130 a.D.
4. al-Mu'izz:	341 - 365 H. 953 - 975 a.D.	11. al-Hâfiz:	525 - 544 H. 1130 - 1149 a.D.
5. al-'Azîz:	365 - 386 H. 975 - 996 a.D.	12. al-Zâhir:	544 - 549 H. 1149 - 1154 a.D.
6. al-Hâkim:	386 - 411 H. 996 - 1021 a.D.	13. al-Fa'iz:	549 - 555 H. 1154 - 1160 a.D.
7. al-Zâhir:	411 - 427 H. 1021 - 1036 a.D.	14. al-'Ãdil:	555 - 567 H. 1160 - 1171 a.D.

The Ayyubids of Egypt

1. Salâh al-Dîn Yûsuf:	576 - 589 H. 1171 - 1193 a.D.	5. al-Kâmil:	615 - 635 H. 1218 - 1238 a.D.
2. al-'Azîz 'Uthmân:	589 - 595 H. 1193 - 1198 a.D.	6. al-'Ãdil II:	635 - 637 H. 1238 - 1240 a.D.
3. al-Mansûr:	595 - 596 H. 1198 - 1199 a.D.	7. as-Sâlih Ayyûb:	637 - 647 H. 1240 - 1249 a.D.
4. al-'Ãdil:	596 - 615 H. 1199 - 1218 a.D.	8. al-Mu'azzam:	647 - 648 H. 1249 - 1250 a.D.

1. 'Abd al-Rahmân ı:	138 - 172 H. 756 - 788 a.D.	9. al-Hakam ıı (al Mustansir):	350 - 366 H. 961 - 976 a.D.
2. Hishâm ı:	172 - 180 H. 788 - 796 a.D.	10. Hisham ıı (al-Mu'aiyad):	366 - 399, 400-403 H. 976 - 1009 1010 - 1013 a.D.
3. al-Hakam ı:	180 - 206 H. 796 - 822 a.D.	11. Muhammad ıı:	399 - 400 H. 1009 - 1010 a.D.
4. 'Abd al-Rahmân ıı:	206 - 238 H. 822 - 852 a.D.	12. Sulaymân:	400, 403 - 407 H. 1009 - 1010 a.D. 1013 - 1016
5. Muhammad ı:	238 - 273 H. 852 - 886 a.D.		
6. al-Mundhir:	273 - 275 H. 886 - 888 a.D.	13. 'Abd al-Rahmân ıv (al Murtaza):	408 H. 1018 a.D.
7. 'Abd Allâh:	275 - 300 H. 888 - 912 a.D.	14. 'Abd al-Rahmân v:	414 H. 1023 a.D.
		15. Muhammad ııı:	414 - 416 H. 1023 - 1025 a.D.
8. 'Abd al-Rahmân ııı (an Nâsir):	300 - 350 H. 912 - 929 a.D. 929 - 961 caliph	16. Hishâm ııı:	418 - 422 H. 1027 - 1031 a.D.

The Mulûk at-Tawâ'if in the eleventh century

Kingdom of Seville: the Banû 'Abbâd

1. Muhammad ibn Ismâ'îl:	1023 - 1042 a.D.
2. 'Abbâd ibn Muhammad al-Mu'tadid:	1042 - 1069 a.D.
3. Muhammad ibn 'Abbâd al-Mu'tamid:	1069 - 1091 a.D.

al-Mu'tamid taken prisoner by the Almoravids.

Kingdom of Cordoboa: the Banû Gahwar

1. Gahwar ibn Muhammad ibn Gahwar:	1031 - 1043 a.D.
2. Muhammad ibn Gahwar:	1043 - 1064 a.D.
3. 'Abd al-Malik and 'Abd al-Rahmân:	until 1070

Cordoba annexed to the Kingdom of Seville.

4. Idrîs ıı ibn Yahyâ ibn 'Alî ibn Hammûd al-Âli:	1042 - 1047 a.D.
5. Muhammad ı ibn Idrîs al-Mahdî:	1047 - 1054 a.D.
6. Idrîs ıı ibn Yahyâ ibn Idrîs al-Sâmî:	1054 a.D.
7. Idrîs ıı (for the second time):	1054 - 1055 a.D.
8. Muhammad ıı ibn Idrîs ı al-Musta'lî:	1055 - 1057 a.D.

Malaga annexed to the Kingdom of Granada.

Kingdom of Granada: the Banû Zîrî

1. Zâwù ibn Zîrî:	1012 - 1019 a.D.
2. Habbûs ibn Mâksan:	1019 - 1038 a.D.
3. Bâdis ibn Habbûs:	1038 - 1073 a.D.
4. 'Abd Allâh ibn Bâdis:	1073 - 1090 a.D.

Kingdom of Malaga: the Banû Hammûd

1. Idrîs ibn 'Alî ibn Hammûd
   al-Mutra'aiyad: 1035 - 1039 a.D.

2. Yahyâ ibn Idrîs I al-Qâ'im: 1039 - 1040 a.D.

3. Hasan ibn Yahyâ ibn 'Alî ibn
   Hammûd al-Mustansir: 1040 - 1042 a.D.

2. Muhammad ibn 'Abd Allâh
   al-Mudaffar: 1045 - 1063 a.D.

3. Yahyâ ib Muhammad
   al-Mansûr: 1063 - 1067 a.D.

4. 'Umar ibn Muhammad

   al-Mutawakkil: 1067 - 1094 a.D.

Kingdom of Valencia

The Slavs Mubârak,
Mudaffar and Labîb: 1016 - 1021 a.D.

'Abd al'Azîz ibn Abî 'Āmir
al-Mansûr: 1021 - 1061 a.D.

'Abi al-Malik ibn 'Abd al-Azîz
Nidâm ad-dawla: 1061 - 1065 a.D.

Valencia annexed to the Kingdom of
Toledo.

al-Ma'mûn of Toledo: 1065 - 1076 a.D.

Valencia detached from Toledo.

Abû Bakr ibn 'Abd al-'Azîz: 1076 - 1085 a.D.
'Uthmân ibn Abî Bakr: 1085 a.D.

Yahyâ al-Qâdir: 1084 - 1092 a.D.
Ga'far ibn Gahhâf: 1092 - 1095 a.D.

The Cid: 1095 - 1102 a.D.
Almoravid domination of the kingdom.

Kingdom of Murcia

Khairân of Almeria: 1012 - 1028 a.D.

Zuhair in Almeria: 1028 - 1038 a.D.

'Abd al-Azîz al-Mansûr of Valencia: 1038 - 1061 a.D.
'Abd al-Malik al-Mudaffar of Valencia: 1061 - 1065 a.D.

Governor of Murcia in this last period:
Abû Bakr Ahmad Ibn Tâhir: 1063 a.D.

His son Muhammad   1063 - 1078 a.D.

Almoravid domination of the Kingdom.

Kingdom of Badajoz: the Banû l-Aftas

1. 'Abd Allâh ibn Muhammad ibn
   Maslama al-Mansûr: 1022 - 1045 a.D.

2. Muhammad ibn Yahyâ 'Izz
   ad-Dîn: 1041 - 1051 a.D.

3. Fath ibn Khalaf ibn Yahyâ
   Nasîr ad-Dîn: 1051 - 1053 a.D.

Niebla annexed to the Kingdom of
Seville.

Kingdom of Silves: The Banû Muzain

1. 'Isâ ibn Abî Bakr al-Mudaffar: 1048 - 1054 a.D.

2. Muhammad ibn 'Isâ an-Nâsir: 1054 - 1058 a.D.

3. 'Isâ ibn Muhammad al-Mudaffar: 1058 - 1063 a.D.

Silves annexed to the Kingdom of Seville.

Kingdom of Denia and the Balearic Isles

1. Mugâhid al-Muwaffaq: 1009 - 1044 a.D.

2. 'Alî ibn Mugâhid Iqbal ad-dawla: 1044 - 1076 a.D.

Denia annexed to the Kingdom of Saragossa.

Kingdom of Toledo: The Banû Dhi n-Nûn

1. Ismâ'îl ibn Dhi n-Nûn al-Dâfir: 1036 - 1043 a.D.

2. Yahyâ ibn Ismâ'îl al-Ma'mûn: 1043 - 1075 a.D.

3. Yahyâ ibn Ismâ'îl al-Qâdir: 1075 - 1085 a.D.
Toledo taken by Alfonso VI of Castile.

Kingdom of Saragossa: the Banû Tugîb

1. al-Mundhir ibn Yahyâ: 1017 - 1023 a.D.

2. Yahyâ ibn al-Mundhir
   al-Mudaffar: 1023 - 1029 a.D.

3. al-Mundhir ibn Yahyâ ibn
   al-Mundhir Mu'izz ad-dawla: 1029-1039

Kingdom of Saragossa: The Banû Hûd

1. Sulaimân ibn Muhammad ibn
   Hûd al-Musta'în: 1039 - 1046 a.D.

2. Ahmad ibn Sulaimân
   al-Muqtadir: 1046 - 1081 a.D.

al-Mu'tamid of Seville and his viziers
Ibn 'Ammâr and Ibn Rashîq: until 1090 a.D.

Kingdom of Niebla: The Banû Yahyâ

1. Ahmad ibn Yahyâ al-Yahsubî
Tâg ad-Dîn: 1023 - 1041 a.D.

3. Yûsuf ibn Ahmad al-Mu'tamid: 1081 - 1085 a.D.
4. Ahmad ibn Yûsuf al-Musta'în: 1085 - 1110 a.D.
5. 'Abd al-Malik ibn Ahmad
'Imâd ad-dawla: 1110 a.D.

Saragossa taken by the Almoravids in 1110 and conquered by the Christians in 1118.

The Almoravids

1. Yahya b. Ibrâhîm al-Gaddâlî

2. Yahya b. 'Umar
(d. 448 H./1057)

3. Abû Bakr b. 'Umar
(d. 480 H./ 1087-1088)

4. Yûsuf b. Tâshfîn, amîr
al-muslimîn: 453 - 500 H.
1061 - 1107 a.D.

5. Alî b. Yûsuf, amîr al-muslimîn: 500 - 537 H.
1107 - 1143 a.D.

6. Tâshfîn b. 'Alî, amîr
al-muslimîn: 537 - 539 or 541 H.
1143 - 1145 or 1147 a.D.

7. Ibrâhîm b. Tâshfîn, amîr
al-muslimîn: dethroned immediately.

8. Ishâq b. 'Alî, amîr al-muslimîn: killed in the siege of
Marrakesh.

The Almohads

1. Muhammad b. Tumart
al-Mahdî: 515 - 522 H.
1121 - 1128 a.D.

2. Abd al-Mu'mîn, amîr
al-mu'minîn: 522 - 558 H.
1128 - 1163 a.D.

3. Abû Ya'qûb Yûsuf, amîr,
al-mu'minîn: 558 - 580 H.
1163 - 1184 a.D.

4. Abû Yûsuf Ya'qûb al-Mansûr,
amîr al-mu'minîn: 580 - 595 H.
1184 - 1199 a.D.

5. Muhammad al-Nâsir, amîr
al-mu'minîn: 595 - 610 H.
1199 - 1214 a.D.

6. Yûsuf al-Mustansir, amîr
al-mu'minîn: 611 - 620 H.
1214 - 1224 a.D.

7. 'Abd al-Wâhid al-Makhlû', amîr
al-mu'minîn: 620 - 621 H.
1224 - 1224 a.D.

8. al-Âdil, amîr al-mu'minîn: 621 - 624 H.
1224 - 1227 a.D.

9. al-Ma'mûn, amîr al-mu'minîn: 624 - 630 H.
1227 - 1232 a.D.

10. al-Rashîd, amîr al-mu'minîn: 630 - 640 H.
1232 - 1242 a.D.

11. al-Sa'îd, amîr al-mu'minîn: 640 - 646 H.
1242 - 1248 a.D.

12. Al-Murtadâ, amîr al-minîn: 646 - 665 H.
1248 - 1266 a.D.

13. Abû l-'Ulâ' Abû Dabbûs, amîr
al-mu'minîn: 665 - 668 H.
1266 - 1269 a.D.

The Nasrids of Granada

1. Farag Muhammad I: 1237 - 1273 a.D.

2. Muhammad II: 1273 - 1302 a.D.

3. Muhammad III: 1302 - 1309 a.D.

4. Nasr: 1309 - 1314
1314 - 1322 a.D.

5. Ismâ'îl I: 1314 - 1325 a.D.

6. Muhammad IV: 1325 - 1333 a.D.

7. Yûsuf I: 1333 - 1354 a.D.

8. Muhammad V: 1354 - 1359
1362 - 1391 a.D.

9. Yûsuf V: 1445 - 1446 a.D.
September - December 1462

10. Muhammad VI: 1360 - 1362 a.D.

11. Yûsuf II	1391 - 1392 a.D.	17. Yûsuf V:	1445 - 1446 a.D.
12. Muhammad VII:	1392 - 1408 a.D.	18. Muhammad X:	January - June 1445 1446 - 1447 a.D.
13. Yûsuf III:	1408 - 1417 a.D.		
14. Muhammad VIII:	1417 - 1419 1427 - 1429 a.D.	19. Muhammad XI:	1451 - 1452 1453 - 1454 a.D.
15. Muhammad IX:	1419 - 1427 1430 - 1431 1432 - 1445 a.D. 1447 - 1453 1454	20. Sa'd:	1454 - 1462 1462 - 1464 a.D.
		21. Abû Hasan 'Ali:	1464 - 1482 1482 - 1485 a.D.
16. Yûsuf IV:	January 1431 - April 1432	22. Muhammad XII Boabdil):	1482 1486 - 1492 a.D.

Bibliography

General Works

E. Atiyah, *Gli Arabi*, Bologna 1962.

AA.VV. *Arabic Islamic Bibliography*, Hassocks 1977.

M. van Berchem, *Corpus Inscriptionum Arabicarum* (C.I.A.). First part: *Egypte*, I, Cairo 1894-1903; *Egypte*, II Cairo 1929-1930; second part: *Syrie du Nord*, I, Cairo 1909; *Syrie du Nord*, II, Cairo 1954-'56; *Syrie du Sud*, Cairo 1920-'49; third part: *Asie Mineure*, I, Cairo 1910-'17.

R. Blachère, *Histoire de la Littérature Arabe des origines à la fin du* XV *siècle de J.C.*, Paris 1952-'66, 3 vols.

C. Brockelman, *Geschichte der Islamischen Völker und Staaten*, Munich 1943²; Eng. tr. New York 1947; Fr. tr. Paris 1949.

C. Brockelmann, *Geschichte der Arabischen Literatur*, Weimar-Berlin 1898-1902, 2 vols., and 3 vols. of *Supplementbände*, Leiden 1937-1942.

L. Caetani, *Cronografia generale del bacino mediterraneo e dell'Oriente musulmano dal 622 al 1517 dell'Era Volgare*, Rome 1923.

L. Caetani, *Annali dell'Islam*, Milan 1905-'07.

C. Cahen, *Les peuples musulmans dans l'histoire médiévale*, Damascus 1977. *Cambridge (The) History of Islam*, compiled by P.M. Holt-A.K.S. Lambton-B. Lewis, Cambridge 1970, 2 vols.

Encyclopédie de l'Islam, 1st ed. Leiden-Paris 1913-'33, 4 vols. and 1 supplementary vol.; 2nd ed. Leiden-Paris 1954.

R. Ettinghausen, *A Selected and Annotated Bibliography of Books and Periodicals in Western Languages Dealing with the Near and Middle East*, Washington 1952.

F. Gabrieli, *Aspetti della civiltà arabo-islamica*, Rome 1956.

F. Gabrieli, *Gli Arabi*, 2nd ed. Florence 1975.

F. Gabrieli, *Storia della letteratura araba*, Florence 1967.

F. Gabrieli, *Gli Arabi nel Mediterraneo*, Rome 1970.

F. Gabrieli, *L'Islam nella storia. Saggi di storia e storiografia musulmana*, Bari 1966.

G. Gabrieli, *Manuale di bibliografia musulmana*, Rome 1916.

M. Gaudefroy-Demombynes, *Les institutions musulmanes*, Paris 1950.

H.A.R. Gibb, *Arabic Literature*, London 1963².

G.E. von Grunebaum, *Medieval Islam*, Chicago 1954².

H.W. Hazard-H.L. Cooke, *Atlas of Islamic History*, Princeton 1954³.

P.K. Hitti, *History of the Arabs*, London 1956⁶; It. tr. by P. Attendoli, *Storia degli Arabi*, Florence 1966.

M. Jimenez Ocaña, *Tablas de conversión de datas islámicas a cristianas*, Madrid 1946.

S. Lane-Poole, *The Mohammedan Dynasties*, Beirut 1966.

B. Lewis, *The Arabs in History*, London 1950.

K. Miller, *Mappae Arabicae*, Stuttgart 1926-1931, 3 vols.

A. Miquel, *L'Islam et sa civilisation au* VIIᵉ-XXᵉ *siècle*, Paris 1968; It. tr. by A. Francisi, *L'Islam. Storia di una civiltà*, Turin 1975.

A. Miquel, *La littérature Arabe*, Paris 1969.

A. Miquel, *Géographie humaine du monde musulman*, I, Paris 1975.

Occident (L') e l'Islam nell'Alto Medioevo, Spoleto 1965.

F.M. Pareja, *Islamologia*, Rome 1951.

J.D. Pearson, *Index Islamicus*, Cambridge 1958, 1962, 1966.

X. de Planhol, *Les fondaments géographiques de l'histoire de l'Islam*, Paris 1968.

U. Rizzitano, *Studi di storia islamica in Egitto (1940-1952)*, «Oriente Moderno», 33 (1953), 442-456.

F. Rosenthal, *A History of Muslim Historiography*, Leiden 1952.

J. Sauvaget, *Introduction à l'histoire de l'orient musulman*, Paris 1961.

F. Sezgin, *Geschichte des arabischen Schrifttsums*, Leiden 1967.

B. Spuler, *Geschichte der Islamischen Länder*, Vol. 1: *Die Calif enzeit: Entstehung und Zerfall des Islamischen Weltreiches*, Leiden 1952.

B. Spuler - L. Forrer, *Der Vordere Orient in islamischer Zeit*, Berne 1954.

    Studi orientalistici in onore di G. Levi Della Vida, Rome 1956, 2 vols.

    Studi orientalistici offerti a F. Gabrieli nel sessantesimo compleanno, Rome 1964.

G. Vajda, *Album de paléographie arabe*, Paris 1958.

L. Veccia Vaglieri, *L'Islam da Maometto al secolo* XVI, Milan 1974.

G. Weil, *Geschichte der Chalifen*, Stuttgart 1846-'62, 5 vols.

J. Wellhausen, *Das Arabische Reish und sein Sturz*, Berlin 1902.

E. de Zambaur, *Manuel de généalogie et de chronologie pour l'histoire de l'Islam*, Hanover 1927.

On the Birth of Islam and its Initial Expansion

'Abd al-Galîl, *Aspects intérieurs de l'Islam*, Paris 1949.

G.C. Anawati - L. Gardet, *Mystique musulmane*, Paris 1961; It. tr. *Mistica musulmana*, Turin 1960.

T. Andrae, *Muhammed: sein Leben und sein Glaube*, Gottingen 1932; It. tr. by F. Gabrieli, *Maometto, la sua vita e la sua fede*, Bari 1934.

T. Andrae, *Islamischer Mystiker*, Stuttgart 1960.

    Antica (L') società beduina, compiled by F. Gabrieli, Rome 1959.

T.W. Arnold - A. Guillaume, *The Legacy of Islam*, Oxford 1931.

    Atlas of the Arab world the Middle East, London-New York 1960.

A. Bausani, *Il Corano*, Florence 1978.

R. Bell, *The Origin of Islam and its Christian Environment*, London 1926.

R. Blachère, *Le Coran*, Paris 1949-'51, 2 vols.

R. Blachère, *Introduction au Coran*, Paris 1959.

F. Buhl, *Das Leben Muhammads*, Leipzig 1930.

al-Bukhârî, *Sahîh*, edited by L. Krehl - T. Juynboll, Leiden 1862-1908; Fr. tr. *Les Traditions islamiques*, edited by O. Houdas - W. Marçais, Paris 1903-'14, 4 vols.

L. Caetani, *Annali dell'Islam*, Milan 1905-'26, 10 vols.

A. Carra de Vaux, *Les penseurs de l'Islam*, Paris 1921-'26, 5 vols.

R.E. Cheesman, *In unknown Arabia*, London 1926.

E. Dermenghem, *La vie de Mahomet*, Paris 1950; It. tr., *Maometo*, Milan 1964.

C.M. Doughty, *Travels in Arabia Deserta*, London 1922.

R. Eldon, *The Holy Cities of Arabia*, London 1928, 2 vols.

A.A.A. Fyzee, *Introduction to the Study of Mahomedan Law*, London 1931.

F. Gabrieli, *Maometto*, Novara 1972.

F. Gabrieli, *Maometto e le grandi conquiste arabe*, Milan 1967.

L. Gardet, *La Cité musulmane*, Paris 1954.

L. Gardet - M.M. Anawati, *Introduction à la théologie musulmane. Essai de théologie comparée*, Paris 1948.

M. Gaudefroy - Demombynes, *Les institutions musulmanes*, Paris 1921.

I. Goldziher, *Le dogme et la loi de l'Islam*, Paris 1921.

I. Goldziher, *Muhammedanische Studien*, Halle 1889-'90, 2 vols.

C.E. von Grunebaum, *Islam: Essays in the Nature and Growth of a Cultural Tradition*, London 1961.

A. Guillaume, *The Traditions of Islam, An Introduction to the Study of the Hadîth Literature*, Oxford 1924; It. tr., *Islam*, Bologna 1961.

M. Hamidullah, *Le Prophète de l'Islam*, Paris 1959, 2 vols.

M. Horten, *Die Philosophie des Islam*, Munich 1924.

J. Kraemer, *Das Problem der islamischen Kulturgeschichte*, Tübingen 1959.

H. Lammens, *L'Islam, croyances et institutiones*, Beirut 1941.

H. Laoust, *Les schismes dans l'Islam*, Paris 1965.

H. Lammens, *Le berceau de l'Islam. L'Arabie occidentale à la veille de l'Hégire*, Rome 1914.

L. Massignon, *Recueil de textes inédits concernant l'histoire de la mystique en pays d'Islam*, Paris 1929.

C.A. Nallino, *Raccolta di scritti editi e inediti*, 1939-'48, 6 vols.

C.A. Nallino, *Vita di Maometto*, Rome 1946.

S. Noja, *Maometto profeta dell'Islam*, Fossano 1974.

Th. Nöldeke, *Geschichte des Qor'ans*, Leipzig 1909-'38, 3 vols.

Th. Nöldeke, *Geschichte der Perser und Araber zur Zeit der Sassaniden*, Leiden 1879.

D. Santillana, *Istituzioni di diritto musulmano malichita*, Rome 1926.

J. Sauvaget, *Introduction à l'histoire musulmane*, Paris 1961.

J. Schacht, *The Origins of Muhammaidan Jurisprudence*, Oxford 1950.

A.S. Tritton, *Muslim Theology*, London 1947.

K.S. Twitchel, *Saudi Arabia*, London 1947.

A.A. Vasiliev, *Bysance et les Arabes*, Brussels 1935-'50.

Vita e detti di santi musulmani compiled by V. Vacca, Turin 1968.

W.M. Watt, *Free Will and Predestination in Early Islam*, London 1948.

W.M. Watt, *Muhammad at Mecca*, Oxford 1953.

W.M. Watt, *Muhammad at Medina*, Oxford 1956.

W.M. Watt, *Muhammad, Prophet and Statesman*, London 1961.

G. Weil, *Geschichte der Chalifen*, Stuttgart 1846-'62, 5 vols.

A.J. Wensinck, *Handbook of Early Muhammedan Tradition*, Leiden 1927.

A.J. Wensinck, *Concordances et indices de la tradition musulmane*, Leiden 1933.

On the Conquest of Mediterranean Africa

C.H. Becker, *Beiträge zur Geschichte Aegyptens unter dem Islam*, Strasburg 1902-'03.

A. Bel, *La religion musulmane en Berbérie*, Paris 1938.

F. Braundel, *La Méditerranée et le monde méditerranéen à l'époque de Philippe* II, Paris 1949.

R. Brunschvig, *La Berbérie Orientale sous les Hafsides*, Paris 1940-'47, 2 vols.

A.J. Butler, *The Arab Conquest of Egypt and the Last Thirty Years of the Roman Dominion*, Oxford 1902.

M. Caudel, *Les premières invasions arabes dans l'Afrique du Nord*, Paris 1900.

N. Daniel, *Islam and the West*, Edinburgh 1960.

J. Despois, *L'Afrique du Nord*, Paris 1964.

G. Deverdun, *Marrakesh des origines à 1912*, Rabat 1959.

G. Drague, *Esquisse d'une histoire religieuse du Maroc*, Paris 1951.

H. Fournel, *Les Berbères. Etude sur le conquête de l'Afrique par les Arabes d'après les textes arabes imprimés*, Paris 1875-'81.

E. Fritsch, *Islam und Christentum im Mittelalter*, Breslau 1930.

S. Goitein, *The unity of the mediterranean world in the Middle Ages*, «Studia Islamica», 1960.

E.F. Gauthier, *Les siècles obscurs du Maghreb. L'islamisation de l'Afrique du Nord*, Paris 1927.

I. Goldziher, *Materialen zur Kenntnis der Almohadenbewegung in Nord Afrika*, «Zeitschrift der Deutschen Morgenländischen Gesellschaft», 1887, 30-140.

L. Golvin, *Le Magrib central à l'époque des Zirides*, Paris 1957.

S. Gsell-G. Marçais-G. Iver, *Histoire d'Algérie*, Paris 1927.

H.E. Idris, *La Berbérie orientale sous les Zirides* (X^e-XIIe *siècle*), Paris 1959.

C.A. Julien, *Histoire de l'Afrique du Nord (Tunisie, Algérie, Maroc). De la conquête arabe à 1830*, Paris 1956.

J.F.R. Hopkins, *Medieval Muslim Government in Barbary until the Sixth Century of the Hijra*, London 1958.

A. Huici Miranda, *Historia politica del imperio almohade*, Tetuan 1956-1957.

R. Le Tourneau, *Fez in the Age of the Marinides*, Norman 1961.

E. Lévi-Provençal, *Islam d'Occident: études d'histoire médiévale*, Paris 1948.

E. Lévi-Provençal, *Les historiens des Chorfa*, Paris 1922.

B. Lewis, *Naval Power and Trade in the Mediterranean, A.D. 500-1100*, Princeton 1951.

B. Lewis, *The Origins of Ismâ'ilism: a Study of the Historical Background of the Fâtimid Caliphate*, Cambridge 1940.

H. Mamour, *Polemics on the origins of the Fatimi Caliphs*, London 1934.

G. Marçais, *Les Arabes en Berbérie du* XIe *au* XIVe *siècle*, Constantine-Paris 1913.

G. Marçais, *La Berbérie musulmane et l'orient au Moyen Age*, Paris 1946.

W. Marçais, *Comment l'Afrique du Nord a été arabisée*, in *Articles et conférences*, Paris 1961.

L. Massignon, *Le Maroc dans les premières années du* XVIe *siècle*, Algiers 1906.

W. Niemeyer, *Aegypten zur Zeit der Mamluken. Ein kultur-landeskündige Skizze*, Berlin 1936.

F. Quatrèmere, *Histoire des sultans mamelouks*, Paris 1837-1845, 2 vols.

P. Sebag, *La Tunisie*, Paris 1951.

R. Strothmann, *Berber und Ibâditen*, «Der Islam», 1928, 258-279.

H. Terrasse, *Histoire du Maroc des origines à l'établissement du protectorat français*, Casablanca 1949-'50.

P.J. Vatikiotis, *The Fatimid Theory of State*, Lahore 1957.

M. Vonderheyden, *La Berbérie orientale sous la dynastie des Banoût 'l-Arlab, 800-909*, Paris 1927.

T.H. Weir, *The Shaikhs of Morocco in the* XVIth *Century*, Edinburgh 1904.

G. Wiet, *L'Egypte musulmane de la conquête arabe à la conquête ottomane*, Paris 1938.

F. Wüstenfeld, *Die Statthalter von Aegypten zur Zeit der Chalifen*, «Abh.d kön. Ges. d. Wiss. Göttingen», 1875.

F. Wüstenfeld, *Geschichte der Fatimiden Chalifen*, Göttingen 1881.

Saracen Raids in Europe

A. Abbantuono, *I Saraceni in Puglia*, «Japigia», 1931, 318-339.

N. Aberg, *The Occident and the Orient in the Art of the Seventeenth Century. Part.* II. *Lombard Italy*, Stockholm 1955.

R. Basset, *Les documents arabes sur l'éxpédition de Charlemagne en Espagne*, «Revue Historique», 1904, 286-295.

A. Bausani, *Islamic Influences on Italian Culture*, «Pakistan Quarterly», 1966, 45-53.

E. Bertaux, *Les arts de l'Orient musulman dans l'Italie Méridionale*, «Mélanges d'archéologie et d'histoire», 1895, 41-453.

N. Cilento, *I Saraceni nell'Italia meridionale nei secoli* IX *e* X, «Archivio storico per le province napoletane», n.s., 1958, 109-122.

R. Corso, *Tracce arabe in Calabria*, «Archivio storico per la Calabria e la Lucania», 1955, 337-411.

Ch. Daras, *Réflexions sur les influences arabes dans la décoration romane des églises charantaises*, in *Mélanges offerts à René Crozet à l'occasion de son soixante-dixième anniversaire*, Poitiers 1966, 751-753.

A. Dardanelli, *Invasioni arabe in Provenza, Savoia e Piemonte sul finire del secolo* IX *e nel secolo* X, Rome 1904.

C. Enlart, *L'église du West en boulonnais et son portail arabe*, «Gazette des Beaux Arts», 1927, I-II.

A. Fikry, *L'art roman du Puy et ses influences islamiques*, Paris 1934.

F. Gabrieli, *La storiografia arabo-islamica in Italia*, Naples 1975.

F. Gabrieli, *Taranto araba*, «Cenacolo», 1974.

F. Gabrieli, *Gli utlimi Saraceni in Italia*, «Nuova Antologia, 1978, 144-150.

J. Gay, *L'Italie méridionale et l'Empire Byzantin depuis l'avènement de Basile* I *jusqu'à la prise de Bari par les Normands (867-1071)*, Paris 1904.

I. Guidi, *La descrizione di Roma nei geografi arabi*, «Archivio della Società romana di storia patria», 1878, 173-218.

Hasan el-Basha, *A forgotten Islamic influence in the Art of the Renaissance*, «Minbar al-Islam», 1960, 74-81.

H.A.R. Gibb, *The Influence of Islamic Culture on Medieval Europe*, «Bulletin of the John Rylands Library», 1955-'56, 89-98.

C. Inostransev, *Note sur les rapports de Rome et du Califat abbaside au commencent du* Xᵉ *siècle*, «Rivista degli Studi Orientali», 1911-'12, 81-86.

J. Lacam, *Vestiges de l'occupation arabe en Narbonnaise*, «Cahiers archéologiques», 1956, 93-115.

J. Lacam, *Les Sarrazins dans le haut Moyen Age français*, Paris 1965.

P. Lambert, *L'art hispano-mauresque et l'art roman*, «Hespéris», 1933, 29-43.

G. Levi Della Vida, *Berta di Toscana e il califfo Mùktafi*, in *Aneddoti e svaghi arabi e non arabi*, Milan-Naples 1959, 26-44.

G. Levi Della Vida, *La sottoscrizione araba di Riccardo di Lucera*, «Rivista degli Studi Orientali», 1923-'25, 284-292.

B. Lupi, *I Saraceni in Provenza, in Liguria e nelle Alpi Occidentali*, Bordighera 1952.

M.A. Marzouq, *Influences of the Arabian Art on the European Medieval Arts, as portrayed in its Fabrics, Metal-Work, Ceramics preserved in the Museums of the West*, «The Islamic Review», 1970, 23-29.

P. Martini, *Storia delle invasioni degli arabi e delle piraterie dei Barbareschi in Sardegna*, Cagliari 1861.

G. Marçais, *Sur l'inscription arabe de la cathédrale de Puy*, in Mélanges d'histoire et d'archéologie de l'Occident musulman, Algiers 1957, I, 205-210.

A. Molinié-H. Zotenberg, *Invasion des Sarrazins dans le languedoc d'après les historiens musulmans*, in *Histoire générale du Languedoc*, Toulouse 1875, II, 549-558.

U. Monneret de Villard, *Le capiteau arabe de la Cathédrale de Pise*, «Comptes Rendus de l'Académie des Inscriptions et Belles Lettres», 1946, 17-23.

G. Musca, *L'emirato di Bari, 847-871*, Bari 1978.

M. Nallino, *Venezia in antichi scrittori arabi*, «Annali di Ca' Foscari», 1963.

C. Patrucco, *I Saraceni in Piemonte e nelle Alpi Occidentali*, «Biblioteca della Società Storica Subalpina», 1908.

J.T. Reinaud, *Les invasions des Sarrazins en France, en Savoie-Piémont et dans la Suisse*, Paris 1836.

C. Schiapparelli, *Notizie d'Italia estratte dall'opera di Sihâb ad-Dîn al-Umarî, intitolata Masâlik al-absâr*, «Rendiconti della Reale Accademia dei Lincei. Classe di Scienze Morali», 1888, 304-316.

L. Spinelli, *Gli Arabi in Sardegna*, Cagliari 1976.

L. Veccia Vaglieri, *Musulmani e Sardegna*, «Atti del Congresso di Studi nordafricani», Cagliari 1965, 233-240.

Muslim Spain

M. al-'Abbâdî, *Muhammad* v, *al-Ghanî bi-illâh, rey de Granada (755-760 H./ 1354-1359 y 763-793 H./ 1362-1391)*, «Revista del Instituto de Estudios Islamicos», 1963-'64, 209-327; 1965-'66, 43-102; 1967-'68, 139-173.

'Abd al-Wâhid al-Marrâkushî, *al-Mu'gib fî talkhîs ta'rîkh al-Maghrib*, ed. R. Dozy, *The History of the Almohades*, Leiden 1845; Fr. tr. E. Fagnan, *Histoire des Almohades*, Algiers 1893.

Abu-l-Fidâ, *al-Mukhtasar fî akhbâr al-bashar*, Cairo 1325 H., 4 vols.

Akhbâr Magmû'a, ed. and Span. tr. by E. Lafuente y Alcantara, Madrid 1867.

M. Alarcón y Santón - R. Garcia de Linares, *Los Documentos arabes diplomaticos del Archivo de la Corona de Aragón*, Madrid-Granada 1940.

I.S. Allouche, *La vie économique et sociale à Grenade au* XIV *siècle*, in *Mélanges d'histoire et d'archéologie de l'Occident musulman*, Algiers 1957, II/7-12.

R. Arié, *Quelques remarques sur le costume des musulmans d'Espagne au temps des Nasrides*, «Arabica», 1965.

R. Arié, *Les relations diplomatiques et culturelles entre les Musulmans d'Espagne et les Musulmans d'Orient au temps des Nasrides*, in *Mélanges de la Casa de Velasquez*, I, 1965, 87-107.

R. Arié, *L'Espagne musulmane au temps des Nasrides (1232-1492)*, Paris 1973.

E. Ashtor, *History of the Jews in Muslim Spain*, Philadelphia 1969.

E. Ashtor, *Che cosa sapevano i geografi arabi dell'Europa*, «Rivista Storica Italiana», 1969, 453-479.

M. Asin Palacios, *Abenhazam de Cordoba y su historia de las ideas religiosas*, Madrid 1927-'28.

al-Bakrî, *Description de l'Afrique septentrionale*, ed. M.G. de Slane, Algiers 1911; Fr. tr. by de Slane, Algiers 1913.

A. Ballestreros Beretta, *Sevilla en el siglo* XIII, Madrid 1913.

R. Blanchère, *Un pionnier de la culture arabe orientale en Espagne au* Xᵉ *siècle. Sâ'id de Baghdâd*, «Hesperis», 1930, 15-36.

R. Blachère, *La vie et l'œuvre du poète-épistolier andalou Ibn Darrâg al-Qastallî*, «Hespéris», 1923, 99-121.

J. Maurel Bosque, *Geografia urbana de Granada*, Saragossa 1962.

F. Braudel, *La Méditerranée et le monde méditerranéen à l'époque de Philippe* II, *Paris 1966, 2 vols.*

I. Cagigas de las, *Los Mozarabes*, Madrid 1947-'48, 2 vols.

I. Cagigas de las, *Los Mudejares*, Madrid 1948-'49.

G. Chejne Anwar, *Muslim Spain: its History and Culture*, Minneapolis 1975.

F. Codera y Zaidin, *Decadencia y disparicion de los Almoravides en España*, Saragossa 1899.

G.S. Colin, *Quelques poètas arabes d'Occident au* XIVᵉ *siècle*, «Hespéris», 1931, 241-247.

A. Cour, *Un poète arabe d'Andalousie; Ibn Zaidoûn*, Constantine 1920.

N. Daniel, *The Arabs and Medieval Europe*, London-Beirut 1975.

J. Dickie, *The Hispano-Arab garden: its philosophy and function*, «Bulletin of the School of Oriental and African Studies», 1968, 237-248.

L. Di Giacomo, *Une poétesse grenadine du temps des Almohades: Hasfa bint al-Hâjj*, Paris 1949.

R. Dozy, *Histoire des Musulmans d'Espagne jusqu'à la conquête de l'Andalousie par les Almoravides*, Leiden 1932, 3 vols.

R. Dozy, *Recherches sur l'histoire et la littérature des Arabes d'Espagne pendant le Moyen Age*, Leiden 1881, 2 vols.

Ch. E. Dufourcq, *L'Espagne catalane et le Maghrib au* XIIIᵉ *at* XIVᵉ *siècle*, Paris 1966.

Ch. Dufourcq, *La vie quotidienne dans l'Europe médiévale sous la domination arabe*, Paris 1978.

D.M. Dunlop, *The British Isles according to Medieval Arabic authors*, «Islamic Quarterly», 1957, 11-28.

F. Gabrieli, *Arabi e Bizantini nel Mediterraneo centrale*, «Bollettino dell'Istituto Storico Italiano per il Medio Evo e Archivio Muratoriano», 1964, 31-46.

F. Gabrieli, *Arabi di Sicilia e Arabi di Spagna*, «Al-Andalus», 1950, 27-46.

E. Garcia-Gomez, *Cinco poetas musulmanes. Biografias y estudios*, Madrid 1944.

E. Garcia Gomez, *Poemas arabigoandaluces*, Madrid 1930.

E. Garcia Gomez, *Poetas musulmanes cordobeses*, «Boletin de la Real Academia de ciencias, bellas letras y nobles artes de Cordoba», 1929, 145-176.

A. Gonzales Palencia, *Historia de la literatura arabigo-española*, Barcelona 1928.

A. Gonzales Palencia, *Historia de la España musulmana*, Barcelona-Buenos-Aires 1940.

H. Gousson, *Die christlisch-arabische Literatur der Mozaraber*, Leipzig 1909.

G. Graf, *Die christlisch-arabische Literatur bis zum fränkischen zeit*, Freiburg in Breisgau 1905.

G. Graf, *Geschichte der Christlichen arabischen Literatur*, Vatican City 1944-'53, 5 vols.

I. Guidi, *L'Europa Occidentale negli antichi geografi arabi*, in *Florilegium Melchior de Vogüé*, Paris 1909, 263-269.

W. Heyd, *Histoire du commerce dans le Levant au Moyen Age*, Leipzig 1923.

W. Hoenerbach, *Les parentés islamo-chrétiennes dans la diplomatique de l'Espagne médiévale*, Laos 1961.

W. Hoenerbach, *Spanisch-Islamische Urkunden aus der Zeit der narsiden und moriscos*, Berkeley-Los Angeles 1965.

J.F.P. Hopkins, *An Andalusian poet of the 14th Century: Ibn al-Hâgg*, «Bulletin of the School of Oriental and African Studies», 1961, 57-64.

A. Huici Miranda, *Las Grandes Batallas de la Reconquista durante las invasiones africanas*, Madrid 1956.

A. Huici Miranda, *Historia politica del Imperio Almohade*, Tetuan 1956-'57, 2 vols.

Ibn al-Abbâr, *al-Hullat as-siyarâ'*, ed. R. Dozy, *Notices sur quelques manuscrits arabes*, Leiden 1847-'51, 30-260; ed. H. Monès, Cairo 1963.

Ibn 'Abd al-Hakam, *Futûh Misr*, ed. C.C. Torrey, Yale Oriental Series 1922.

Ibn 'Abdûn, *Traité de Hisba; un document sur la vie et les corps de métier à Séville au début du* XIIe *siècle*, ed. E. Lévi-Provençal, «Journal Asiatique», 1934, 177-299. Fr. tr. by E. Lévi-Provençal, *Séville musulmane au début du* XIIe *siècle: Le Traité d'Ibn 'Abdûn*, Paris 1947. It. tr. by F. Gabrieli. *Il trattato censorio di Ibn 'Abdûn sul buon governo in Siviglia*, «Rendiconti della R. Accademia nazionale dei Lincei. Classe di Scienze morali, storiche e filologiche», 1935, 878-935.

Ibn al-Athîr, *al-Kâmil fî ta 'rîkh*, ed. Torberg, Leiden- Uppsala 1850-'74 - 12 vols; abridged Fr. tr. by E. Fagnan, *Annales du Maghreb et de l'Espagne*, Algiers 1901.

Ibn Bassâm, *adh-Dhahîra fî mahâsin ahl al-gazîra*, Cairo 1939, 1940, 1947.

Ibn Battûta, *Rihla: Voyages*, Arabic text and Fr. tr. by Ch. Defrémery and B.R. Sanguinetti, Paris 1853-'59, 5 vols.

Ibn Fadl Allâh al'Umarî, *Masâlik al-absâr fî mamâlik al-amsâr: l'Afrique moins l'Egypte*, abridged Fr. tr. by M. Gaudefroy- Demombynes, Paris 1927.

Ibn Haiyân, *Muqtabis: Kitâb al-Muqtabis fî ta 'rîkh rigâl al-Andalus*, abridged ed. by P. Melchor M. Antuña, *Chronique du règne du calife umaiyade 'Abd Allâh à Cordoue*, Paris 1937. Ed. E. Lévi-Provençal for the part relative to the reigns of al-Hakam I and of 'Abd al-Rahmân II, Alexandria. Ed. P. Chalmeta for the reign of 'Abd al-Rahmân al-Nâsir, Madrid 1979. Ed. 'Abd al-Rahmân for the period 360-374 H., Beirut 1965.

Ibn Hawqal, *Kitâb al-masâlik wa-l-mamâlik*, Leiden 1873; 2nd ed. J.H. Kramers, Leiden 1938, 2 vols. Fr. tr. by De Slane, *Description de l'Afrique*, «Journal Asiatique», 1842, 153-196; 209-258.

Ibn Hazm, *Tawq al-hamâma fî-l-ulfa wa-l-ullâf*, ed. D.K. Pétrof, Leiden 1914. Fr. tr. by L. Bercher, *Le Collier du Pigeon ou de l'Amour et des Amants*, Algiers 1949, Eng. tr. by A.R. Nykl, *The Dove's Neck-Ring about Love and Lovers*, Paris 1931. Span. tr. by E. Garcia Gomez, *El Collar de la Paloma, tratado sobre el Amor y los Amantes*, Madrid 1952. It. tr. by F. Gabrieli, *il Collare della Colomba sull'Amore e gli Amanti*, Bari 1949.

Ibn Hazm, *Djamhara: Kitâb Djamharat ansâb al'Arab*, ed. E. Lévi-Provençal, Cairo 1948.

Ibn Khaldûn, *al-Muqaddima: les Prolégomènes. ed. Quatrèmère, Paris 1858-'68*, Fr. tr. by de Slane, Paris 1862-'68, Eng. tr. F. Rosenthal, New York 1958, 3 vols.

Ibn Khaldûn, *Kitâb al 'Ibar wa dîwân al-mubtada' wa-l-khabar fî ayyâm al' Arab wa-l-'Agan wa-l-Barbar wa man 'âsara-hum min dhawî as-sultân al-akbar*, Bûlâq 1284, 7 vols.

Ibn Khaldûn, *Histoire des Berbères, extraite du Kitâb al-'Ibar*, ed. M.G. de Slane, Algiers 1847-'51, 2 vols; Fr. tr. de Slane, Paris 1852-'56, 4 vols.

Ibn Khaldûn, *Histoire des Benou l'Ahmar, rois de Grenade, extraits du Kitâb al-'Ibar (Livre des Examples)*, Fr. tr. by M. Gaudefroy-Demombynes, «Journal Asiatique», 1898.

Ibn al-Khatîb, *Kitâb A'mal al-a'lâm fîman bûyi'a qabl al-ihtilâm min mulûl al-Islâm wa mâ yagurr dhalik min shugûn al-kalâm*, abridged ed. by E. Lévi-Provençal, *Histoire de l'Espagne musulmane*, Rabat 1935, Beirut 1956.

Ibn al-Khatîb, *al-Ihâta fî ta'rîkh Gharnâta*, abridged ed. Cairo 1347 H., 2 vols.

Ibn al-Khatîb, *Correspondencia diplomatica entre Granada y Fez (siglo* XIV*)*. Extracotos de la Raihamal al-Kuttab de Lisân aldîn Ibn al-Jatîb al-Andalusi, ed. and Span. tr. by M. Gaspar Remiro, «Revista del Centro de Estudios Historicos de Granada y su reino», Granada 1911-'16.

Ibn Gubair, *Rihla al-kinâni*, ed. and It. tr. by C. Schiaparelli, Rome 1906.

Ibn 'Idhârî, *Kitâb al-Bayân al-mughrib fî akhbâr mulûk al-Andalus wa-l-Maghrib*, ed. R. Dozy, Leiden 1848-'51; Fr. tr. by E. Fagnan, Algiers 1901-'04; vol. III, ed. E. Lévi-Provençal, Paris 1930.

Ibn al-Qâdî, *Durrat al-higâl fî ghurrat asmâ' al-rigâl*, ed. I.S. Allouche, Rabat 1934.

Ibn al-Qiftî, *Ta'rîkh al-hukamâ'*, ed. J. Lippert, Leipzig 1903.

Ibn Qutaiba, *ash-shi'r wa-sh-shu' arâ'*, ed. M.J. De Goeje, Leiden 1904.

Ibn al-Qutiyya, *Iftitâh: Ta'rîkh iftitâh al-Andalus*, ed. by P. De Gayangos - E. Saavedra - F. Codera, Madrid 1968; Span. tr. by J. Ribera, Madrid 1926.

Ibn Quzmân, *Dîwân: Cancionero*, abridged ed. and tr. by A.R. Nykl, Madrid - Granada 1933.

Ibn ars Rûmîi, *Dîwân: Extraits choisis*, ed. Kâmil Kîlânî, Cairo 1342 H./ 1924.

Ibn Rusta, *Description du Maghreb et de l'Europe du* IXe *siècle*, ed. and Fr. tr. by M. Hadj - Sadok, Algiers 1949.

H.R. Idrîs, *Le mariage en Occident musulman d'après un choix de fatwâs médiévales extraites du Milyâr d'al-wansharîsi*, «Studia Islamica», 1970, 157-165.

Al-Idrîsî, *Nuzhat al-mushtâq. Description de l'Afrique et de l'Espagne*, ed. and Fr. tr. by R. Dozy - M.J. de Goeje, Leiden 1866.

S.M. Imamuddin, *Some aspects of the socio-economic and cultural History of Muslim Spain, 711-1402 A.D.*, Leiden 1965.

Al-Kushani, *Qudat Qurtuba: Ta'rîkh qudat Qurtuba*, ed. and Span. tr. by J. Ribera, *Historia de los jueces de Cordoba*, Madrid 1914.

E. Lafuente y Alcantara, *Inscripciones arabes de Granada*, Madrid 1859.

H. Lapeyre, *Géographie de l'Espagne morisque*, Paris 1959.

E. Lévi-Provençal, *L'Espagne musulmane au* X^e *siècle. Institutions et vie sociale*, Paris 1932.

E. Lévi-Provençal, *Histoire de l'Espagne musulmane*, Paris-Leiden 1950-'53, 3 vols.

E. Lévi-Provençal, *Le Cid de l'histoire*, in *Islam d'Occident*, Paris 1948, 155-185.

E. Lévi-Provençal, *La Péninsule ibérique au Moyen Age d'après le Kitâb al-Rawd al-mi'târ d'Ibn 'Abd al-Mun'im al-Himyarî*, Arabic and Fr. texts by E. Lévi-Provençal, Leiden 1938.

E. Lévi-Provençal, *Documents arabes inédits sur la vie sociale et économique en Occident musulman au Moyen Age. Trois traités hispaniques de hisba*, Cairo 1955.

E. Lévi-Provençal, *Inscriptions arabes d'Espagne*, Leiden-Paris 1931.

T. Lewicki, *L'apport des sources arabes médiévales (IXᵉ-Xᵉ) à la conaissance de l'Europe centrale et orientale*, in *L'occidente e l'Islam nell'Alto Medioevo*, I, Spoleto 1965, 461-486.

B. Lewis, *The Muslim discovery of Europe*, «Bulletin of the School of Oriental and African Studies», 1957, 409-416.

P. Longas, *Vida religiosa de los moriscos*, Madrid 1915.

M.A. Makkî, *Ensayo sobre las aportaciones orientales y su influencia en la formacion de la culture hispano-arabe*, «Revista del Instituto de Estudios Islamicos», 1961-'62, 65-231.

Al-Maqqarî, *Nafh at-tîb min ghusn al-Andalus ar-ratîb wa dhikr wazîrihâ Lisân ad-Dîn Ibn al-Khatîb*, Bûlâq 1279 H./ 1862, 4 vols. Abridged ed. Leiden 1855-'61, 2 vols.

Marmol Carvajal (Luis de), *Historia de la rebelion y castigo de los moricos del reino de Granada*, Madrid 1798, 2 vols.

Mas-Latrie (L. de), *Traités de paix et de commerce concernant les relations des Chrétiens avec les Arabes de l'Afrique Septentrionale au Moyen Age*, Paris 1866.

L. Massignon, *Recherches sur Shushtarî, poète andalou enterré à Damiette*, in *Mélantes William Marçais*, Paris 1950, 251-276.

R. Menendez Pidal, *Historia de España*, Madrid 1966.

J. Monroe, *A curious morisco appeal to the Ottoman Empire*, «Al-Andalus», 1960, 281-303.

A. Nafis, *Muslim contribution to Geography*, Lahore 1947.

E. Neuvonen, *Los arabismos del español en el siglo XIII*, Helsinki 1941.

Al-Nubâhî, *Kitâb al-Marqata al-'ulyâ fî man yastahiqq al-qadâ' wa-l-fitya Histoire des juges d'Andalousie)*, ed. E. Lévi-Provençal, Cairo 1947.

Al-Nuwairî, *Nihâyat al-arab fî funûn al-adab*, Cairo 1923-'49, 15 vols; ed. and abridged Span. tr. by M. Gaspar Remiro, *Historia de las Musulmanes de España y Africa*, «Revista del Centro de Estudios historicos de Granada y su reino», Granada 1917-'19, 2 vols.

P. Nwiya, *Ibn Abbâd de Ronda (1332-'90)*, Beirut 1961.

H. Pérès, *La poésie andalouse en arabe classique au XIᵉ siècle; ses aspects généraux et sa valeur documentaire*, Paris 1953.

F. Pons Boigues, *Ensayo bio-bibliografico sobre los historiadores y geografos arabigo-españoles*, Madrid 1898.

A. Prieto y Vives, *Los reyes de taifas. Estudio historico numismatico de los musulmanes españoles en el siglo V de la hegira (XI de J.-C.)*, Madrid 1926.

Ramirez de Arellano - R. Diaz de Morales, *Historia de Cordoba desde su fundacion hasta la muerte de Isabel la Catolica*, Ciudad Real 1915-'17, 2 vols.

J. Ribera, *Historia de la conquista de España*, Madrid 1926.

E. Saavedra, *Estudio sobre la invasion de los Arabes en España*, Madrid 1892.

Cl. Sanchez Albornoz, *Estampas de la vida de Leon hace mil años*, Madrid 1926.

L. Seco de Lucena Paredes, *Documentos arabigo-granadinos*, Arabic text and Span. tr., Madrid 1961.

M.K. Shabâna, *Yûsuf al-awwal Ibn al-Ahmar, sultân Gharnâta (733-755 H.)*, Cairo 1969.

F.J. Simonet, *Historia de los Mozarabes de España*, Madrid 1897-1903.

F. Simonet, *Descripcion del reino de Granada bajo la dominacion de los Naseritas*, Granada 1872.

M. Souabah, *Une élégie andalouse sur la guerre de Grenade*, Algiers 1914-'19.

M. Steinschneider, *Die arabischen Literatur der Juden*, Frankfurt 1902.

S.M. Stern, *Les chanson mozarabes*, Oxford 1964.

H. Terrasse, *Le royaume nasrides dans la vie de l'Espagne du Moyen Age. Indications et problèmes*, in *Mélanges offerts à Marcel Bataillon par les hispanistes français*, Bordeaux 1963, 253-260.

D. de Valera, *Cronica de los Reyes Catolicos*, Madrid 1927.

W.M. Watt - P. Cachia, *Islamic Spain*, Edinburgh 1965.

J. Zurita, *Anales de la Cronaca de Aragon*, Saragossa 1610.

The General Characteristics of Art in the Muslim World

M. Aga-Oglu, Remarks on the Character of Islamic Art, «The Art Bulletin», 1954, 175-202.

T.W. Arnold, *Painting in Islam. A Study of the place of Pictorial Art in muslim culture*, Oxford 1928.

T.W. Arnold, *The Influence of Poetry and Theology on Painting*, in *Survey of Persian Art*, III, London 1909-'10.

T.W. Arnold, *Painting in Islam*, Oxford 1965.

Bishr Farès, *Essai sur l'esprit de la décoration islamique*, Cairo 1952.

E. Blochet, *Musulman Painting*, London 1927.

M.S. Briggs, *Muhammadan Architecture in Egypt and Palestine*, Oxford 1914.

N. Brunow, *Über einige allgemeine Probleme der Kunst des Islams. Kritische Bibliographie Islamischer Kunst 1914-'27*, «Der Islam», 1928, 121-248.

K.A.C. Creswell, *Early Muslim Architecture*, Oxford 1932-'40, 2 vols.

K.A.C. Creswell, *A Bibliography of Muslim Architecture of Egypt*, Cairo 1957.

K.A.C. Creswell, *A Bibliography of Muslim Architecture in North Africa*, Paris 1957.

K.A.C. Creswell, *The Lawfulness of Painting in Early Islam*, in *Ars Islamica*, XI-XII, Chicago 1946.

E. Diez, *Die Kunst der Islamischen Völker*, Berlin 1915.

M. Dimand, *L'arte dell'Islam*, Florence 1972.

R. Ettinghausen, *La Peinture Arabe*, Geneva 1962.

H. Glück - E. Diez, *Die Kunst des Islam*, Berlin 1925.

L. Golvin, *La Mosquée, ses origines, sa morphologie, ses diverses functions, son rôle dans la vie musulmane, plus spécialement en Afrique du Nord*, Algiers 1960.

L. Golvin, *Essai sur l'architecture religieuse musulmane*, Paris 1970-'73, 3 vols.

O. Grabar, *The formation of Islamic Art*, Yale University Press 1973.

L. Hautecoeur - G. Wiet, *Les Mosquées du Caire*, Paris 1932.

E. Herzfeld, *Die Genesis der Islamischen Kunst*, «Der Islam», 1910, 27-63; 105-1044.

C. Huart, *Les Calligraphes et les Miniaturistes de l'Orient musulman*, Paris 1908.

E. Kühnel, *Die Kunst des Islams*, Stuttgart 1962; It. tr. *L'Arte islamica*, Milan 1964.

E. Kühnel, *Die Moschee*, Berlin 1949.

E. Kühnel, *Islamic Art and Architecture*, Ithaca 1966.

E. Kühnel, *Die Arabeske*, Wiesbaden 1949.

G. Marçais, *L'art de l'Islam*, Paris 1946.

G. Marçais, *La question des images dans l'art musulman*, in *Mélanges d'histoire et d'archéologie de l'Occident Musulman*, I, Algiers 1957, 67-79.

L. Massignon, *Les méthodes de réalisation artistique des peuples d'Islam*, «Syria», 1921, 47-53; 149-160.

G. Migeon, *Manual d'art musulman*, Paris 1927, 2 vols.

A. Papadopoulo, *L'Esthétique de l'art musulman. La Peinture*, Paris-Lille 1972, 6 vols.

A. Papadopoulo, *L'Islam et l'art musulman*, Paris 1976.

J.D. Pearson - D.S. Rice, *Islamic Art and Archeology. A Register of Works Published in 1954*, London 1956.

A.M. Raymond, *L'art islamique en orient*, Paris 1926, 2 vols.

E. Richmond, *Moslem Architecture*, London 1926.

J. Sauvaget, *La mosquée omeyyade de Médine*, Paris 1947.

U. Scerrato, *Islam*, Milan 1972.

B. Spuler-J. Sourdel Thomine, *Die Kunst des Islam*, Berlin 1973.

D. Talbot-Rice, *Islamic Art*, London 1964.

G. Wiet, *Condidérations dur l'art musulman*, «Revue du Caire», 1938.

G. Wiet, *La valeur décorative de l'alphabet arabe*, «Arts et Métiers Graphiques 1935.

G. Wiet, *Les mosquées du Caire*, Paris 1966.

The Islamic Art of al-Andalus

Ahmad 'Isâ Bey, *Histoire des Bimaristan à l'époque islamique*, Cairo 1928.

Aleya Ibrâhîm el-Enany, *Tres telas granadinas*, «Revista del Instituto de Estudios Islamicos», 1954, 149-159.

S.A. Almagro y Cardena, *Estudio sobre las inscripciones arabes de Granada, con un apendice sobre su madrasa o Universidad arabe*, Granada 1879.

R. Amador de los Rios, *Inscripciones arabes de Cordoba*, Madrid 1880.

R. Amador de los Rios, *Inscripciones arabes de Sevilla*, «Museo Español de Antigüedades», 1875, 321-380.

R. Amador de los Rios, *Las pinturas de la Alhambra*, Madrid 1891.

Arco Ricardo (del), *La Aljaferia de Zaragoza*, «Arte español», 1924, 162-173.

J. Bermudez Pareja, *La fuente de los leones*, «Cuadernos de la Alhambra», 1967, 21-29.

C. Bernis, *Tapiceria hispanomusulmana (siglos IX-XI)*, «Archivio Español de Artel», 1954, 189-211; 1956, 95-115.

R. Brunschwig, *Urbanisme médiévale et droit musulman*, «Revue des Etudes Islamiques», 1947, 127-155.

Kh. Bukhari, *Calligraphy*, «Iqbal», 1959, 53-63.

P.B. Cott, *Siculo-Arabic Ivories*, Princeton 1939.

M.S. Dimand, *Two Fifteenth Century Hispano-Mauresque Rugs*, «Bulletin of the Metropolitan Museum of Arts», 1964, 341-352.

R. Ettinghausen, *Arab Painting*, Geneva 1962.

R. Ettinghausen, *Notes on the Lustreware of Spain*, «Arte Orientalis», 1954, 133-156.

A.W. Frottingham, *Spanish Glass*, London 1964.

E. Garcia Gomez - J. Bermudez Pareja, *La Alhambra; la Casa Real*, Granada 1968.

J.A. Gaya Nuño, *Gormaz, castillo califal*, «Al-Andalus», 1943, 431-456.

M. Gomez Moreno, *El Arte Arabe hasta los Almohades. Arte Mozarabe*, Madrid 1951.

M. Gomez Moreno, *Alhambra*, Barcelona 1922, 2 vols.

E. Guidoni, *Urbanistica islamica e città medievali europee*, «Storia della città», 1978, 4-10.

G. Hardendorff Burr, *Hispanic furniture from the 15th through 18th Century*, New York 1968.

A.H. Hourani, *The Islamic City*, Oxford 1970.

E. Kühnel, *Islamic Art and Architecture*, London 1966.

J. Lafond, *L'orientation des mosquées musulmanes*, «Bulletin de la Société Nationales des Antiquaires de France», 1945-'46-'47, 216-217.

E. Lafuente y Alcantara, *Inscriptiones arabes de Granada*, Madrid 1959.

E. Lambert, *Les mosquées de type andalou en Espagne et en Afrique du Nord*, «Al-Andalus», 1949, 273-289.

I.M. Lapidus, *Muslim Cities in the Later Middle Ages*, Cambridge, Mass. 1967.

L.M. Llubia, *Ceramica medieval española*, Barcelona 1967.

G. Marçais, *L'architecture musulmane d'Occident. Tunisie, Algérie, Maroc, Espagne et Sicile*, Paris 1955.

L.F. May, *Hispano-Mauresque Rugs*, «Notes Hispanic», 1945, 30-69.

L.F. May, *Silk Textiles of Spain: eighth to fifteenth Century*, New York 1957.

J.V. McMullan, *Islamic Carpets*, New York 1965.

G. Mehrez, *Las pinturas murales musulmanas en el Partal de la Alhambra*, Madrid 1951.

L.A. Meyer, *Islamic armourers and their works*, Geneva 1962.

G. Migeon, *Manuel d'art musulman*, Paris 1906.

A.R. Nykl, *Inscripciones arabes de la Alhambra y del Generalife*, «Al-Andalus», 1936, 174-194.

A.R. Nykl, *Arabic inscriptions of Portugal*, «Ars Islamica», 1946, 167-183.

G.J. Osma de, *Azulejos sevillanos del siglo* XIII, Madrid 1902.

B. Pavon, *Las almenas decorativas hispano-musulmanas*, Madrid 1967.

J. Sauvaget, *Introduction à l'étude de la céramique musulmane*, «Revue des Etudes Islamiques», 1965, 1-68.

U. Scerrato, *Metalli Islamici*, Milan 1966.

A. Schimmel, *Islamic Calligraphy*, Leiden 1970.

V. Strika, *Origini e sviluppi dell'urbanistica islamica*, «Rivista degli Studi Orientali», 1968, 53-72.

S. Tamari, *Aspetti principali dell'urbanesimo musulmano*, «Palladio», 1966, 45-82.

H. Terrasse, *L'art hispano-mauresque des origines au* XIIIᵉ *siècle*, Paris 1932.

H. Terrasse, *Les forteresses de l'Espagne musulmane*, Madrid 1954.

H. Terrasse, *La Grande Mosquée almohade de Séville*, in *Mémorial Henri Basset*, II, 249-266.

L. Torres Balbas, *Arte Almohade - Arte Nazari - Arte Mudejar*, Madrid 1949.

L. Torres Balbas, *Arte almoravide y almohade*, Madrid 1955.

L. Torres Balbas, *La Mezquita Real de la Alhambra y el baño frontero*, «Al-Andalus», 1945, 213-214.

L. Torres Balbas, *Plantas de casas arabes en la Alhambra*, «Al-Andalus», 1934, 380-387.

L. Torres Balbas, *La Alhambra*, Madrid 1953.

L. Torres Balbas, *Dâr al' arûsa y las ruinas de palacios y albercas granadinos situados por encima del Generalife*, «Al-Andalus», 1948, 185-203.

L. Torres Balbas, *El-Maristan de Granada*, «Al-Andalus», 1944, 481-498.

L. Torre Balbas, *La torre del Oro de Sevilla*, «Al-Andalus», 1934, 372-373.

J. Torres Ferrandis, *Alfombras antiguas españolas*, «Revista española de arte», 1933, 355-367.

J. Torres Ferrandis, *Muebles hispanoarabes de taracea*, «Al-Andalus», 1940, 13-21.

Muslim Sicily

'Abd al-Wahhab - F. Dachraoui, *Le régime foncier en Sicilie au Moyen Age* (IXᵉ-Xᵉ *siècle*). *Edition (Arabic text) and translation of a chapter of the Kitâb al-amwâl d'al-Dâwûdî*, in *Etudes d'orientalisme dédiés à la mémoire de Lévi-Provençal*. Paris 1962, II, 401-444.

Ahmad Aziz, *A History of Islamic Sicily*, Edinburgh 1975.

A. Airoldi, *Codice diplomatico di Sicilia sotto il governo degli Arabi*, Palermo 1789-'92, 3 vols.

M. Amari, *Storia dei musulmani di Sicilia*, Rome 1937.

M. Amari, *Biblioteca arabo-sicula*, Leipzig 1857-'87; It. tr., Turin-Rome 1880-'81.

M. Amari, *Le epigrafi arabiche di Sicilia*, Palermo 1879-'85.

G. Bellafiore, *La Zisa di Palermo*, Palermo 1978.

S. Braida Santamaura, *Il castello di Favara. Studi di restauro*, «Architettura di Sicilia», 1965.

S. Braida Santamaura, *Il palazzo ruggeriano di Altofonte*, «Palladio», 1973, 185-197.

M. Canard, *Quelques notes relatives à la Sicile sous les premiers califes fatimides*, in *Studi medievali in onore di Antonino De Stefano*, Palermo 1956, 569-576.

G.B. Caruso, *Biblioteca Historica Regni Siciliae*, Palermo 1723.

Centenario della nascita di Michele Amari, Palermo 1910, 2 vols.

G.M. Columba, *Per la topografia antica di Palermo*, in *Centenario...*, II, 395-426.

S. Cuccia, *I bagni di Cefalà Diana*, Catania 1965.

S. Cusa, *I diplomi greci ed arabi di Sicilia pubblicati nel testo originale, tradotti e illustrati*, Palermo 1868-'82.

A. De Simone, *Palermo nei geografi e viaggiatori arabi del Medioevo*, «Studi Maghrebini», 1968, 129-189.

A. De Stefano, *La cultura in Sicilia nel periodo normanno*, Bologna 1954.

G. Di Stefano, *Monumenti della Sicilia normanna*, Palermo 1955.

F. Gabrieli, *Ibn Hawqal e gli Arabi di Sicilia*, «Rivista degli Studi Orientali», 1961, 245-253.

F. Gabrieli, *Normanni e Arabi in Sicilia*, in *Saggi Orientali*, Caltanissetta 1960.

F. Gabrieli, *Arabi di Sicilia e Arabi di Spagna*, «Al-Andalus», 1950, 27-47.

F. Gabrieli, *Federico II e la cultura musulmana*, in *Dal mondo dell'Islam*, Milan-Naples 1954.

F. Gabrieli, *Ibn Hamdis*, Mazara 1948.

F. Gabrieli, *La storiografia arabo-islamica in Italia*, Naples 1975.

W. Krönig, *Il castello di Caronia in Sicilia*, Rome 1977.

B. Lagumiña, *Catalogo delle monete arabe esistenti nella Biblioteca Comunale di Palermo*, Palermo 1892.

E. Lévi-Provençal, *Une héroine de la résistance musulmane en Sicile au début du XIIIᵉ siècle*, «Oriente Moderno», 1954, 283-288.

U. Monneret de Villard, *Le pitture musulmane al soffitto della Cappella Palatina in Palermo*, Rome 1950.

I. Perri, *Uomini, città e campagne in Sicilia dall'XI al XIII secolo*, Bari 1978.

M. Reinaud, *Histoire de la sixième croisade et de la prise de Damiette d'après les écrivains arabes*, «Journal Asiatique», 1826, 18-40; 88-110, 149-169.

U. Rizzitano, *Un compendio dell'Antologia di poeti arabo-siciliani intitolata ad-Durrah*, «Memorie dell'Accademia Nazionale dei Lincei», 1958, 335-378.

U. Rizzitano, *Il Libro di Ruggero*, Palermo 1966.

U. Rizzitano, *Asad ibn al-Furât, giureconsulte dell'Ifriqia*, in *Storia e cultura della Sicilia saracena*, Palermo 1975, 3-17.

U. Rizzitano, *Nuove fonti arabe per la storia dei musulmani di Sicilia*, «Rivista degli Studi Orientali», 1957, 531-555.

U. Rizzitano, *La cultura araba nella Sicilia saracena*, Verona 1961.

A.M. Schmidt, *La fortezza di Mazzallaccar*, «Bollettino d'Arte», 1972, 90-93.

A. Saliñas, *Trafori e vetrate nelle finestre delle chiese medievali di Sicilia*, in *Centenario Amari*, 495-507.

D.M. Smith, *Storia della Sicilia medievale e moderna*, Bari 1970.

C. Waern, *Medieval Sicily: Aspects of Life and Art in the Middle Ages*, London 1910.

P. Wiegler, *The Infidel Emperor and his struggle against the Pope*, London 1930.

G. Wolf, *Stupor Mundi, Zur Geschichte Friedrichs II*, Darmstadt 1966.

Th. C. Van Cleve, *The Emperor Frederick II of Hohenstaufen, Immutator Mundi*, Oxford, 1972.

The Legacy of Islam to Europe

A. Abel, *De l'alchimie arabe à l'alchimie occidentale*, Rome 1969.

M.M. Antuña, *Una version arabe compediada de la «Estorca de España» de Alfonso el Sabio*, «Al-Andalus», 1933, 105-134.

R. Arié, *L'Espagne musulmane au temps des nasrides (1232-1492)*, Paris 1973.

M. Asin Palacios, *Aben Masarra y su escuela. Origines de la filosofia hispano-musulmana*, Madrid 1914.

M. Asin Palacios, *La espiritualidad de Algazel y su espiritu cristiano*, Madrid 1934-1941, 4 vols.

A. Badawi, *La transmission de la philosophie grecque au monde arabe*, Paris 1968.

W.C. Bark, *Origins of the Medieval World*, Stanford 1958.

W.J. Bishop, *Cirurgia historica*, Barcelona 1963.

F. Bliemitz-Rieder, *Abelhard von Bath*, Munich 1935.

M. Bloch, *Pour une histoire comparée des sociétés européennes*, in *Mélanges historiques*, I, Paris 1963.

G. Bofitto - C. Melzi d'Eril, *Almanach Dantis Alighieri sive Prophacii Judae Montispessulani*, Florence 1908.

B. Boncompagni, *Vita e opere di Gherardo cremonese traduttore del secolo duodecimo e di Gherardo da Sabbianetta astronomo del secolo decimoterzo*, Rome 1851.

F. Cantera, *La canción mozárabe*, Santander 1957.

G. Carbonelli, *Sulle fonti della chimica e dell'alchimia in Italia*, Rome 1925. *Catalogue of Latin and Vernacular Alchemical manuscripts in Great Britain and Ireland dating from before the 16th Century*, Brussels 1928-'31, 3 vols.

E. Cerulli, *The «Kalilah wa-Dimnah» and the Ethiopic «Book of Barlaam and Josaphat»*, «Journal of Semetic Studies», 1964, 75-100.

E. Cerulli, *Il «Libro della Scala» e la questione delle fonti arabo-spagnole della Divina Commedia*, the Vatican 1949.

V. Chauvin, *Bibliographie des ouvrages arabes ou relatifs aux arabes publiés dans l'Europe chrétienne de 1810 à 1885*, Leiden 1892-1922, 2 vols.

M. Clagett, *Archimedes in the Middle Ages*, Madison 1964.

M. Danton - G.E. Grimm, *Fibonacci on Egyptian fractions*, «Fibonacci Quarterly», 1966, 339-354.

P. Dronke, *Medieval Latin and the rise of the European love-lyric*, Oxford 1968.

C.E. Dubler, *Die «materia medica» unter der Muslimen des Mittelalters*, 1952, 329-350.

L. Ecker, *Arabischer, prvenzalischer und deutscher Minnesang, eine motivgeschichtliche Untersuchung*, Berne-Leipzig 1934.

E.L. Fackneheim, *A Treatise of Love by Ibn Sînâ*, «Medieval Studies», 1945, 208-228.

T. Fahd, *La divination arabe*, Leiden 1966.

G. Furlani, *Le antiche versioni araba, latina ed ebraica del «De partibus animalium» di Aristotele*, «Rivista degli Studi Orientali», 1922, 237-257.

F. Gabrieli, *Federico II e la cultura musulmana*, «Rivista Storica Italiana», 1954, 5-18.

F. Gabrieli, *La poesia araba e le letterature occidentali*, «Belfagor», 1954, 377-386.

S. Garcia Franco, *Historia del arte y ciencia de navegar*, Madrid 1947.

E. Garcia Gomez, *La lirica hispanoarabe y la aparición de la lirica románica*, Rome 1956.

E. Garcia Gomez, *Poesia arabigoandaluza. Breve sintesis*, Madrid 1952.

A. Gonzales Palencia, *El arzobispo don Raimundo de Toledo*, Barcelona 1942.

M. Hartmann, *Das Arabische Strophengedicht: I, Das Muwashshah*, Weimar 1897.

C.H. Haskins, *The Sicilian Translations of the Twelfth Century*, «Howard Studies in Classical Philology», 1910, 99-102.

C.H. Haskins, *The Reception of Arabic Science in England*, «English Historical Review», 1915, 5-7.

C.H. Haskins, *La rinascita del dodicesimo secolo*, Bologna 1972.

J. Heers, *L'occident aux XIVᵉ et XVᵉ siècle*, Paris 1962.

W.H. Hein - K. Sappert, *Die Medizinalordnung Friedrichs II. Eine Pharmazie historische Studie*, Eutin 1957.

G. Hilty, *La poésie mozarabe*, 1970.

A. Hottinger, *Kalila und Dimna*, Berne 1958.

Kâlila wa Dimna, Fr. tr. A. Miquel, Paris 1957.

P. Le Gentil, *La strophe zadjalesque, les khardjas et le problème du lyrisme roman*, «Romania», 1963, 1-27; 209-250.

R. Lemay, *Dans l'Espagne du XIIIᵉ siècle. Les traductions de l'arabe au latin*, «Annales, Economies, Sociétés, Civilisations», 1963, 639-665.

M. Levey, *Influence of Arabic pharmacology on Medieval Europe*, Rome 1969.

E. Lévi-Provençal, *La «Mora Zaida»*, in *Islam d'occident*, Paris 1948, 139-151.

I.B. Madkour, *L'Organon d'Aristote dans le monde musulman*, Paris 1934.

F. Marcos Marin, *Poesia narrativa arabe y epica hispanica*, Madrid 1971.

J. Martinez Ruiz, *La tradicion hispanoarabe en el «Libro del Buen Amor»*, Barcelona 1973.

R. Mendizabal Allende, *Averroes. Un Andaluz para Europa*, Madrid 1971.

R. Menedez Pidal, *Cantos romanicos andalusies*, «Boletin de la Real Academia Española», 1951, 187-270.

R. Menedez Pidal, *Poesia arabe y poesia europea*, Madrid 1941.

M. Meyerhof, *Esquisse d'histoire de la pharmacologie et botanique chez les musulmans d'Espagne*, «Al-Andalus», 1935, 1-41.

M. Meyerhof, *Thirty-three Chemical observations by Rhazes*, «Isis», 1935.

A. Mieli, *La science arabe et son rôle dans l'évolution scientifique mondiale*, Leiden 1938.

J.M. Millas, *Estudios sobre Azarquiel*, Madrid 1943-'50.

J.M. Millas, *La poesia sagrada hebraicoespañola*, Madrid 1940.

J.M. Millas, *Las traducciones orientales en los manuscritos de la Biblioteca Catedral de Toledo*, Madrid 1942.

J.M. Millas, *Selomó ibn Gabirol como poeta y filosofo*, Barcelona 1945.

J.M. Millas, *El literalismo de los traductores de la corte de Alfonso el Sabio*, «Al-Andalus», 1933, 155-187.

J.M. Millas, *Las tablas astronomicas del rey don Pedro el Ceremonioso*, Barcelona 1962.

A.R. Nykl, *La poesia a ambos lados del Pirineo hacia el año 1100*, «Al-Andalus», 1933, 357-408.

A.R. Nykl, *Hispano Arabic Poetry and its relations with the old Provençal troubadours*, Baltimore 1946.

A.R. Nykl, *El cancionero de Aben Guzmán*, Madrid 1933.

A. Pagliaro, *Riflessi di poesia araba in Sicilia*, Rome 1956.

F.M. Pareja, *El libro del ajedrez, de sus problemas y sutilezas*, Madrid 1933.

E. Patzelt, *Die fränkische Kultur und der Islam*, Brunn 1932.

G.B. Pellegrin, *L'elemento arabo nelle lingue neolatine con particolare riguardo all'Italia*, in *L'occidente e l'Islam nell'Alto Medioevo*, Spoleto 1965, 697-790.

J. Ribera, *La enseñanza entre los musulmanes españoles*, Madrid 1928.

J. Ribera, *Epica andaluza romanceada*, Madrid 1928.

J. Ribera, *La musica de Las Cantigas de Santa Maria*, Madrid 1922.

M. de Riquer, *La leyenda del graal y temas epicos medievales*, Madrid 1968.

M. Rondison, *Les influences de la civilisation musulmane sur la civilisation européenne médiévale dans les domaines de la consommation et la distraction: l'alimentation*, Rome 1969.

D. Romano, *Le opere scientifiche di Alfonso X e l'intervento degli ebrei*, Rome 1969.

A. Roncaglia, *La lirica arabo-ispanica e il sorgere della lirica romanza fuori della Penisola Iberica*, Rome 1956.

V. Ronchi, *L'influenza dell'ottica araba sulla cultura dell'Occidente nel Medioevo*, Rome 1969.

J.C. Russel, *Hereford and Arabic Science in England*, «Isis», 1932, 14-18.

J. Ruska, *Arabische Alchemisten*, Heidelberg 1924.

J. Ruska, *Das Buch der Alaume und Salze. Ein Grundwerk der spätlateinische Alchemie*, Berlin 1935.

E. Saez - J. Trenchs, *Juan Ruiz de Cisneros (1295/1296 - 1351/1352), autor del «Buen Amor»*, Barcelona 1973.

A. Sanchez Romeralo, *El villancico (Estudios sobre la lirica popular en los siglos XV y XVI)*, Madrid 1969.

G. Sarton, *Introduction to the History of Sciences*, Baltimore 1927-'49, 3 vols.

H. Schippergers, *Die Assimilation der arabischen Medizin durch das lateinische Mittelalter*, Wiesbaden 1964.

L. Seco de Lucena, *Investigaciones sobre el romancero. Estudio de tres romances fronterizos*, Granada 1958.

M. Steinschneider, *Die europäischen Übersetzungen aus dem Arabischen bis Mitte des 17. Juhrhunderts*, Graz 1956.

M. Stainschneider, *Die arabischen Übersetzungen aus dem Griechischen*, Leipzig 1889-'91, 3 vols.

M. Steinschneider, *Die hebräische Übersetzungen des Mittelalters*, Berlin 1893.

H. Suter, *Die Mathematiker und Astronomen der Araber und ihre Werke*, Leipzig 1900.

H. Suter, *Beiträge zu den Beziehungen Kaiser Friedrichs II zu zeitgenössischen Gelehrten des Ostens und Westens zu dem arabischen Enzyklopädisten Kamâl ed-Dîn ibn Jûnis*, Erlangen 1922.

H. Sutherland, *Islam and the Divine Comedy*, London 1926.

M. Ullmann, *Die Natur und Geheimwissenschaften in Islam*, «Handbuch der Orientalistik», 1972.

J. Vernet, *Tradiction e innovacion en la ciencia medieval*, Rome 1969.

J. Vernet, *Copernico*, Barcelona 1974.

C. Villanueva, *La farmacia arabe y su ambiente historico*, «Miscelanea de Estudios Arabes y Hebraicos, 1958, 29-83.

D.S. Wingate, *The medieval Latin versions of the Aristotelian scientific corpus, with special reference to biological works*, London 1931.